How OTTAWA SPENDS

1990 - 91

Tracking the Second Agenda

How Ottawa Spends

1990-91

Tracking the Second Agenda

EDITED BY

KATHERINE

A. GRAHAM

Carleton University Press
Ottawa, Canada
1990

© Carleton University Press Inc. 1990

ISBN 0-88629-107-0
Printed and bound in Canada
Carleton Public Policy Series #1

The National Library of Canada has catalogued this publication
as follows:

Main entry under title:

How Ottawa spends

1983-
Prepared at the School of Public Administration,
    Carleton University.
Issues for 1983-   constitute 4th-   eds.
Edited by: 1983, G. Bruce Doern; 1984, Allan M. Maslove;
    1985-1987, Michael J. Prince; 1988- Katherine A. Graham.
Publisher varies: 1983, Lorimer; 1984-1987, Methuen;
    1988-   , Carleton University Press.
Includes bibliographical references.
ISSN 0822-6482

    1. Canada--Appropriations and expenditures--Periodicals. I.
Carleton University. School of Public Administration.

HJ7663.S6   354.710072'2   C84-30303-3 rev.

Distributed by: Oxford University Press Canada
                  70 Wynford Drive
                  Don Mills, Ontario
                  Canada M3C 1J9
                  (416) 441-2941

Cover design: Robert Chitty

Acknowledgements

Carleton University Press gratefully acknowledges the support extended to its publishing program by the Canada Council and the
Ontario Arts Council.

Contents

Preface

This is the eleventh edition of *How Ottawa Spends*. Like previous editions, it focusses on particular departments and policy initiatives of the federal government. This year's edition also deals with some of the internal management issues that have emerged as important in the government's quest for efficiency and productivity. Beyond evaluating past actions, the book is intended to offer informed comment on prospects for the future in the areas it explores.

This is the second edition since the re-election of a Conservative majority government in November 1988. We now have an opportunity to assess the direction of the second Tory agenda. It seems important to start this assessment by asking some very basic questions: Is there a discernible government agenda? To what extent can we see similarities and differences in the direction of Conservative initiatives when we compare their first and second terms? What accounts for any similarities and differences that emerge? What are the implications of the direction of government initiatives? These questions are given broad treatment in the book's first chapter, which focusses largely on the February 1990 Budget and the federal Estimates for the 1990-91 fiscal year. That analysis is intended to set the stage for the more specific discussions of the federal agenda which follow.

How Ottawa Spends is produced by the School of Public Administration at Carleton University. On behalf of the contributors, I would like to thank the government officials, academic colleagues and administrative staff at Carleton who have assisted us. We are especially indebted to the staff at the School of Public Administration, without whom this annual volume would not appear. Sarah Bradshaw, Reeta Sanatani and Ann Wilson were very helpful as research assistants for this year's edition. The staff at Carleton University Press, especially David Knight and Pauline Adams were once again very helpful and enthusiastic. Nancy Warren, our copy editor, also provided invaluable assistance.

This is my last year as editor of *How Ottawa Spends*. I would like to give special thanks to Margaret Bezanson and Martha Clark who have masterminded the production of the book over the past three years. Their dedication and unfailing good humour made my work much more enjoyable. I would also like to thank my family for their understanding and support during my three year preoccupation with *How Ottawa Spends*.

Katherine A. Graham
Ottawa
March 1990

CHAPTER 1

TRACKING THE SECOND AGENDA:

ONCE MORE WITH FEELING?

Katherine A. Graham

Résumé

Dans ce chapitre on soutient que les conservateurs, au cours de leur deuxième mandat, ont un programme perceptible suivant lequel ils se concentrent de plus en plus sur le contrôle des dépenses et sur la réduction du rôle de l'état fédéral dans l'édifice social et économique du pays. On explore les implications de ce programme tel qu'il ressort du Budget 1990-91 et des Prévisions 1990-91. Parmi les conclusions, le rôle prédominant du ministre des finances dans l'élaboration de tout ce programme. Si les objectifs de ce programme se réalisent, certains segments de la société canadienne seront avantagés sur le plan économique, alors que d'autres groupes tels que les strates socio-économiques inférieures, les autochtones et les autres défavorisés risquent d'être délaissés, au grand détriment de nous tous à long terme.

It has now been over a year and a half since the Conservative Party was re-elected to its second term in Ottawa. The time has come to take stock and see if we can get some sense of where the Tories are taking us as we move into the last decade of the twentieth century. The period 1989-90 was characterized by widespread and dramatic change in the world which frequently overshadowed domestic events. Some of those changes in the international world, as well as the challenges Canada has faced domestically, make it important to evaluate the current government and address four basic questions:

°   Is there a discernible government agenda?

°   To what extent can we see similarities and differences in the direction of Conservative initiatives when we compare their first and second terms?

°   What accounts for any similarities and differences that emerge? and

°   What are the implications of the direction of the government's agenda?

This chapter argues that we can answer the first question in the affirmative. There is a discernible government agenda as the Conservatives move through their second term. The chapter's exploration of the remaining questions gives us an idea of the extent to which the Tories have learned from experience and observation, both on the domestic and international fronts. As will be seen, the government's agenda has become increasingly focussed on expenditure control and reducing the role of the federal state in both the social and economic fabric of Canada. The implications of this agenda, as it is manifested in the 1990-91 Budget, the 1990-91 Estimates and in the more specific policy and program sectors reviewed in this volume, are that some segments of Canadian society may benefit in economic terms. However, other segments of our society may be left behind, to the long-term detriment of us all.

The individual chapters in this volume address some important specific initiatives of the Mulroney Conservatives as they move through their second term. Among their conclusions:

°   The Goods and Services Tax (GST), as currently structured, represents a retreat from some of the government's original proposals. For example, the tax is only partially visible and is no longer intended to be revenue neutral. Nevertheless, the GST still represents a substantial improvement over the tax that it will replace. Despite this fact, certain characteristics of the GST and the public policy environment related to tax reform have resulted in a much rougher ride for the Conservatives over the GST than they received when they reformed the income tax system.

°   In some respects, the structure and mandate of Industry, Science and Technology Canada (ISTC) have sensible features which reflect the Conservatives' desire to focus on international competitiveness and link science and technology policy with industrial policy at the federal level. However, ISTC will not become Canada's flagship department in making microeconomic policy unless there is greater continuity in leadership and unless the Conservatives also give it the mandate to fashion some active industrial policy. Such a policy would provide mechanisms (now lacking) for ISTC to deal with key Canadian firms in an increasingly global world.

o   In light of the political fall-out from the free trade debate, the government had no option but to undertake some form of work force adjustment initiative. The Conservatives' emphasis in their adjustment package has been to try to shift expenditures from Unemployment Insurance and other programs in the labour market policy envelope, rather than to commit new resources to the adjustment challenge. The second element of their adjustment policy is to shift the emphasis from equity to efficiency. One danger associated with this shift is that a "polarized" economy will result, with a core of workers benefiting from enhanced training and job mobility, while another portion of the labour force will be left to languish.

o   The Conservatives' interest in environmental policy tracks the attitudes of the Canadian population quite closely. In terms of specific initiatives, the government's ethos seems to lean towards market-based approaches to dealing with environmental issues. Environment Canada is beginning to demonstrate an interest in using approaches other than direct command and control of polluters to achieve its policy objectives. This, combined with an enhanced capability in the department to develop positions on environmental issues using "harder" techniques, such as cost benefit analysis, suggest that Environment Canada will be better able to get political support for its policy proposals than in the past.

o   Over the 1984-88 period, the Mulroney government achieved only modest progress in implementing its agricultural policy agenda. While helping to stabilize and even augment Prairie farm incomes during a period of crisis, safety net programs have not solved the farm debt problem and they have had distributional effects which raise the issue of equity among farmers. The legacy of the 1984-88 record, combined with some of the policy reforms under discussion in the extensive review of agriculture policy launched by the Tories in 1989, suggest a much greater likelihood of federal-provincial and inter-regional conflict over Canadian agriculture policy in the Conservatives' second mandate.

° The Conservative government does not accept that it has betrayed a commitment to the universality of social programs, including those aimed at children. However, the changes to various family and child assistance programs have resulted in a decline in the value of benefits for many families. This has been accompanied by a marked increase in the complexity of how child benefit programs are administered. The efforts of various social sector organizations to influence the Finance Minister on child care and related issues have met with limited success. Despite the Prime Minister's commitments to the contrary, universality in child benefits has effectively disappeared without a public debate.

° Although the movement towards improved public sector management cannot be attributed exclusively to the Conservatives, there has been far more stress on management improvement since their election in 1984. The Tories' emphasis on a more business-like approach to government has generally (although not always) been supported by managers in the public service. At times, these same managers have been the proponents of specific reforms. The results of efforts to improve the management effectiveness and productivity of government are, of necessity, not immediate. The danger is that the Conservatives' commitment to reforms of this kind will be sidetracked by short-term political considerations.

° The related problems of low morale and productivity in the federal public service are fearful in and of themselves. If they are not dealt with, they will become increasingly vexatious in the 1990s, as the public service is mandated with increased responsibilities. The creation of the Public Service 2000 task force by the Prime Minister late in 1989 signals some government concern for the health of the public service. However, it would be a mistake for this task force to focus, as it seems set to do, on efficiency-type solutions to the problems at hand. The government also needs to address demographic problems, the future pattern of specialization in employment and other problems of leadership and communication within the public service.

Beyond these policy or department-specific findings, the assembled chapters and the 1990-91 Budget and Estimates point to a broad, but discernible agenda for this Mulroney government. That agenda has five distinct (but sometimes interrelated) elements:

○ Gaining control of the debt and the deficit. This is a cornerstone of the government's efforts, as will be seen in the subsequent discussion in this chapter on the 1990-91 Budget and Estimates. It is also evident in the shift in approach from introducing the GST as a revenue neutral tax to making it a deficit fighter. The political implications of this change are discussed by Allan Maslove in chapter two.

○ Reducing the role of the federal state as an intervener in markets and as an agent of command and control. Bruce Doern and Michael Prince discuss the Conservatives' approach to market intervention in their respective chapters on ISTC and agriculture policy, while Douglas Smith examines some of the alternative approaches the government has embraced for reducing pollution other than by ordering polluters to cease and desist and backing such orders with government inspections.

○ Reducing the role of the federal state as an intermediary or engine of adjustment as Canada faces a changing global economy. Rianne Mahon's chapter on employment adjustment, as well as the chapters by Doern and Prince point to this policy stance. Certain provisions of the Budget and Estimates related to regional development, and the reduction of subsidies to business also suggest that this is a government priority.

○ Maintaining (perhaps reducing) the boundaries of the social welfare state, as it is supported by the federal government. While the Conservatives are retaining the major institutions of the welfare state, they are reducing the federal financial commitment to supporting central programs, such as unemployment insurance. In addition, there are strong signals that the government is axing its support for citizen participation, a major institutional underpinning of the evolution of social policies and programs in Canada. The relevant provisions of the 1990-91 Budget, including those related to the Canada Assistance Plan (CAP) and Established Programs Financing (EPF), will be discussed in this chapter. Moreover, the chapters by Rianne Mahon and Allan Moscovitch also suggest that this is part of the Tories' second agenda.

○ Enhancing the efficiency and productivity of government. The chapter by Lloyd Brown-John ascribes an enhanced concern with productivity and efficiency to the Conservatives since they came into office. The chapter by David Zussman points out the pitfall of exclusive concern with these issues in terms of the broader issues facing the public service.

This agenda has at least two interesting characteristics. It is not driven by substantive policy issues, such as the environment, broadcasting or child care, that are most often the stuff of electoral politics. In addition, our typically Canadian preoccupation with federal-provincial relations emerges only in an oblique fashion. The strong federal effort to achieve "national reconciliation," so front and centre in the early years of the first Mulroney government, seems to have faded. Instead we have an apparently determined ethos to restrict the role of the federal government and to create the image both nationally and internationally that what the federal government does, it does in a fiscally responsible manner. That is ostensibly what the 1990-91 Budget and Estimates are all about. It is important to examine both of these before we turn to the three remaining questions about the government's agenda.

THE 1990-91 BUDGET: SIX YEARS OF ACCUMULATED SMARTS

On February 20, 1990, Michael Wilson brought down his sixth consecutive Budget as Minister of Finance. His budget speech did not begin with a statement of how much the government would spend in the fiscal year 1990-91. Instead, his first major pronouncement was that "the deficit for this year is on track at $30.5 billion."[1] The fact that "the magic number" of the size of the 1989-90 deficit was the first highlight of the budget speech is indicative of the unique policy environment surrounding the making of the 1990-91 Federal Budget. Although the Conservatives and some interest groups have been on the deficit/debt reduction trail since 1984, the period 1989-90 marks the first time when a political consensus began to emerge that attacking the debt and the deficit should be top priority, and that expenditure control by the federal government should become the way to achieve this end.

In what has become a predictable pattern, the run up to the 1990-91 Budget was accompanied by strenuous lobbying on the part of Canada's organized business community over the need for tougher expenditure reduction measures.[2] However, public opinion polls and other sources also suggested a more widespread concern among Canadians about the deficit and public debt. This concern was refined by an increasing unwillingness to support deficit/debt reduction and other government initiatives through increased taxes. The public debate over the GST in the period leading up to the Budget heightened Canadians' realization that taxation had been, to date, a major tool in the government's deficit/debt reduction efforts.[3] This confluence of opinion on the domestic front was reinforced by an awareness that there was some concern in the international community about the competitiveness of Canada and its attraction as a place to invest. The Conservative's policies of fiscal restraint, divestment, trade liberalization and "supply side social policy"[4] had been winning praise (with cries of "more") in international quarters.[5] However, there were concerns in international money markets whether the government could stay on its course.

Prior to the budget, the government tried to send out a number of signals that federal expenditure control was the way of the future. In December, the President of the Treasury Board, Robert de Cotret, announced spending cuts of $1.4 billion over the next three years. In addition to Mr. Wilson's customary pre-budget warnings, the Prime Minister opined publicly in the run up to budget day that a tough budget was needed.[6] Expenditure restraint definitely seemed to be in the cards. The role of taxation in the upcoming federal budget was more ambiguous.

When it was unveiled, the 1990-91 Budget emerged as very well crafted in terms of the political needs of the federal government. In fact, it was as much a political document as an economic one. The essence of the budget is a continued effort to fight the debt and deficit by federal expenditure control and by passing on part of the burden of the fight to other levels of government. The support of individual Canadians for this strategy has been bought by ostensibly leaving them alone. Indeed, one might wonder whether the majority of Canadians "tuned out" when they heard Michael Wilson pronounce early in his budget speech: "There will be no new taxes in this budget."[7] Furthermore, transfers to persons, in the form of old age security, family allowances, unemployment insurance benefits and the like were also left untouched, thus adding to the "good news" image of this budget. The reality, however, is that individual Canadians will pay for the initiatives contained in the budget. The only difference is that they will be holding their respective provincial government (or, in some cases, local government) accountable as services are reduced or taxes are increased. In the aftermath of this federal budget, the most relevant question is very much "How do governments spend?" rather than "How does Ottawa spend?"

One has to read through the first 102 pages of the main budget document before finding out what the federal government is actually planning to spend in 1990-91. The highlights of the government's expenditure plan are found in Table 1.1.

Table 1.1
Budgetary Expenditures

	1989-90	1990-91	1991-92
	(millions of dollars)		
A. Major transfers to persons	32,380	34,965	37,255
B. Major transfers to other levels of government [1]	24,645	23,985	24,475
C. Major subsidies/other major transfers	10,465	9,890	9,935
D. Payments to major Crown corporations	5,410	4,745	4,650
E. Defence	11,310	11,870	12,460
F. Official Development Assistance	2,445	2,565	2,695
G. Other government operations	16,845	17,330	18,105
H. Reserves net of lapse	-	1,275	1,675
I. Program spending	103,500	106,625	111,250
J. Public debt charges	39,400	41,150	41,500
K. Total budgetary expenditures	142,900	147,775	152,750

	(per cent change from previous year)		
A. Total budgetary expenditures	7.7%	3.4%	3.4%
B. Public debt charges	18.7%	4.4%	0.9%
C. Program spending	4.0%	3.0%	4.3%
D. Consumer price index (CPI)	5.0%	4.7%	5.1%
CPI excluding one-time impact of 7% GST	5.0%	4.7%	3.9%
E. Gross domestic product (value)	7.5%	5.2%	6.4%

[1] Certain transfers to other levels of government are made as a combination of cash and a transfer of tax points. Program spending includes only the cash transfer component as well as adjustments to program entitlements for prior years. Total transfer entitlements, including cash and tax transfers but excluding prior-year adjustments, are as follows:

	1989-90	1990-91	1991-92
	(millions of dollars)		
Cash and tax transfer entitlements to other levels of government	35,050	36,100	37,150

Source: Department of Finance, *The Budget* (Ottawa: February 20, 1990), p. 103.

It shows that total budgetary expenditures for 1990-91 are set at $147,775 million, an increase of 3.4 per cent from last year. Although public debt charges are to increase by 4.4 per cent from 1989-90, they are supposed to remain constant as a percentage of total budgetary expenditures, staying at 28 per cent of the total.

The most interesting component of the budget deals with the government's plans to reduce expenditures and enhance revenue through more efficient money management. These plans, summarized in Table 1.2, include the initiatives announced by Mr. de Cotret in December 1989. They reveal a complex set of political trade-offs involving both statutory and discretionary expenditures by the federal government.

One of the most important elements of this budget is the federal government's attempt to constrain statutory payments to the provinces through the budgetary process. The payments affected are made under two programs, Established Programs Financing (EPF) and the Canada Assistance Plan (CAP).

EPF transfers provide equal per capita financial assistance to all provinces. This program was initiated in 1977 to replace conditional grant programs whereby the federal government contributed to meeting the costs of health care and post-secondary education. The mythology is that the provinces continue to use EPF funds for these specific purposes. However, there has been a sustained sense in Ottawa that some provinces have been using EPF funds for other purposes at the same time as post-secondary institutions and health care providers have been pleading impoverishment. EPF transfers are the largest single form of federal assistance to provinces, having grown from $14.5 billion in 1984-85 to about $20 billion in 1989-90. This represents an average annual growth rate of about six per cent since the Conservatives came to power.[8]

Table 1.2
Expenditure Reductions and Management Initiatives -
December 1989 and February 1990

	1990-91	1991-92	Five-year savings
	(millions of dollars)		

A.   Expenditure control plan
  1. Key exempt programs
   ° Major transfers to persons; old age security, guaranteed income supplement, spouses' allowances, family allowances, veterans' pensions and allowances and unemployment insurance benefits.
   ° Major transfers to provinces: equalization and Canada Assistance Plan for the equalization-receiving provinces.

  2. Programs constrained to 5% annual growth for two years

	1990-91	1991-92	Five-year savings
° Science and technology	38	1	39
° Indian and Inuit Programs	50	50	100
° Canada Assistance Plan (non-equalization-receiving provinces)	75	80	155
° Defence	210	270	658
° Official Development Assistance	116	190	558

  3. Programs frozen for two years

	1990-91	1991-92	Five-year savings
° Established Programs Financing (per capita)	869	1,541	7,364
° Public utilities income tax transfers	16	34	50
° Canadian Broadcasting Corporation	5	15	20
° Telefilm Canada	6	7	13
° Export Development Corporation	25	50	100
° Marine Atlantic	4	5	24

  4. Programs reduced

	1990-91	1991-92	Five-year savings
° Grants and contributions			
Secretary of State	23	23	113
National Health and Welfare	12	12	44
° Small craft harbours	4	5	29
° Canada Mortgage and Housing Corporation	16	35	165

5. Programs/projects eliminated

° Canadian Exploration Incentives Program	50	125	811
° OSLO	-	46	602
° Polar	84	62	373

6. Management measures

° Crown corporations and agencies	401	125	679
° Management initiatives			
Enhanced collection of accounts receivable	167	230	1,237
Acceleration of Bank of Canada remittances	400	-	400
Management efficiencies	12	24	556

7. Associated public debt charge savings	200	400	2,600
8. Total expenditure control plan fiscal savings	2,782	3,329	16,689
B. December 1989 expenditure reductions and management improvements	246	450	2,806
C. Total fiscal impact of measures	3,028	3,779	19,495

[1] Figures may not add due to rounding.

Source: Department of Finance, *The Budget 1990-91* (Ottawa: February 20, 1990), p. 74.

       This budget freezes the per capita EPF transfers to all provinces at the 1989-90 level for the next two fiscal years. However, the majority of the provinces have been mollified by two related budget announcements. Equalization payments, which are received by every province except Ontario, Alberta and British Columbia, are untouched. In addition, the "have-not" provinces were excluded from the federal government's other statutory program initiative which is to place a ceiling of five per cent on CAP transfers to Ontario, Alberta and B.C. The Canada Assistance Plan provides for open-ended federal-provincial cost sharing for social assistance benefits and services. CAP funding is demand driven, in the sense that expenditures are related to the number of individuals who require assistance. Ironically, the rate of growth in expenditures has been highest in Ontario, with an average increase of about 14 per cent per year over the past five years despite Ontario's strong economy.

In political terms, the poorer provinces' objections to the EPF initiative have been bought off by leaving equalization and their level of CAP support untouched. The "have" provinces, particularly Ontario, look like fat cats who have been put on a diet for their own health.[9] Mr. Wilson took great pains in his budget to portray the provinces as hitherto weak partners in the deficit/debt battle. He compared federal and provincial government debt charges and found the provinces getting off easily.[10] He compared federal and provincial public sector wage settlements and found the provinces to be generally less tight-fisted.[11] Implicit is the suggestion that the provinces should consider themselves lucky to get off as easily as they did.

In terms of regional politics, there were also trade-offs in this budget. Donald Savoie argues that, at least into the mid-1980s, the federal government's inability to cut back existing programs is rooted in the regional nature of Canada. Every region wants its own share and more, if possible.[12] This time, the Prairies and B.C. lost more. Cancellation of the federal commitment to the oil sands OSLO project in Northern Alberta beyond 1991 and the Canadian Exploration Incentives Program does have an affect on the western economy, as does cancellation of the Polar 8 icebreaker project in the case of B.C.[13] However, the west was spared cuts in the agricultural subsidy system, at least for the moment.[14] Atlantic Canada will have to bear the consequences of the freeze in federal subsidies to Marine Atlantic for the operation of ferries, and the reduction in the budget of the Small Craft Harbours Program may also have an effect. However, it appears that business grants to Atlantic enterprises by the Atlantic Canada Opportunities Agency (ACOA) will not be subject to the "lean and mean" philosophy of converting forgivable business grants to loans announced by Mr. Wilson in his budget.[15]

When we consider the impact of the EPF freeze and the CAP ceiling on Ontario, it would seem that every region, with the possible exception of Quebec, is being required to shoulder a little extra burden. However, on the surface the burdens can be portrayed as relatively equal. The fact that Quebec emerges most unscathed is a possible reflection of its electoral importance to the Conservatives and a desire not to give nationalist forces further fuel. As of budget day, the Meech Lake impasse continued.

Much has been written about interest group politics in Canada. Indeed, one of the theses put forward in the last edition of *How Ottawa Spends* is that interest group politics would be a prominent feature of the second Conservative government.[16] On the surface, the budget reflects a similar distribution of the burden of restraint among different types of interests. The business sector, for example, is going to have to deal with the conversion of federal grants and subsidies to repayable loans. Women's, Aboriginal and multicultural groups are going to have to cope with reduced funding from the Secretary of State and National Health and Welfare. Clients for social housing will have to shoulder the impact of a 15 per cent reduction in the federal commitment to social housing.

The budget suggests a philosophy that everyone should do their part. However, a review of the impact of the budget on different interest groups suggests a different reality. Specifically, it appears that the government has used the budget to placate some interests and muffle others. As noted by Bruce Doern in his chapter on ISTC, business has generally supported the withdrawal of the government from business grant and subsidy schemes, especially in the post-free trade era. Thus it would seem that the cost to business of this move is somewhat illusory, especially given the special arrangements for small business in Atlantic Canada noted earlier. The impact of budget cuts to Aboriginal organizations, women's groups and others who rely on federal support for sustained funding and grants for special initiatives which are not inherently marketable is more severe.

The 1990-91 Budget announced cuts in grants and contributions to groups by the Secretary of State and National Health and Welfare totalling $35 million for each of the next two fiscal years. The 1990-91 Estimates, tabled by the President of the Treasury Board two days after the Budget, indicate that the cuts will be specifically directed at voluntary groups, professional organizations and institutions active in cultural development, citizenship, Native communication and friendship centres, heritage, child care advocacy, welfare advocacy, fitness and community and public health. In addition, National Health and Welfare's contribution to the National AIDS Program has been slashed from $20 million to $7.8 million.[17]

Susan Phillips has argued that federal funding cutbacks for voluntary interest groups hurt them considerably.[18] One result of such cutbacks is that these groups are forced to chase after money from disparate sources, which is something they are ill-equipped to do. The search for funding to survive diverts their already scarce resources from their basic functions of advocacy and the enhancement of a collective identity among their constituent membership. Predictably then, the reaction of organizations on the receiving end of the cuts was one of objection and dismay. The Grand Chief of the Assembly of First Nations went public to say that the cut in his organization's core funding would effectively silence a national voice for Aboriginal Peoples.[19] On

March 13, 1990, for the first time since the budget, a number of women's organizations and child care advocacy groups met with the minister responsible for women's issues . Although their objections to the cutbacks were both articulate and passionate, to the point of causing the minister considerable discomfort, she could not give any assurances of a brighter future. Fundamentally, she had no authority to give such assurances; her role was as a "flack-catcher."

One characteristic of the post-budget lobbying of groups affected by expenditure restraint is that their efforts have not received widespread attention. They are observed and sometimes supported by those who have a special interest in the B.C. shipbuilding industry, social issues or Aboriginal affairs, but there has not been any ground swell of broad public resistance to the cutbacks affecting specific interests, particularly in the social sector. Perhaps, as Allan Moscovitch suggests, this is a result of the characteristics of social sector lobby groups. It may also signal that the budget's appeal to individual self-interest (no new federal taxes and no changes to transfers to individuals) overwhelms our sense of collective identity or interest affiliation. In the short term, this is very smart as a political strategy for the government. It is also consistent with the overall Tory views of the importance of free markets and individual self-reliance. However, one must question the long-term consequences of this for Canadian society where, historically, distinct groups have faced systemic barriers to equality and self-reliance. To a large extent, it is advocacy and voluntary assistance groups for these particular sectors of Canadian society that have been adversely affected by this budget.

To a considerable degree, the 1990-91 Budget was a success for Michael Wilson. His agenda of expenditure control and deficit/debt reduction is predominant. He succeeded in muting domestic objections to specific restraint measures by appealing to individual self-interest and by passing on the political burden of some decisions related to service reduction or tax increases stemming from this budget to other levels of government. Some provinces are aggrieved; others are being stoic. Local governments are still collecting themselves and have to await the trickle down impact from their respective provincial governments to react. By then, their objections to changes as ultimately resulting from federal budgetary initiatives may well be lost. The budget was successful on the international front, at least in the short term, in the sense that it did not result in a run on the Canadian dollar or appear to otherwise decrease investor confidence. Mr. Wilson seems to have gambled correctly that international money markets care not a whit about the fiscal structure of Canadian federalism.[20]

The overall sense that the Conservative government is trying to convey in this budget is that it is not spending much. Indeed, the budget placed considerable emphasis on the fact that the government now has an operating surplus; it is taking in more in revenue than it is spending on programs.[21] The 1990-91 Estimates, tabled by the President of Treasury Board were intended to reinforce the budget's message by emphasizing that when the government spends, the government spends smart.

THE ESTIMATES

The Estimates are the government's detailed spending plan for the forthcoming fiscal year. On a department-by-department and agency-by-agency basis, they set out the amount allocated to different programs and the amount allocated to meet other financial commitments, such as transfer payments to other levels of government and other organizations. The Estimates also indicate the Person Year (PY) allocation to each department or agency and deal with particular initiatives in the operation of government which are thought to be important.

Michael Wilson and Robert de Cotret are a tag team remarkable for their longevity. This year marked Mr. Wilson's sixth budget and Mr. de Cotret's fifth set of Estimates. The relevant provisions of the 1990-91 Estimates for those departments and agencies dealt with in this volume are treated in their respective chapters. However, there are some interesting general characteristics of this year's Estimates that should be considered here.

Perhaps the most important characteristic of this year's Main Estimates is that they do not give a truly accurate picture of how the government is planning to spend in 1990-91. The reason for this is the expenditure control exercise. Departments and agencies prepare their version of their Estimates some months before the final version of the budget is concluded.[22] With the government's current emphasis on cutting, rather than spending, some departments proceeded to develop their Estimates knowing that there was an environment of restraint, but unaware of the specific effects of the expenditure control measures, such as the five per cent ceiling on specific programs announced in the February budget. This is not to suggest that departments and agencies were inflating their expenditure Estimates; however, all of the cuts cannot be accounted for by looking at the Estimates.

For example, the Minister of Finance announced a $12 million cut in grants and contributions by National Health and Welfare, which was echoed by the President of Treasury Board when he tabled the Estimates. However, in Part II of the Estimates, a review of the chapter dealing with Health and Welfare suggests only about $4.2 million in cuts, if the AIDS Program is excluded and a $16.4 million reduction in grants and contributions if the AIDS Program is added in. This presents a confusing picture. A similar review of the cuts in grants and contributions by the Secretary of State indicates that the Estimates show $1 million less in cuts than the $23 million announced at budget time.[23]

This does not suggest that the Estimates are deliberately being "cooked" to mislead. It is more likely a symptom of the highly political and compressed expenditure review process leading up to the budget. The role of the Cabinet Expenditure Review Committee would seem to be important here. As part of the routine reporting machinery of government, the Estimates process simply cannot not keep up. In terms of program expenditures, it seems that departments and agencies are now conditioned to cutting. For example, it is interesting to note, at least in the case of the Secretary of State, the extent to which the nature of the cuts to grants and contributions had already worked itself through the ministry's own budgetary process by the time Mr. Wilson rose to deliver the full budget. However, the government (most likely represented by the Expenditure Review Committee) exercised the option of undertaking additional surgery as the budget neared.

The second important announcement in the Estimates (it was also announced in the budget but it has received more attention from Mr. de Cotret) is that the operating and maintenance budgets of all departments and agencies will be held to a two per cent cap on inflation adjustment for an additional two years. This limit, initially announced in 1989, will now be extended to 1994-95. It represents a real cut in the spending power of departments and agencies, if the government's own estimate that the rate of inflation will continue to be higher than two per cent per year holds up. As in the past, all departments and agencies will not necessarily receive even two per cent. It is a maximum figure going only to those with "demonstrated need."[24] This suggests that the government plans to continue to squeeze all departmental budgets in the hope of saving money and achieving innovation through adversity.

A major Conservative initiative, since the party came into office in 1984, has been to reduce the size of the public service. Since that time, considerable attention has been focussed on the nature of public service cutbacks, the extent to which they have been "real," in terms of actually saving the government money, and their implications in terms of the morale and rejuvenation of the public service.[25] The chapters in this volume by Lloyd Brown-John and David Zussman address some of these same themes.

The 1990-91 Estimates indicate the results of the government's initiative to reduce the size of the public service by 15,000 Person Years (PYs) between 1985-86 and 1990-91. The actual net reduction achieved was 12,377.[26] The fact that the government achieved somewhat less than its original target is, at least in part, a reflection of the government's realization that the public service was being cut quite close to the bone, and that adequate personnel were required to meet the government's responsibilities. The Estimates plan a further net reduction in the size of the public service of 781 PYs in 1990-91. This is a relatively small cut compared to recent years. In addition, the Estimates indicate that there will be some real growth areas in public service employment in the coming year. The most spectacular is in National Revenue Taxation, which is forecast to grow by 1,027 PYs in 1990-91.[27] Much of this growth is attributable to planned implementation of the GST.

Another important characteristic of this year's Estimates is the considerable attention paid to the importance of management initiatives in the public service as a vehicle to realize economies and foster innovation and high morale in the public service. The nature and implications of these initiatives are dealt with in the chapters by Lloyd Brown-John and David Zussman. Suffice to note here that an entire chapter of Part I of the Estimates is devoted to "productive management" which is described in terms of: restraining the cost of operations; using improved management practices; finding better ways to deliver programs; stressing results-oriented management; and building a revitalized public service.[28] This is an indication of how integral changes in this area are to the government's agenda.

As a final note, it should be remembered that the Main Estimates, delivered in February, are only one part of the government's detailed expenditure plan. Later in the year, Supplementary Estimates will be tabled to acknowledge unanticipated spending requirements. The government typically sets aside a reserve fund for the Supplementary Estimates when the Main Estimates are brought down. The amount of the reserve set aside this year is $2,392 million or two per cent of the $147,775 million total budgetary expenditures in the fiscal plan. This is a very small reserve indeed. Compare it, for example, to the $4,300 million reserve set out in the 1989-90 Estimates which were brought down prior to the last federal election campaign. A reserve of this size suggests that the squeeze in spending is really on, especially since this is unlikely to be an election year.

THE EVOLVING CONSERVATIVE AGENDA: FOCUSSING IN

Having identified the current Conservative agenda, as revealed in the selected chapters in this volume and the 1990-91 Budget and Estimates, it is worthwhile to consider the extent to which we can see similarities and differences in the direction of Conservative initiatives when we compare their first and second terms. Have the Tories changed their agenda? What accounts for any similarities and differences that emerge? Finally, what are the implications of the direction of government initiatives? We can now turn our attention to these questions.

Writing at a similar stage in the Conservatives' first term of office, my predecessor as editor of *How Ottawa Spends,* Michael Prince, came to four main conclusions after tracking the first Tory agenda. In his view:

°   The Conservatives had a definite idea of where they wanted to go in terms of economic and foreign policy and, to a lesser extent, social policy.

°   Their strategy was to shift federal policies and expenditures in a right wing, small-c conservative direction.

°   The agenda was not fully consistent, nor was the government fully in control of it.

°   The Conservative agenda was not a complete break with the Liberals in the sense that the Liberals had started to move in a rightward direction. But the Mulroney government's style was different, especially in its efforts to be conciliatory with the provinces rather than confrontational.[29]

It is worthwhile briefly to consider each of these conclusions in turn, in light of the observations and conclusions about the second Conservative agenda contained in this volume.

The Conservatives now seem to have established a consistent course in social policy, as well as in economic and foreign policy.[30] The established direction in social policy has been to follow the lead of restraint policies for government expenditure. One of the first manifestations of this agenda was the government's abandonment of the non-tax elements of its proposed national child care program in the 1989-90 Budget. It is now evidenced by the retreat from universality in social programs and the approaches to labour market adjustment (including changes to the unemployment insurance program) discussed in this volume. Although they were made in the name of restraint, the government's cutback in funding for social advocacy groups signals dissolution of the social policy network which has helped spur previous governments to small-l liberal innovations in the social welfare state. The amount of money saved by these latter cutbacks was relatively small; however, their broader impact is very significant.

In terms of economic policy per se, the Tories are continuing their emphasis on private sector vitality and using market-based approaches wherever possible. For example, subsidies to agriculture flourished in the first Conservative term; however, as Michael Prince points out, the government has begun to send signals to the agriculture sector that it wants to increase the exposure of that sector to free market forces. Michael Wilson's reference to the government's forthcoming environmental strategy in the 1990 Budget Speech was no accident. As Douglas Smith points out, it is very likely that the government's strategy will view the environment through the prism of neo-classical economics, rather than command and regulation. These observations about the general direction of the Conservatives' economic policy in their second term sustain Michael Prince's second conclusion that the government's agenda is to shift federal policies in a right wing, small-c conservative direction.

Is the government's agenda constant and is the government fully in control of it? In the first term, a succession of political scandals and apparent confusion in the political operation of the government achieved prominence and threatened to overwhelm the government agenda. This time around, while scandals and political crises have not abated, the government seems more prepared to clench its teeth and carry on. For example, the severe situation in the Atlantic fishery has not resulted in major promises of special remedial aid from the federal government. In some respects, this lack of action, even symbolic action, is reminiscent of the days of R.B. Bennett. But in the context of the present government, it demonstrates a rather remarkable degree of political resolve, at least among the major forces in Cabinet. As of now, the resolve to keep to the agenda of restraint and free market economics seems to be sustained, even in the face of dreadful opinion poll results for the government. This suggests that some members of the inner Cabinet, now somewhat long in the tooth in the job, see themselves as people with a mission, more than as politicians out to maximize votes.

In terms of Michael Prince's fourth conclusion, it is evident that the Conservatives have moved the direction of government considerably to the right of where the Liberals had taken it by the time they left office in 1984. (It is moot to question how much farther right the Liberals would have gone had they won the 1984 or 1988 elections.) But what about the conciliatory style of the Mulroney government in federal-provincial relations that was noted early in its first agenda? The first observation that should be made is the apparent decline in the symbolic importance of federal-provincial relations this time around. As this is being written, federal politicians other than the Minister of State for Federal-Provincial Relations, seem strangely removed from the goings-on in the Meech Lake impasse. Given his role in reaching the original Meech Lake Accord, the Prime Minister's failure as a public advocate for its adoption is surprising. In other instances where federal-provincial relations are prominent, conflict rather than reconciliation has become more evident. For example, as Alan Maslove points out in his chapter on the GST, negotiations between the Minister of Finance and provincial treasurers over the GST have not been smooth. At least two provinces are taking the federal government to court over the 1990 Budget. Finally, the aspirations of some provinces for Senate reform and, more specifically, the intent of Alberta to elect its own senator have met with federal silence.

In short, the Conservative agenda has become more consistent and more focussed in the second term. Why has this occurred, especially given the reduced majority accorded the Conservatives in the last election? The answer would seem to lie in the key role of a few members of Cabinet in shaping the government's agenda. The most important of these is the Minister of Finance, Michael Wilson. Mr. Wilson is the longest serving Canadian Minister of Finance in memory. In 1984, he came to the position with a small-c conservative business-oriented background and philosophy that have been sustained and augmented as he has become more familiar with the dominant rules of international economics and public finance. He has worked hard in his portfolio and has been able to master, from his own ideological perspective, the major issues outstanding. His success with income tax reform and his consistent attention (except, perhaps for a brief lapse during the 1988 election) to the agenda of restraint, fiscal reform and fighting the debt have energized the Finance Department to the point where it has re-emerged as the dominant force in Ottawa. His sustained effort has also overwhelmed any doubting colleagues at the Cabinet table. Bruce Doern has written about the debilitating effect of revolving ministers on the achievement of a policy agenda in this volume and elsewhere.[31] The case of Michael Wilson exemplifies what can be achieved when the opposite approach is taken when filling a key Cabinet portfolio.

It is not outlandish to suggest that Mr. Wilson's agenda has become the government's agenda. At least to this point in the Conservatives' second mandate, his influence seems to have restrained the Prime Minister and other Cabinet colleagues who might have more profligate tendencies. The final question, however, concerns the implications for sustaining this course. This question has to be dealt with on at least two levels: What are the implications for Canada and what are the implications for the Conservatives?

Mr. Wilson, and indeed the government, argue strenuously that the economic course of restraint and free market-based development will lead to the long-term economic and social health of the country. The argument that the size of the public debt has a potentially crippling influence on our future has gained currency over the past six years. The prescription of the government spending less than it receives in revenue to reduce the debt is easily understood as a sensible one for most households, as well as for a country like Canada. Accordingly, tightening our belts and contributing our fair share seem like reasonable things to do, especially when we can do so seemingly without paying more tax and still receive the government transfers to which we have become accustomed. If that is the national priority, so be it. However, this analysis of the budget suggests that the real impact of the Conservatives' approach is that, in relative terms, some pay more than others. Those who will be paying more through reduced services, opportunities and social support tend to be the less advantaged in Canada. It is an open question how resilient these sectors of our society will be as we move into the new economic age that the Conservatives hold before us.

For the Conservatives, the 1990-91 Budget and Estimates, as a manifestation of the government agenda must be called a short-term political success. As suggested above, it may also result in sound economic results. However, historically in Canada, sound economics does not necessarily make good politics.[32] Traditionally, Canadians look to their governments to do things rather than take things away, and are loath to link strong economies with votes for the party in power. If this pattern holds, the Conservatives will be under pressure to move away from their current agenda into a more activist and perhaps even interventionist approach as they move toward the next election.

As of now, the Conservatives' second agenda seems to be driven by a particular perception of the possible impact of the forces of international economics (and their political manifestations in other countries, like Britain and the U.S.) on Canada. These influences should not be dismissed out of hand. However, Canadians need to hear some solid arguments from our national leaders (of whatever party or venue) which speak to the unique nature of our society and attempt to reconcile that with the "global" forces which may now seem so overwhelming. The fact that these arguments are not now being made, combined with the government's view of its current mandate, account for the current pattern of how Ottawa spends.

Notes

I would like to thank my colleagues Frances Abele, Allan Maslove and Susan Phillips who read an earlier draft of this chapter. Their comments were stimulating and helpful. However, I bear sole responsibility for the arguments and any errors of fact contained in this final version.

1   Michael Wilson, *The Budget Speech*, February 20, 1990, p. 1.

2   See, for example, Don McGillivray, "Business indignation over budget a warning to Tories," *The Ottawa Citizen*, January 23, 1990.

3   See, for example, Joan Cohen, "Federal Tories grow arrogant," *Winnipeg Free Press*, October 30, 1989, and Alan Freeman, "New decade begins in a host of higher taxes," *The Globe and Mail* [Toronto], December 30, 1989.

4   See Michael J. Prince and Jim J. Rice, "The Canadian Jobs Strategy: Supply Side Social Policy," in Katherine A. Graham (ed.), *How Ottawa Spends, 1989-90* (Ottawa: Carleton University Press, 1989), pp. 247-289.

5   See Madelaine Drohan, "Ottawa wins praise from OECD," *The Globe and Mail* [Toronto], December 4, 1989.

6   Jane Wilson, "Budget a tough one: PM," *The Ottawa Citizen*, January 30, 1990.

7   *Budget Speech*, p. 3.

8   *The 1990-91 Budget*, p. 78. It should be noted that the federal government also transfers tax points to the provinces as part of EPF. For a more extended review of CAP and EPF, see Allan Maslove and Bohodar Rubashewsky, "Cooperation and Confrontation: The Challenges of Fiscal Federalism," in Michael J. Prince (ed.), *How Ottawa Spends: 1986-87* (Toronto: Methuen, 1986), pp. 95-118 and Allan Moscovitch, "The Canada Assistance Plan: A Twenty Year Assessment, 1966-1968," in Katherine A. Graham (ed.), *How Ottawa Spends, 1988-89* (Ottawa: Carleton University Press, 1988), pp. 269-301.

9   In the aftermath of the budget, Ontario and B.C. announced that they were taking the federal government to court over the CAP ceiling. They argue that the federal government did not give them the required one-year notice before making the change. There is also the issue of whether the federal government can discriminate across provinces in a program like CAP.

10   *The 1990-91 Budget*, p. 126. According to Mr. Wilson's calculation, the provinces spent an average of 11.8 cents of each revenue dollar to cover debt charges while the federal government spent 35.1 cents in 1989-90.

11   *The 1990-91 Budget*, p. 128.

12   Donald J. Savoie, *The Politics of Public Spending in Canada* (Toronto: University of Toronto Press, 1990).

13   In the aftermath of the budget, the B.C. shipbuilding industry mounted a lobbying campaign to save the Polar 8 project, arguing that its cancellation would cripple the industry and B.C.'s economic well-being.

14   As Michael Prince points out in his chapter, the 1990 Budget was silent about agriculture. However, the Main Estimates for the agriculture ministry indicate an almost 30 per cent decline in Agriculture Canada's expenditures from 1989-90 to 1990-91. Nonetheless, a systematic revision of the agriculture safety net is still pending.

15   See "Except this one, and that one, and those," *The Globe and Mail* [Toronto], March 1, 1990. It should be noted that the 1990-91 Main Estimates for ACOA indicate a nine per cent decrease in its budget. Also, at the time of writing, the federal government was still noncommittal about its intentions for dealing with the difficulties in the Atlantic fishery.

16   See Katherine A. Graham, "Discretion and the Governance of Canada: The Buck Stops Where?" in Katherine A. Graham (ed.), *How Ottawa Spends, 1989-90* (Ottawa: Carleton University Press, 1989), pp. 12-22.

17   *1990-91 Estimates*, Part II (Ottawa: Minister of Supply and Services Canada, 1990), pp. 19-7 to 19-11 and 24-5 to 24-9.

18   Susan Phillips, "Managing Voluntary Political Organizations: The Illusory Glow of Davids and Goliaths," a paper to be presented to the Canadian Political Science Association annual meeting, Victoria, May 1990.

19   Deborah Dowling, "Muzzling dissent," *The Ottawa Citizen*, March 14, 1990.

20   My colleague Allan Maslove perceptively made this observation in the immediate aftermath of the budget.

21   *The 1990-91 Budget*, p. 3.

22   These comprise the individual volumes of Part III and contribute to the ministry by ministry summaries in Part II of *The Estimates*.

23   *The Main Estimates*, Part II, pp. 19-7 to 19-11 and pp. 24-5 to 24-9.

24   The Hon. Robert de Cotret, *Managing Government Expenditures* (Ottawa: Minister of Supply and Services, February 22, 1990), p. 57.

25   These and other issues related to cutbacks have been reviewed in many places. One of the seminal articles in this regard is by Sharon Sutherland, "The Public Service: Surviving the Pinch Test," in Michael J. Prince (ed.), *How Ottawa Spends, 1987-88* (Toronto: Methuen, 1987), pp. 38-128.

26   *The Estimates*, Part I, p. 39.

27   *Managing Government Expenditures*, p. 23.

28   *The Estimates*, Part I, p. 20.

29   Michael J. Prince, "The Mulroney Agenda: A Right Turn For Ottawa?" in Michael J. Prince (ed.), *How Ottawa Spends, 1986-87* (Toronto: Methuen Press, 1986), pp. 1-60.

30   The conduct of Canadian foreign policy is largely outside the scope of this review. For a contemporary analysis of Canadian foreign policy initiatives, see Maureen Appel Molot and Fen Osler Hampson (eds.), *Canada Among Nations* (Ottawa: Carleton University Press, 1990).

31   In addition to Bruce Doern's chapter on Industry, Science and Technology Canada in this volume, see G. Bruce Doern, "Consumer and Corporate Affairs: The Dilemma of Influencing Without Spending," in Katherine A. Graham (ed.), *How Ottawa Spends, 1988-89* (Ottawa: Carleton University Press, 1988), pp. 233-268.

32   Calum Carmichael, "Economic Conditions and the Popularity of the Incumbent Party in Canada," *Canadian Journal of Political Science*, forthcoming.

CHAPTER 2

THE GOODS AND SERVICES TAX:
LESSONS FROM TAX REFORM

Allan M. Maslove

Résumé

Suivant son désir de renforcer l'efficacité du système fiscal canadien, le gouvernement Mulroney mettra sur pied une nouvelle taxe sur les produits et services (TPS) en 1991. Une grande partie du revenu généré par la TPS remplacera la taxe fédérale sur les ventes des fabricants, qui sera éliminée du même coup. Comparée à l'ancienne taxe, la TPS doit s'appliquer à une plus grande gamme de biens et services, être prélevée à un taux uniforme et être plus visible aux consommateurs. De plus, en 1991, un crédit pour la TPS sera mis en place pour les familles à bas revenu.

Le projet de la TPS a suscité un grand débat public sur des questions telles que l'efficacité, les effets distributionnels, les impacts macro-économiques, la visibilité, le mécanisme administratif et la neutralité quant au revenu. Divers milieux déplorent également que jusqu'ici il n'y ait pas eu d'accord avec les provinces sur une taxe de vente coopérative.

Les problèmes politiques que le gouvernement a vécus peuvent être attribués à plusieurs facteurs: 1) la TPS substitue une taxe invisible à une taxe qui est partiellement visible; 2) le désir du gouvernement de rehausser son revenu (face aux pressions venant du déficit) soulève des difficultés politiques, puisqu'il a l'air de vouloir mettre la main sur notre argent; 3) la question de la TPS a su concentrer les griefs qui s'étaient accumulés contre le gouvernement au cours des cinq dernières années; 4) certains analystes dignes de foi ont pu mettre en doute l'analyse du gouvernement; 5) aucun rôle catalyseur n'est joué par les Etats-Unis, comme c'était le cas pour la réforme fiscale.

Somme toute, la TPS représente une nette amélioration dans le régime fédéral des taxes de vente. Le crédit pour la TPS vient compléter l'appareil administratif nécessaire à l'instauration d'un régime d'impôt sur le revenu négatif. Cela sera peut-être un legs surprise de la TPS.

The Mulroney government formally launched its tax reform initiative in June 1987 with the release of a White Paper.[1] At that time it was announced that the reform process would be split into two phases. The first would deal with the income tax system, and the second with the indirect or commodity tax system.

The general thrust of the government's tax reform efforts has been to strengthen the efficiency properties of the tax system. Expressed somewhat differently, the goal has been to reduce the influence of tax considerations on market behaviour, including spending, saving and investment decisions. Seen in context, the government's tax reform initiative constituted an integral part of its broader strategy of limiting the role of government and strengthening the play of market forces.[2]

The reforms of the income tax system (Phase I) were enacted and became effective for the 1988 taxation year. Broadly speaking, these reforms were of three types: several deductions or exemptions in the calculation of taxable income were converted to credits. To a limited extent, preferential tax measures were eliminated, thereby broadening the tax base; and the rate schedule was changed to create three tax brackets (rather than the former 10), with the highest being lowered considerably. As well, refundable tax credits for low income individuals and families were enriched.

While development work was obviously underway earlier, the reform of the federal commodity tax system was deferred until after the 1988 election. Phase II has proved to be much more difficult and politically contentious for the government than was the income tax reform. In this chapter some of the factors accounting for this difficulty are discussed, along with a review of the reform process in this area. First, however, it is necessary to review the problems with the old commodity tax system, and the substantive issues raised in moving from the old to the new system.

THE FEDERAL MANUFACTURERS' SALES TAX

Virtually everyone who has examined the Canadian tax system agrees that the federal manufacturers' sales tax (MST) needs to be replaced. This tax, which was first enacted in 1924, is levied on a narrow range of goods, accounting for about one-third of total consumer spending. Indeed, a group of goods that constitutes 15 per cent of total consumer spending generates 40 per cent of the total MST revenues. Because the tax is levied at the manufacturers' level, it is embedded in the prices of goods that are input into the production of other goods, with the result that tax is paid on earlier tax (tax cascading).[3] While one basic rate is applied to most commodities (currently 13.5 per cent), significant groups of others are taxed at a lower (e.g. construction materials) or a higher rate (e.g. tobacco and alcohol).

The litany of complaints goes on. Because of the variable rates, the narrow base, and the application of the tax at an early stage in the production process, it is virtually impossible for taxpayers to determine the amount of tax they are actually paying when they purchase manufactured commodities. In fact, in these terms the MST is almost certainly the most invisible tax levied by any government in Canada. For reasons of simple accountability of democratic government, invisible taxes are undesirable.

The MST distorts private decisions in several ways that impact negatively on the efficiency and growth of the Canadian economy. It increases the cost to firms undertaking investment. Even though investment is directly tax-exempt, the MST is embedded in the prices of goods that enter firms' investment spending. Likewise, the cost of goods exported from Canada is similarly affected, even though exports themselves are tax-exempt. Imports also tend to be taxed less than domestic substitute goods. The MST is levied at the point of importation. In many instances associated costs (such as marketing) are not included in the import price of goods, but are included in the prices of domestic goods when they are taxed. Further, domestic production tends to be subject to more tax cascading than imported products. As a result, foreign goods are treated favourably in comparison to domestic.

While these problems make the MST a poor tax, they are not new. The Carter Royal Commission on Taxation recognized many of these problems in 1966.[4] Work on the development of alternatives to the MST had been going on within the Department of Finance for many years. It may not be possible to identify why the reform of the MST emerged on the public agenda at this time, but two factors do appear to be relevant. First, increasing international trade competition (in-cluding the Canada-U.S. Free Trade Agreement), and the Mulroney government's overall concern with efficient markets made the shortcomings of the MST loom larger. Second, the revenue flows generated by the MST were becoming increasingly uncertain as global markets became more competitive. Increasing competition was acting as an impetus for manufacturers to try to avoid the tax and, thus, the incentives to tax avoidance increased. Third, the MST, with its narrow base and distortionary effects stood in the way of the government's apparent intention to alter the balance between income-based and consumption-based taxes. A broad-based, more neutral, and more reliable revenue source was required to achieve this shift.

THE EVOLUTION OF THE GOODS AND SERVICES TAX

In theory, one could contemplate several potential alternatives to the existing MST. For example, one could argue that the federal govern-ment should abandon the field of commodity (indirect) taxation to the provinces, and replace the MST revenues (estimated by the Finance Department to be $18.5 billion in 1991) with increased revenues from the income tax system and/or by re-instituting wealth/estate taxation in Canada. Alternatively, one could argue for a general consumption tax that could be administered using the collection apparatus of the in-come tax system.[5]

In fact, some version of a value-added tax (VAT) appears to be the only option seriously considered by the government. Value-added taxation is well established in several industrialized economies, notably in Western Europe and recently in New Zealand. There were thus models and experience on which to draw. Perhaps the major complica-tion that arises when introducing a VAT to Canada is the existence of two levels of government taxing consumption. Therefore, it became necessary to consider the integration of the federal and provincial sales tax systems, or to consider the option of running two systems side by side. (It is interesting to note that in pursuing the VAT option, the Canadian government has not followed the lead of the United States which does not have a general commodity tax system at the federal level. This is a marked contrast to the role played by the U.S. model in income tax reform.)

The federal government's VAT proposal was first outlined in the June 1987 White Paper. At that time, two alternatives for a multi-stage sales tax were advanced, the preferred alternative being a sales tax integrated with the provinces, and the other a purely federal system. While sales tax reform was deferred to a second round following income tax reform, the White Paper did provide a number of principles and details of the government's thinking at that time. Several of these points have since returned to haunt the government.

First, the intention was clearly stated that the base of the new tax was to be set to include virtually all consumption spending. The White Paper was vague, however, on items to be included or excluded. Whether food was to be taxed was not specified, probably intentionally to test the waters.

Second, it was made clear that the new tax was to be visible to taxpayers. This means that taxpayers would be clearly aware that they were paying the tax and the amount of tax they were paying could also be readily determined. Achieving this goal would have been straightforward with a tax integration arrangement with the provinces; the federal tax would then have been equally as visible as the existing provincial sales taxes.

Third, it was clearly stated that the new tax, and the associated changes taken as a package, were meant to be revenue neutral. While there was always some ambiguity surrounding the meaning of this term over the long run, it was taken by all parties to mean that at least in the first year, the net fiscal position of the government would not change. The tax rate required to generate this amount of revenue was not stated explicitly, but sample calculations were provided using eight per cent as the illustrative rate.

Finally, among the associated changes in the Phase II reform package, the White Paper clearly stated that there would be certain income tax offsets at the time of the enactment of the new sales tax. Specifically, the government announced its intention to remove the personal and corporate income tax surcharges, and to offer some further reduction in tax rates, notably for the new middle personal income tax bracket. In addition, the enriched sales tax credit that was an integral part of the sales tax reform package, was to be funded from sales tax revenues. In total, these offsets represented a significant shift from income-based to consumption-based taxation in the federal revenue system.

Given the initial focus on income tax reform, the proposed sales tax package received little attention until the spring of 1989 when the government announced several significant changes to its plan.[6] Ottawa announced that it had broken off negotiations with the provinces, and would implement a federal Goods and Services Tax (GST). In the Budget of April 1989, it announced that the GST rate would be set at nine per cent. At this rate the tax would generate sufficient revenues in 1991 to replace the MST, to fund the proposed sales tax credit and to reduce the middle personal income tax rate by one percentage point. In addition, the federal government's budgetary position would improve by about $1 billion.[7] The removal of the surtaxes on personal and corporate income taxes that had been promised earlier as an accompaniment to sales tax reform had been dropped. Further details were released in August[8] and draft legislation was published in October.

Finally, in December 1989 the Minister of Finance announced a further round of modifications. This was ostensibly the government's response to the report of the Commons Standing Committee on Finance (Blenkarn Committee)[9] but more directly it was the government's response to the wave of criticism being directed at the GST proposal from virtually all sectors of the economy.[10] The main change announced at that time was, of course, the reduction in the rate from nine per cent to seven per cent. In addition, the basic amounts for the refundable sales tax credit were adjusted downward to correspond to the lower tax rate (from $275 to $190 per adult; for children, the credit remained unchanged at $100 per child), as was the rebate for purchases of newly constructed houses. The government also argued that in order to help pay for the lower revenue that would be generated by the lower sales tax rate, it was necessary to eliminate the planned reduction in the middle personal income tax bracket, and to raise the high income surtax from three per cent to five per cent. The threshold level for application of the surtax was also lowered.

While the December 1989 amendments addressed several of the issues of contention, by no means did they put to rest all (or even most) of the political opposition to the GST. These main points of contention that have been raised in the GST debate are reviewed in the next section.

MAJOR ISSUES OF DEBATE

When the public debate over the Goods and Services Tax finally got underway, it was intense. Many economic and social interest groups became involved, public opinion was surveyed, and the parliamentary opposition took up the cause. In several communities, groups of individuals came together for the sole purpose of mounting protests against the government's GST proposals. The more formal non-political opposition was channeled largely through submissions to the Blenkarn Committee as it toured the country in the course of its hearings in the fall of 1989. In short, the GST generated popular opposition ranging from disagreement with specific design features of the proposal to general dissatisfaction with some vaguely articulated, money-grabbing "big government." The parliamentary opposition tended to follow rather than lead this popular uprising against the GST.

While each opposing group obviously chose to focus on its own concerns, the opposition can really be described in terms of several distinct (but interrelated) issues. These are discussed below. To provide a perspective on these issues, however, it is worthwhile to reiterate that the government's GST proposal is a package that includes three separable components. First, it will replace the existing MST which is currently levied at 13.5 per cent. Most of the GST revenues - over three-quarters of the amount raised in 1991 - will replace the MST. Second, the GST will, when all effects are taken into account, improve the government's fiscal position by about $1 billion in the first year.[11] Third, the refundable sales tax credit is redesigned and enriched. This new GST Credit is projected to cost about $2.5 billion in 1991.

Efficiency

The first topic of debate concerns the allocational or efficiency impact of the GST. For the most part, it is desirable to design a tax to minimize its impacts on economic decisions; in other words, one does not want to distort decisions that economic agents would otherwise make.[12] In these terms the GST is a marked improvement on the MST because it taxes a much broader range of consumer goods and it taxes them more uniformly. Therefore it will create fewer distortions between categories of goods. It will be essentially neutral with respect to the tax treatment of imported goods compared to domestically produced substitutes. In addition, because the tax that is now embedded in investment goods and intermediate goods is effectively eliminated, the distortions in investment decision-making that the MST creates will disappear. This will produce an efficiency gain, and in addition, if it increases the rate of investment, it will lead to higher growth and incomes in the future.

Distribution

The second area of concern is whether the GST is a progressive or regressive tax. The GST is likely to have a favourable distributional impact relative to that of the old MST. The conventional wisdom is that the MST is a regressive tax, essentially because the goods involved constitute a higher proportion of a household's expenditures as household income declines. The GST is likely to be less regressive because it will also tax services. The consumption pattern for most services is more progressive than the pattern for goods currently taxed by the MST. Therefore the GST, in relative terms, will impact more heavily than the MST on the consumption spending of higher income individuals. Thus, if the GST revenues were simply to replace those generated by the MST (the first of the three components of the package noted above), the switch would almost certainly be progressive (that is, the new system would be less regressive) because the tax would be spread over a larger range of commodities in a manner that would have a greater impact on households as their incomes increased.

However, that is not the end of the story. As noted earlier, the new sales tax system is going to be used to generate more revenue than the old one, not simply to replace revenues (the second component) and to fund the GST Credit (the third component). Overall, a higher proportion of federal revenues will come from this tax and a smaller share will come from income taxes. This shift is regressive. Even though the GST is less regressive than the MST, it is still regressive compared to the income tax. The net outcome from all these changes is unclear. To a large degree the government is taking one step forward and another step backward.[13]

In assessing the distributional impacts we must also take into account the proposed enrichment of the refundable sales tax credit for the lowest income families (the third component). In 1990 the values of these credits are $140 per adult and $70 per child for families eligible for full benefits. Under the current GST proposal, these values will increase to $190 and $100 respectively. In addition, the income threshold above which benefits begin to be reduced will increase from $18,000 to about $25,000. These changes will clearly benefit families at the lower end of the income spectrum. Other changes, such as more frequent payment of the credit, will also work to their benefit. On the downside, the credits are indexed to increases in the Consumer Price Index (CPI) after three per cent. Therefore, as long as inflation is at this level or higher, the real value of the credits will erode at three per cent per year.[14]

The government has always maintained that these credit enrichments were an integral part of the GST. They have been largely successful in maintaining this linkage in public perceptions. However, as already noted, analytical changes to the sales tax credit are quite distinct from changes to the structure of the sales tax system. There is nothing to prevent the government from introducing the credit improvements while keeping the MST or introducing the GST while not adjusting the credits. In determining overall distributional impacts one must, of course, examine all the changes. However, at the same time it is worthwhile to keep in mind that these two reforms are conceptually distinct.

Macroeconomic Impacts

A third area that has elicited a great deal of discussion is the macroeconomic impact of the GST. Over the longer term, the prospects for increased growth and higher incomes seem quite strong. Because the buried tax on investment goods will be removed, the level of investment in the economy should be boosted permanently. Similarly, the GST will not tax exports (as the current tax does implicitly), and will tax imports more neutrally relative to domestic substitutes. These two changes together are predicted to substantially improve the trade balance, which will also boost the level of incomes in Canada.

The short run macroeconomic impacts were originally much murkier. Independent analyses of the GST (cited earlier) predicted that introduction of the GST at nine per cent would have generated an initial shock to the CPI of between two and three per cent. If this price level increase was a one-time event, consumer spending would have been reduced as a result of the lower real incomes, but the impact would have been relatively short-lived. The positive impacts of the change in the sales tax system would soon have overtaken the price level effects.

The uncertainty that entered this scenario revolved around the possible reactions of economic agents to the initial price level increase. For example, it was likely that labour unions would have attempted to recoup some of their lost real wages as a result of the price increase. Even in 1989 some unions were clearly indicating that they would be pursuing such a strategy. If these unions were to be even partially successful, the question is raised of the policy response to this increasing cost pressure. In particular, based on recent history, it would seem likely that the Bank of Canada would have sought to head off inflation resulting from these cost increases by raising the level of interest rates above what they otherwise would have been.

Higher interest rates would, in turn, have muted the positive impacts of the GST. For example, investment activity would have been reduced. In addition, the higher interest rates would have raised the exchange value of the Canadian dollar and the positive trade effects would also have been dampened or perhaps reversed. Finally, higher interest rates would have increased the federal government's budgetary deficit, and would probably have prompted some combination of spending cuts and higher taxes in response. In short, responses to the initial price shock could have created a chain of events that would have significantly delayed the positive effects of the tax reform.

In December 1989, when the Finance Minister announced the GST rate had been revised down to seven per cent, he removed most of this short term uncertainty. The initial price level impact of the GST at this lower rate will likely be in the neighbourhood of one per cent. The response of labour unions and other economic agents will probably be less, and the transition period correspondingly easier.

Visibility

A fourth issue of concern is the visibility of the new GST. As noted earlier, visible taxes are desirable because the accountability of governments to the electorate is presumably improved as a result. The initial promise accompanying the GST proposal in 1987 was that the new tax would be fully visible. That promise, in combination with the hoped-for national sales tax system (integrated federal and provincial), created the expectation that the federal tax would appear explicitly on consumers' sales receipts as is now the case with provincial sales taxes. The government did nothing to quash this expectation.

This version of visibility began to fall by the wayside in early 1989 when Ottawa announced the failure of negotiations with the provinces. (Reasons for this failure are suggested below.) Shortly thereafter, the government raised the question of whether it could compel retailers to collect the GST in the form of an addition to the sale price, and suggested that the tax would likely be embedded in the posted price of goods and services. Visibility would be maintained, it was argued, by placing a sign in all establishments stating that prices include the GST.

If visibility is taken to mean that consumers are aware not only of the existence of a tax, but also of the amount they are paying, the government has retreated substantially from its initial promise. The GST will still be more visible than the old MST because it will be applied uniformly across broad categories of goods and services, and therefore, tax liabilities will be easier to calculate for anyone inclined to do so. However, compared to the level of visibility originally expected, this outcome represents a clear retreat.

Administration

The administrative costs and complexity that the GST will impose on retail establishments are other areas of contention. Concern about administrative complexity, in large part, stems from the failure to co-ordinate collection with the provinces. The need to operate two sales tax systems simultaneously means that retailers, acting as tax collectors for two separate governments, will be required to manage two tax bases that are defined differently. The federal base will be the broader; provincial bases are largely subsets of the more extensive federal base. There will be many commodities that are taxable by one level of government (federal) and not by the other (provincial), and these differences will themselves vary from province to province. This complexity accounts for much of the opposition that has been directed towards the GST by the retail and small business interest groups.

Revenue Neutrality

Finally, in the White Paper of 1987, the government pledged that tax reform would be revenue neutral. That is, the reformed tax system was to raise no more revenue (net) than the old system. Clearly this objective has been abandoned as details of the GST emerged over the course of 1989. In the technical paper released by the Finance Department in August of that year, the first reason given for the reform of the sales tax system was to reduce the federal deficit.

The main reason for this shift was the fact that despite expenditure cutbacks that were politically very painful for the government, and despite increasing tax burdens (the MST was raised to 13.5 per cent in the April 1989 Budget, while in June 1987, when tax reform was launched, the rate was 12 per cent), the budgetary deficit did not decline during this period. Given the government's continuing and prominent concern with the deficit, the goal of generating more revenue that could be applied against the deficit was added to the original tax reform objective of reducing inefficiencies in the tax system.

During this period, the main factor that prevented the deficit from declining as the government had hoped (and forecast) was the failure of interest rates to decline. Indeed, they increased. Therefore, the cost of servicing the accumulated debt rose, offsetting any savings generated by spending restraint and tax increases.[15] It is beyond the scope of this chapter to discuss the Bank of Canada's high interest rate, anti-inflation policy. However, it is interesting to note how this policy, in combination with the government's focus on the deficit, resulted in a significant change in focus to its tax reform efforts. In particular, most of the earlier promised income tax offsets were abandoned. This change to a revenue-enhancing tax reform was another factor behind the political difficulties encountered over the GST.

TAX HARMONIZATION WITH THE PROVINCES

A significant part of the government's retreat from its original objectives in sales tax reform can be attributed to the failure to achieve a harmonized system with the provinces. While such an agreement may ultimately emerge, Ottawa broke off the negotiations in early 1989, presumably because the prospects for an agreement in time for 1991 implementation were poor. The reluctance of the provinces to enter into a sales tax agreement with Ottawa can be attributed to several factors.

Possibly the least significant reason for this is that an agreement with Ottawa would turn the provinces into tax collectors for the federal government. The agreement would presumably compensate the provinces financially for administrative costs, but not for the political costs. A combined federal-provincial sales tax would have resulted in tax rates greater than 12 per cent in most provinces. If consumers fail to distinguish between a provincial and federal portion of this tax, they might attribute it all to the collector (the province) and therefore direct their dissatisfaction completely to the province. In effect, the sales tax system would be the reverse of the existing income tax system. In all provinces except Quebec the federal government acts as the collector of the provincial personal income tax. The difference between the two systems is that the income tax forms clearly distinguish between the federal and provincial portions of the tax, but a combined sales tax could be less distinct, and therefore the possibility that the collector would "take the heat" is increased.

More seriously, a harmonized sales tax system would mean that the provinces would be required to include more goods and services in their tax bases to make them identical with that of the federal government. In this sense, federal-provincial co-ordination implies a certain degree of coercion. Provinces now define their own sales tax bases, and some provinces have used this power as a policy lever.[16] Quebec, for example, has designed its tax base to favour commodities manufactured in the province. Ontario has, from time to time, altered its base to achieve economic stabilization objectives. The determination of a joint tax base that is defined very broadly would limit strategies such as those pursued by Quebec, and would prevent individual provincial adjustments such as those used by Ontario.

The provinces would tend to view this cost as especially onerous because the sales tax is the largest revenue source that they control independently of Ottawa. If provincial treasurers are to be asked to cede this policy lever, they are likely to demand significant compensation in return. Presumably that compensation would be in the form of higher revenues from the new sales tax. Viewed in this way it would seem that the potential for eventual harmonization still remains. At the time of writing, in fact, several provinces had dropped "hints" that they would be willing to co-operate if suitable agreements were reached.

Closely related is the issue of how changes in the base would be determined. The provinces would be reluctant to enter into another agreement like the income tax agreement in which the federal government unilaterally controls the base. In the case of the income tax, provincial governments are often left in the position of having to adjust to revenue changes imposed upon them without notification by a decision in Ottawa to change the income tax base. They presumably would not wish to be in the same circumstance with respect to a national sales tax.

LESSONS FROM THE TAX REFORM EXPERIENCE

Relative to earlier tax reform attempts, implementing the Phase I income tax reform (which became effective in the 1988 taxation year) was relatively straightforward for the government and was quite clearly a political success. Strong opposition to the Phase I changes did not emerge, and the government's standing in the polls was not damaged by the tax reform exercise. In contrast, Phase II has proved to be politically contentious. Strong opposition is being mounted from a variety of interest groups in the economy, and informal evidence indicates that the GST is extremely unpopular among the general electorate. What accounts for the difference? In this section we discuss some of the key differences between the two reform exercises and the lessons to be learned from the GST initiative to date.

1.   Replacing an invisible tax with a less invisible tax is politically
        costly.

        The old MST is almost totally invisible. Few taxpayers are
aware that they are paying the tax. Fewer still have any real notion of
how much they are paying in the form of the MST. This is because the
base of the tax — what is taxed — is complicated and unclear. Some
commodities are taxed while very close substitute commodities are not.
The tax rate that is applicable varies; it is not the same for all taxed
commodities. Finally, because the tax is levied at an early stage in the
production chain, its total impact on the price of the goods is very
difficult to determine. One has to know something about the post-tax
stages in the production chain in order to be able to estimate the net
impact on price in any reliable fashion. To further complicate the
situation, on some goods such as imports, the tax is applied at a
different stage and therefore its overall impact on price is different.

        The GST, when it was originally proposed, was intended to be
highly visible, compared to the provincial sales taxes which are added
explicitly to sales invoices at the retail level. In a tax system such as
this, one can readily determine what is taxed, the rate of tax, and the
dollar cost of the tax to the taxpayer.

        The GST, as it is now proposed, will, with few exceptions, be
imposed at one rate on all taxable goods and services, and it will not
enter the mark-up policies of suppliers. While there will still be grey
areas in which close substitutes are sometimes taxed and sometimes
not, these ambiguities will be less prevalent than in the current tax.
Moreover, because the GST will apply to almost all goods and services
there will be less uncertainty and confusion over whether a particular
commodity is taxed. What has been withdrawn from the original plan,
and this is an important change, is the intention to have the tax shown
explicitly on the sales invoices at the retail level. At the retail level, the
tax will now be incorporated into the price of the commodity. Thus
while the GST is less visible than the government originally promised,
it is still more visible than the existing MST.

        The comparison that is now relevant is the replacement of an
almost completely invisible MST with a moderately visible (or
moderately invisible) GST. To at least some taxpayers this must appear
as the enactment of a completely new form of taxation rather than the
replacement of one type of commodity tax with another. The government thus appears to be engaged in a massive tax grab.

2.   Tax reform is almost always viewed by taxpayers as a zero-sum game and therefore the probability is high that reform will be highly contentious.

Taxpayers tend to view a tax in a static world. While they may contemplate their own behavioral response to a change in taxation, they seldom recognize the macro effects of similar responses occurring throughout the economy. Therefore, for example, it is very difficult for the government to sell a tax proposal in terms of its efficiency properties. The argument that the tax change will generate higher national output and income is difficult to sustain. People tend to see only the initial impact, that is, "How much more tax will I pay?" They are much less likely to recognize that their real incomes may change as a result of the tax change.

2a.   Corollary: Tax changes that are revenue enhancing are guaranteed to invite trouble.

Since taxpayers fail to recognize the dynamic growth effects of tax change, and see only winners and losers (with the gains and losses summing to zero), a revenue enhancing tax change sets the government up as the biggest winner. The other side of the coin, of course, is that taxpayers as a group see themselves emerging as net losers. A major part of the difficulty encountered by former Finance Minister Allan MacEachen in his ill-fated budget of 1981, was that about half of the revenue to be generated by the tax reforms he proposed was to be kept by the government rather than returned to taxpayers in the form of lower rates.

The GST proposal ran into similar trouble when it appeared that Finance Minister Michael Wilson was backing away from his initial pledge that the reform would be revenue neutral. When sales tax reform was initially proposed, the existing MST rate was several points lower than it is now. The pledge of revenue neutrality made at that time now sounds somewhat hollow, since the old tax rate has gone from 12 per cent at the time of the White Paper to 13.5 per cent currently.[17]

Further, the August 1989 technical paper on the GST begins with the statement that the "GST will contribute to the deficit reduction effort..." One cannot reduce the deficit with the new tax if it is fiscally neutral.

2b.   Corollary: It is important that the taxpayers who are the winners be politically influential.

If tax change is going to be viewed in terms of the competing interests of winners versus losers, it is important that the winners who will be on your side be politically more powerful than the losers. In the first phase of tax reform, which focussed on income taxes, the primary winners were high income earners. Indeed, the largest gainers were the top one per cent of the income earning households. Their support was important to the relative ease with which those reforms were enacted. With the GST (and the associated refundable credits) the only clear winners appear to be those at the lowest end of the income spectrum — those eligible for the full tax credits.[18] Virtually all other groups will pay more because the new GST is being used to raise substantially more revenue than the MST it replaces. As well, by taxing services the GST will apply to substantially more spending by upper income groups than did the old tax on manufactured goods.

It would appear, then, that the lower income beneficiaries of the shift to the GST (accompanied by the enriched tax credit) are less useful political allies than the upper income beneficiaries of the income tax reform.

2c.   Corollary: The risk of tax reform should only be taken on by a new government with a reservoir of good will (political capital) on which to draw.

The Mulroney government is nearing the completion of its sixth year in office. It is a government that has increased taxes several times and has undertaken a number of highly unpopular expenditure cuts. The GST proposal has, as a result, been something of a "lightning rod" for the grievances that have been building up against the government. The fact that the GST is somewhat revenue enhancing (Corollary 2a) and the wrong but apparently strong perception that it is almost all "new taxation" adds to this sense of grievance. In retrospect, perhaps both phases of tax reform should have been carried out at the same time while the government was still young.

3.   It is more difficult to convince all of the people when some of the people have the capacity to conduct independent analyses that are as credible as your own.

It is not that many years ago that the analyses and projections of the Department of Finance were accepted as data by most participants in taxation and budgetary debates. This "monopoly" conferred on the department enormous power. It meant that all critics were playing on the department's home field. The favoured position this created was not lost on the department. In the early 1970s the prestige of the Finance Department, its deputy and even its minister were put on the line in order to prevent the formation of a competing economic analysis unit in the Privy Council Office/Prime Minister's Office.

Over time this monopoly has been eroded, not from within the government but from the outside. Private research organizations, consulting firms, and even individual researchers with the aid of rapidly advancing computer technology, have been able to develop models to simulate and predict economic and fiscal variables. And they have developed track records which are as good as those of the Finance Department itself and, in some cases, better. The department's analyses no longer occupy a place of prominence, but are now taken as simply one of a group. Albeit they still represent the "official" data of the government, but in the media and in public debates the competing analyses of independent organizations are cited with equal authority.

In the GST debate, for example, it was the independent analyses that were largely responsible for calling attention to the transitional difficulties (discussed earlier) likely to accompany the GST's introduction at nine per cent. These problems, in turn, were at least one reason why the government amended its plans and dropped the initial rate to seven per cent.

4.   As a role model, New Zealand is a poor substitute for the United States.

The relevance to Canada of what happens in the U.S. is clear. Therefore there is a strong argument for tax consistency with the U.S., especially when it comes to the corporate and personal income taxes, because of the mobility of the tax bases. This factor was an important catalyst to the success of Phase I; the Minister of Finance was able to trade heavily on the argument that it was important to eliminate quickly some of the major discrepancies between the Canadian income tax system and the American system which had been reformed in 1986.

The government's case for the GST has suffered in comparison because of the absence of a similar catalyst. This is true in two senses. First, arguments for international comparability are inherently weaker with respect to consumption taxes than to income taxes because the base is less mobile internationally. That is, consumption spending tends to be diverted less to other countries in response to taxes than is income earning activity, especially capital investment. Secondly, the path taken by our major trading partner cannot be cited as a model in the case of the GST. The example cited most often in the GST debate has been the experience of New Zealand. That is simply not very convincing. New Zealand is not a major trading partner of Canada, it is of marginal significance to the Canadian economy, and most Canadians do not view the experience of New Zealand as being relevant to this country. It is of some interest to note, however, that the government has made very little use of the European experiences with value-added taxes (VAT) as a model for Canada.

CONCLUSION

The Goods and Services Tax, as currently structured, represents a retreat from some of the government's original proposals. In particular, the tax is only partially visible and the failure to achieve sales tax intregration with the provinces contributes to its complexity and administrative cost. Nevertheless, the GST still represents a substantial improvement over the MST that will be eliminated. The GST is more efficient; it will stimulate investment and exports, and it will make domestic products more competitive with imports.

With respect to distribution, the government has largely met its stated commitment to reducing tax burdens on lower income families, at least initially. However, the partial indexing of the GST Credit means that its real value will erode over time.

Perhaps the most significant aspect of the GST Credit is that it largely completes a structure that was begun in 1978 with the introduction of the Refundable Child Tax Credit. Should we wish to move in that direction, the administrative apparatus to deliver a Guaranteed Annual Income (GAI) by means of a Negative Income Tax (NIT) is now essentially in place. The system will include an anonymous/confidential eligibility determination (means test) based on the filing of an income tax return, benefits keyed to family size and to the ages of the children, provision included for single parent families, and a system for making frequent payments.

The point is not that an adequate GAI/NIT will exist (maximum benefits for a family with two children will initially be $2000-2500), but that the mechanism will be in place if some future government wishes to move in that direction. In fact, a future government could turn the prospect into reality simply by enriching benefits without ever raising the issue explicitly. In the 1970s it proved impossible to overcome the obstacles to a GAI/NIT when the federal and provincial governments tried to do so directly.[19] Perhaps it will be the "surprise" legacy of the GST.

Notes

1   Michael H. Wilson (Minister of Finance), *The White Paper: Tax Reform 1987*, June 18, 1987.

2   Allan M. Maslove, *Tax Reform in Canada: The Process and Impact* (Ottawa: Institute for Research on Public Policy, 1989).

3   To illustrate, if a $10 item is sold by a manufacturer to another producer, that item costs the purchaser $11.35 ($10.00 + $1.35 MST @ 13.5 per cent). Subsequently, when the second producer sells its product and applies the MST, tax is, in effect, levied on the tax already included in the cost of the input. Hence, we have "tax cascading." In the same way, MST can be hidden in consumer goods and services that are nominally tax exempt.

4   Report of the Royal Commission on Taxation, Volume 5 (Ottawa: Queen's Printer, 1966). It is interesting to note that the Commission's preferred reform of the sales tax system was very similar to the proposed GST (including the refundable credits). The only reason this scheme was not formally recommended was that the technology did not exist at that time to administer the refundable credits efficiently and confidentially.

5   A tax of this type would essentially eliminate all the administrative complications that have arisen over the GST. A general consumption tax could be administered through the existing income tax system, could have a progressive rate schedule, and would tax all consumption. The major administrative problem this creates is the need to value assets on an annual basis.

6   The major exception to this statement was an announcement by the Minister of Finance in 1987 that food purchased for home consumption would not be subject to the new sales tax.

7   This was not reported by the government itself, but was roughly the average estimated by several independent macroeconomic forecasts including those of The Conference Board of Canada, the Economic Council of Canada, Informetrica Limited, the Institute for Policy Analysis at the University of Toronto, and the WEFA Group.

8   Minister of Finance, *Goods and Services Tax Technical Paper*, August 1989.

9   The Standing Committee on Finance, *Report on the Technical Paper on the Goods and Services Tax*, November 1989.

10   Minister of Finance, *Goods and Services Tax*, December 19, 1989.

11   See note 7 above.

12   There are exceptions to this general rule. For example, we may wish to use a tax strategically to influence (distort) decisions. In the case of the sales tax, higher than normal rates of tax on tobacco and alcohol may be deliberately intended to restrain consumption of these products.

13   This effect is actually less marked than it would have been had the government been able to implement its original plan. The continuation (and for some, the increase) of the income surtaxes and the elimination of the reduction of the middle tax rate, considerably reduce the extent of the shift between income-based and consumption-based taxes.

14   One of the design features of the credit has drawn criticism for its apparent "perversity." Single adults maintaining their own households can claim an additional credit of up to $100 providing their net income is greater than $6,169. The credit increases at the rate of two per cent of income in excess of that threshold, reaching its maximum value when income is $11,169. The intent is to target this credit to individuals maintaining their own household and not dependent on others for support. However, the phasing in of the full $100 credit does introduce an "upside-down" element to the redistributive intent.

15   The government's fiscal restraint policies were sufficiently biting to produce a primary budget surplus by the 1989-90 fiscal year. This means that revenues were greater than program expenditures.

16   See Allan M. Maslove (ed.), *Budgeting in the Provinces: Leadership and the Premiers* (Toronto: Institute of Public Administration of Canada, 1989).

17   In 1984 when the Conservative government was first elected, the basic MST rate was nine per cent.

18   The Finance Department's documents state that families with incomes under $30,000 will be better off with the GST. Independent studies that have addressed the issue of distribution support this claim.

19   See R. Van Loon, "Reforming Welfare in Canada," *Public Policy*, v. 27, no. 4, Fall 1979, pp. 469-504.

CHAPTER 3

THE DEPARTMENT OF INDUSTRY, SCIENCE AND TECHNOLOGY: IS THERE INDUSTRIAL POLICY AFTER FREE TRADE?

G. Bruce Doern

Résumé

Dans ce chapitre on explore le mandat et les activités d'Industrie, Sciences et Technologie Canada, en examinant trois questions. Premièrement, l'article demande si l'accord sur le libre-échange représente la véritable politique industrielle des conservateurs, ou si une forme de politique d'industries cibles sera essentielle. On soutient que les conservateurs se verront probablement forcés par les événements de développer une forme quelconque de politique industrielle réactive et axée sur certaines entreprises clefs. Au début, cela pourrait survenir si des compagnies canadiennes clefs passaient aux mains d'étrangers. Une politique industrielle active sera sans doute nécessaire également, malgré la difficulté reconnue qu'il y a de concevoir de telles actions sur des industries cibles dans le milieu institutionnel actuel.

Ce chapitre explore également la question à savoir si on peut faire d'ISTC une entité cohérente où seraient abordées les nouvelles interdépendances entre la technologie et la compétitivité. On en conclut qu'ISTC donne une certaine espérance. Il n'en reste pas moins que la marge de manoeuvre d'ISTC est limitée à cause du manque de fonds, même si elle préfère compter sur le savoir et les services plutôt que sur les subventions industrielles.

Troisièmement, on demande si ISTC dispose de certaines as-
sises institutionnelles fondamentales lui permettant de réaliser son
mandat global actuel, sans parler d'un programme comprenant des
politiques industrielles réactives ou actives. On tire la conclusion qu'il
manque à ISTC une continuité dans sa direction au niveau ministériel
et bureaucratique qui lui permettrait d'être une vedette du gouvernement. En outre, on soutient que le gouvernement devra trouver les
moyens de développer des institutions élaborant des politiques qui
s'occupent d'entreprises clefs plutôt que de simples groupes d'intérêt
représentant des secteurs industriels.

In the midst of the free trade negotiations in 1987, the Mulroney
government announced the formation of a department to be called
Industry, Science and Technology Canada (ISTC). Formed out of a
merger between the non-regional remnants of the Department of
Regional Industrial Expansion (DRIE) and the Ministry of State for
Science and Technology (MOSST), the new department was hailed by
the Tories as Canada's "flagship" department of the microeconomy.[1] It
would meld, as its name implies, industrial with science and technology
policies. What the Department of Finance is to macroeconomic policy,
ISTC would hopefully be to microeconomic policy.

This chapter explores the mandate and early activities of ISTC
by focussing on three questions. First, we ask whether the Free Trade
Agreement is the Tories' real industrial policy, or is some form of
targeted industrial policy going to be essential, whether the Conservatives want it or not or whether they choose to call it that or not? With
respect to this first question, we argue that the Conservatives will likely
be compelled by events to develop some form of firm-specific **reactive**
industrial policy. Initially, this could arise from foreign takeovers of
key Canadian firms. An **active** industrial policy will probably also be
necessary despite the acknowledged difficulty of devising such targetted actions in the current institutional milieu.

Second, we ask whether the conflicting cultures, habits, and
priorities of the old DRIE and MOSST can be forged into a coherent
entity in which the new interdependencies between technology and
competitiveness are actually addressed. On this point, the chapter
concludes that ISTC exhibits some promise. However, we also conclude that despite its preference for a greater reliance on knowledge
and services rather than industrial grants, ISTC is still limited in what
it can do because of the absence of enough money.

The third question asked is whether ISTC possesses some of the basic institutional underpinnings needed to carry out its current overall mandate, let alone one with either reactive or active industrial policies. We conclude on this point that it lacks the continuity of ministerial and bureaucratic leadership to be Ottawa's flagship. In addition, we argue that ISTC must find ways to develop policy institutions capable of dealing with key firms, rather than just sectoral industrial interest groups.

The analysis proceeds in three steps. First, we outline the ISTC mandate. The second step consists of a capsule historical review of the three policy trails — science policy, trade policy and industrial policy — which converge to form the new mandate. Finally, we look at the mandate in action over its early years of operation.

ISTC OBJECTIVES AND MANDATE

The objectives and mandate of ISTC were set out in 1988 by its then minister, Robert de Cotret, as follows:

°   to promote international competitiveness and industrial excellence in Canada;

°   to renew and expand Canada's scientific, technological, managerial and production base;

°   to bring together in a concerted way the talents of Canadians to guarantee Canada's place in the first rank of industrial and commercial nations in the twenty-first century; and

°   to act as a reasoned advocate for sound industrial and technological development through its influence on the policies of other government departments and agencies where they affect the environment for business development in Canada.[2]

In various consultations with business and in statements to Parliamentary committees, ISTC officials spelled out other key working assumptions regarding the reasons for the new mandate and how it would affect the culture of the new department.[3] These assumptions were that:

°   Industrial progress was now more dependent on scientific, technological and managerial adaptability and responsiveness than on earlier bases such as abundant natural resources and ready access to markets.

° International competition was no longer coming just from other western countries and newly industrialized countries, but was coming from less developed countries as well.

° Canadians had to face the reality of a materials revolution. This referred to the replacement of traditional production materials, which Canada has in abundance, with new materials including optic fibres for copper, and plastics and ceramics for wood and metal products.

° Compared to the departments that preceded it, ISTC would have to "shift away from trying to be all things to all people, away from trying to address every industrial problem with some kind of financial assistance package."[4]

° ISTC activities would have to be consistent with international trade obligations to reduce the prospect of countervail.

° ISTC would have to strengthen and give far more emphasis to enhancing its information and expertise about markets and innovative technological activities. It would greatly de-emphasize funded programs and would instead supply a program and service mix focussing on the "upstream" end of the production cycle in advance of manufacturing.

° Only those existing programs with a proven record of achievement in developing greater sophistication in Canadian industry would continue. These include programs such as the Defence Industry Productivity Program and the Technology Outreach Program.

This mandate and set of assumptions were indeed different from those which had ostensibly driven ISTC's predecessor departments.

On October 28, 1988 Prime Minister Mulroney announced what were described as the "cornerstone programs" of ISTC. Three programs were announced — strategic technologies, sector competitiveness initiatives, and business information and development services. Some $400 million was to be allocated during the next four years to these programs, about half going to strategic technologies. In outlining the details of these programs, ISTC Minister Robert de Cotret stressed their differences from previous DRIE programs. What he did not stress was that these resources are still dwarfed by the larger budgets under the control of the two regional industrial agencies hived-off from ISTC — the Atlantic Canada Opportunities Agency (ACOA) and the Western Diversification Department (WD).

The strategic technologies program would involve information technology, biotechnology, and advanced materials (the last of these is discussed further below). In the process of helping industry develop, acquire or supply these technologies, de Cotret stressed that firms "will be encouraged to make alliances and create networks, thereby sharing the costs and risks."[5] The sectoral competitiveness initiatives would develop individually tailored action plans to assist sectors to become more internationally competitive. These could range from "export promotion drives, selective investment promotion, and technology applications for new and enhanced products."[6]

The new programs were a "fundamental break from the past" because, in de Cotret's words, "traditionally government industrial assistance has concentrated on the production portion of the continuum" of business activity.[7] ISTC's new programs would spread resources more evenly "along the continuum from science to marketing." These statements certainly suggest a change in emphasis but they do not tell us concretely whether the focus will be on service provision or on actual research and development.

It is clear from this first brief look at the ISTC mandate and its cornerstone programs that it indeed has a new mandate. But before proceeding to our assessment of the mandate, we need to have more of a sense of how three policy trails—science policy, trade policy and industrial policy—have converged to form the ITSC mandate and organizational culture.

THREE POLICY TRAILS TO THE ISTC MANDATE

Science Policy

The first policy trail concerns science policy. More specifically, it involves the former Ministry of State for Science and Technology (MOSST). Formed in 1971, MOSST had valiantly but unsuccessfully carried the banner of science policy.[8] It suffered from the "minister a year" syndrome but its lack of impact arose primarily from its lack of any program clout and from successive governments which were interested in science rhetorically for its "announcement effect" but not in actual practice. Its ministers routinely promised that Canada's research and development (R&D) spending as a percentage of Gross National Product (GNP) would be increased. As expenditure restraint took hold for most of the 1980s, federal science budgets were reduced in real dollar terms. In 1989-90 it was 3.5 per cent of federal spending, compared to 3.9 per cent in 1980-81.[9] MOSST also sought to ensure that other federal R&D departments and agencies contracted out their R&D activities. Canada was unique among Western countries in that the largest part of its R&D activity was carried out by government rather than by industry. From its earliest days, MOSST tried to reverse this situation. But it had little leverage over the line departments and certainly no real responsibility for determining the federal science budget. MOSST had also tried to come to grips with federal funding of academic research through federal granting bodies such as the Social Science and Humanities Research Council (SSHRC) and the Natural Sciences and Engineering Research Council (NSERC). It had some success on this front in the mid-1980s when it secured a new five-year budget framework that included new opportunities for matching private and public funding.

MOSST spent much of its time exhorting but few people in the Ottawa labyrinth were listening. Even though many of its essential arguments were those of favouring markets to increase industrial innovation and product development, it was not seen in Ottawa as an economic department. Rather it was seen as being composed of earnest "science" types.

In the last days of the Trudeau Liberal government, serious consideration was given to ending MOSST's existence. But MOSST was given a new lease on life in the early months of the Mulroney government. Several events and pressures contributed to its revival in the 1984-86 period. First, Prime Minister Mulroney had given great emphasis to "high technology" in the 1984 election campaign and had promised to increase Canada's committment to R&D to 2.5 per cent of GNP, virtually double its 1984 rate. His chief policy advisor in the Prime Minister's Office (PMO), Charles MacMillan, was a key impetus for this focus. He was an academic with expertise on Japan and on industrial organization. The Mulroney government's first science minister, Thomas Siddon, was himself a scientist and therefore was the first science minister with any kind of a technical background. A further catalyst in the MOSST revival was the work of the Nielsen Task Force on Program Review. It uncovered several areas where R&D program co-ordination was lacking. By co-ordination, the Nielsen group did not mean efforts to promote a co-ordinated industrial R&D policy. Rather, it meant that there was duplication and overlap. As a result the Cabinet started asking MOSST to take the lead in dealing with these items. These included areas such as Canada's space program, science sub-agreements with the provinces and international science agreements. MOSST was also given a budget review role. This occurred because, with a huge federal deficit, it was realized that the promised new money for science would have to come, in part, from the base of existing departmental R&D spending.

For the first time in its history MOSST was given a formal written mandate by the Prime Minister that was communicated by him to other departments. This included, in addition to the items above, responsibility for developing a consultation exercise and a national science and technology strategy. Among other things, the consultation exercise with the provinces, industry and the technical community showed the need for high level political recognition of the importance of science and technology. One result of this was the establishment in 1986 of the National Advisory Board for Science and Technology (NABST), chaired by the Prime Minister.

Thus, by the time of ISTC's formation in 1987, MOSST had enjoyed a brief burst of influence. Its views were also eventually aided by two further external voices and pressures. One came from the Wright Report which stressed how critical it was for Canada to ensure that technology transfer occur and that both government and university laboratories be made more relevant to actual commercial product development.[10] A second came from an increasingly mobilized science and technology lobby. Centred especially in the Canadian Advanced Technology Association (CATA), a lobby group dominated by smaller Canadian high technology firms, MOSST had for the first time some semblance of a supportive and organized policy community. The concerns of this lobby were given extra impetus in the first Conservative budget. The 1985 budget announced that the former Liberal government's Scientific Research Tax Credit (SRTC) was being abolished. It had resulted in a billion dollar bleeding of the federal treasury due to unforeseen loopholes in the scheme. A substitute R&D refundable tax credit would be offered to Canadian firms but the CATA-led lobby was pressuring several key ministers to ensure that the government's promise of increased R&D support was honoured. A further vehicle for industrial pressure was that MOSST had a small advisory panel which met regularly with the minister. It included Walter Light who was just ending his term as chief executive officer of Northern Telecom, the firm which alone does over one quarter of Canada's industrial R&D.

Trade Policy

The trade policy trail had three main implications for ISTC. The first was that ISTC retained a vital role as a trade policy advisor. This was part of its necessary horizontal or "reasoned advocate" role; but paradoxically, it lacked trade expertise. This is because, in the 1982 reorganization which had lead to the formation of DRIE, the trade function, primarily the Trade Commissioner Service, had been transferred to the Department of External Affairs.[11] For most of the post-war period, Canadian trade policy had been made through a triumvirate of departments, Trade and Commerce (under its various departmental names), Finance, and External Affairs. The trade function had been transferred to External Affairs in 1982 in part out of a desire to bring trade policy, especially regarding the Canada-U.S. relationship, to the forefront of foreign policy.

For ISTC, a trade policy advisory role, advising External Affairs and the Cabinet, is now even more essential. But it must obtain most of its expertise at "arms-length" from another department rather than as a normal part of its internal intelligence activities. ISTC has some good trade experts but it has basically had to find new ways of developing a critical mass of expertise in the trade policy field.

The second impact of the 1980s trade policy trail on the ISTC mandate stems from the historic Canada-U.S. Free Trade Agreement (FTA). It represents a policy on the part of the Conservative government which says, in effect, that free trade policy is its industrial policy. The free trade initiative was built (partly with the aid of the Macdonald Royal Commission) on the proposition that Canada's manufacturing sector faced a serious productivity gap that could only be addressed by the cold shower of being exposed to full competition and by obtaining more secure access to its biggest market, the United States.[12]

A third element of trade policy with important implications for the ISTC role is the lingering fear, only partly addressed in the FTA, that many Canadian industrial policy actions used in the past will be subject to countervail challenges under American trade law on the grounds that they are trade distorting subsidies.[13] While the FTA mandates a new second round of negotiations over a five to seven year period to obtain a subsidies agreement and hence reduce or eliminate countervail threats, its impact is already clear in the ISTC mandate.

This impact is found in the way in which ISTC defines its mandate as being (a) more service- and knowledge-oriented rather than grants-oriented, (b) focussed on the front end or "pre-competition" or pre-production stage, and (c) non-firm-specific. All of these emphases in the new mandate are intended to increase the probability that federal actions will not be subject to successful countervail action. These trends were further accentuated in the 1990 Budget Speech when the government indicated that all of its grants to business would be changed to repayable loans.

Industrial Policy

While a journey through the first two policy trails is essential to any understanding of the genesis and content of the ISTC mandate, not all of the mandate can be attributed either to "high tech" worries or to the FTA juggernaut. A third partially independent industrial and regional policy trail is also embedded in the ISTC mandate set by the Conservatives.

Over their first three years in office it became clear that the Conservatives, by dint of both ideology and experience, subscribed to the adage that no industrial policy was the best economic policy.[14] This stance emerged gradually but unmistakably in a series of actions and statements. The Conservative's autumn 1984 economic renewal statement set a general pro-market tone. It stressed the importance of getting the basic framework policies right (e.g. taxation, deficit reduction, education and training, general R&D incentives). Prime Minister Mulroney's speeches declaring Canada "open for business" and the conversion of the Foreign Investment Review Agency (FIRA) into Investment Canada with its reduced screening role marked a 180 degree turn from previous Liberal policy. The Nielsen Task Force studies on industrial incentives, combined with the Macdonald Royal Commission critique of past failed industrial policies, were among the reasons for the Conservative decision to gradually reduce the use of grants and to move towards a more knowledge- and service-oriented approach to assisting business. The severe federal deficit also made it easier to conclude that grants or the spending approach was increasingly a non-starter in Tory Ottawa.

In addition, the decisions to establish the two main regional policy agencies, ACOA and WD, were partly driven by long-term frustrations with how regional decisions were made and with the fact that they were made in Ottawa rather than in Atlantic Canada and Western Canada. The formation of the Western Diversification Department in particular reflected the fact that the Mulroney Cabinet had more Western ministers in senior Cabinet positions than any federal government since the 1930s. At the same time, however, the need to ensure that the new ISTC was not overwhelmingly politicized by Canadian regional pressures was also a part of the calculus of reorganization and of policy. In short, the government was convinced that ISTC had to be less concerned with regional issues so that it could give its undivided attention to issues of international competitiveness and technology.

But also lurking in the subconscious of at least some federal industrial policy advisors was the debate concerning the efficacy of industrial policy over the previous two decades. A good place to begin an appreciation of the recent phases of this debate is with the internal deliberations of the Macdonald Royal Commission. One of the Commission's studies that received the most discussion by the commissioners was done by Richard Harris, an economist from Queen's University.[15] The Harris study supported the concept of free trade but also argued that there was a good **economic** case for the practice of an active targetted industrial policy and that such an industrial policy was especially necessary for small open trading nations such as Canada. In simplified form, the argument is as follows.

The standard theory of international trade is based on the concept of comparative advantage. But this theory assumes that all countries have access to identical technologies. Moreover, it assumes that factors of production are immobile internationally but mobile domestically among sectors of the economy. But as Harris pointed out in his review of research on both trade and industrial organizations, countries do not possess identical technologies and therefore differences in the diffusion of technologies are a significant determinant of trade patterns. Technologies were in this sense public goods and therefore there was a good rationale for governments to help "shape comparative advantage."[16]

But thus far, this was an argument only for broad framework policies. The more specific economic case for **firm-** or **sector-specific** policies — in other words for real industrial policy — resided in the notion that some product development cycles were characterized by both increasing returns to scale and imperfect competition. Therefore, in theory, a case exists for government to help capture some of these greater gains from trade (an active industrial policy) or to prevent a country from losing out entirely (a reactive industrial policy).

The Harris position advocating an industrial policy as a complement to free trade was essentially rejected on several grounds by a large majority of Macdonald Royal Commission members. First, other commission research studies by economists pointed out that the capturing of these theoretical gains was problematical at best for most countries.[17] This was because many countries would practice similar policies and potentially compete away any possible gains. The corollary to this view, which was given short shrift in the economics research, is that countries that fail to engage themselves at all face the danger of losing out entirely. The economics research was also extremely skeptical about the technical capacity of government, and its slow politicized speed of response, to actually fashion the right mix of policy instruments and to deliver **and withdraw** them on time.

In contrast to the economics research for the Macdonald Royal Commission which advised, in essence, that the federal government should stick to good framework economic policies and avoid industrial policy making, the research by the Commission's political scientists tended implicitly to be more supportive of industrial policies.[18] But this support was not couched in some active "here's how to do it" sense. Rather, it came in the form of saying that industrial policy of some kind is politically inevitable. Moreover, this research tended to suggest that the past array of policies was not all that wasteful if one took into account the complex interplay of interests, a wider range of political values than just efficiency and Canada's regional realities. The research on the politics of industrial policy also tolerated a much wider definition of industrial policy. It could at times include just about anything that government did that influenced, directly or indirectly, sectors or firms. This looseness, plus its lack of prescriptive content, made it susceptible to attack.

But the question remains, despite the increased skepticism about the capacity to practice industrial policy, and despite the fulsome preference for free trade, whether there is or ought to be room for an industrial policy, active or reactive, as a complement to the FTA and to trade liberalization in general. The industrial policy trail at the point of ISTC's establishment seems to point unambiguously to the demise of industrial policy, to reliance on free trade, and to the desire to hive-off and perhaps reduce regional policy considerations. But there remains the nagging doubt about whether an industrial policy is needed, a point which we explore further in the next section. There are also doubts about how much one can "de-regionalize" industrial policy.

The three policy trails surveyed briefly in this section all converge in the policy and organizational crossroads of ISTC and generate directly and indirectly the three questions which we now pose to help us assess the ISTC mandate in action. We stress immediately that this approach does not give us a complete picture of what ISTC does. ISTC is also a diverse organization with numerous field offices and with other program responsibilities such as tourism and small business entrepreneurship, which we do not examine.[19]

THE ISTC MANDATE IN ACTION

Will There Or Should There Be Industrial Policy After Free Trade?

The first question to be posed about the ISTC mandate is whether in fact an industrial policy—defined as targeted measures aimed at key firms and sectors—is emerging or is likely to emerge as a complement to free trade. The way the ISTC mandate has been expressed would certainly indicate that the Conservatives want no part of an industrial policy—even an industrial strategy defined in terms of mega-project spin-offs as the Liberals espoused in 1981. But just what is emerging requires a need to explore more fully the distinctions between an active and reactive industrial policy.

An active industrial policy refers in essence to the Harris proposition examined earlier, where a co-ordinated array of instruments is targeted at key firms or sectors with a view to assisting particular new or innovative products in penetrating foreign markets and capturing some of the rents that theoretically exist. This requires a high level of product and technological knowledge, as well as marketing and financial co-ordination. It assumes a sophisticated shared effort between a core of experts in ISTC (or elsewhere in the government) and the firm or firms involved. In short, it requires a level of political-technical-entrepreneurial capacity and cohesion that simply does not exist and certainly has not been tried in Canada. In this sense, the Conservatives are right in eschewing an active industrial policy. ISTC may well aspire to be a more strategic knowledge-based department but it clearly lacks any semblance of the political requisites for such positive ventures.

The political requisites here are at least two-fold in nature. The first is cohesion and capacity defined in terms of ministerial and senior official cohesion in alliance with other key centres of power in the government. The second is a capacity to bring key firms and key elements of its interest group structure into a supportive alliance for any ISTC policies or actions. As Atkinson and Coleman have shown, this latter capacity is also rudimentary at best—not just because it is difficult to do but because the Canadian political system, with its strong regional pressures and jealousies, does not produce enough sustained consensus.[20]

But even if these conditions were met, there is still the practical task, technically and entrepreneurially, of picking the right products or product lines and niches to support. This is difficult for single firms to do, and is even more difficult when a government entity is involved especially if it, in turn, cannot act as a single economically **and** politically purposeful player. All of this lends credence to the Conservative's basic instinct not to try active industrial policies of this kind. ISTC is pursuing several sectoral initiatives but these are much more general service-oriented activities geared to the front end of the innovation-production cycle. They are certainly not targeted to key firms.

What then can be said about ISTC and a so-called reactive industrial policy? Pressures for such policies and actions could easily arise in response to future foreign takeovers of Canadian firms. The question here is what policy would ISTC and its Minister, in collaboration with Investment Canada, have if any one of the following firms were taken over: Northern Telecom? Bombardier? Canadian Pacific? These firms are picked for illustrative purposes because they span different kinds of industries and regional/political coalitions of interest. Northern Telecom is a Canadian high tech communications firm centred in Ontario but with much of its production already spreading to the U.S. Bombardier is a world-class transportation and manufacturing company with a power base closely linked to Quebec. Canadian Pacific is a mature "heritage" Canadian firm whose takeover would create a public outcry.

The 1989 travails over the takeover of Connaught BioSciences is a possible precursor of the policy difficulties ahead. But the difficulty of the above examples would be magnified several-fold, politically and economically, compared to the Connaught case.[21] The Free Trade Agreement gradually raises the threshold level at which takeovers can be screened but all of the above firms would still fall within the screening process threshold. The test of "net benefit" to Canada would be undertaken by Investment Canada but such a test in no way addresses the issues inherent in the type of argument made by Harris. Part of that argument stresses as well that industrial policy may be needed to prevent Canada from being shut out entirely from different key technological products since these are the ones that help produce future high wage industries.

Thus, the industrial policy aspect of the ISTC mandate suggests a kind of cruel dilemma. On balance, economic evidence suggests that the Tories are, in many important ways, probably correct under present circumstances not to attempt an active industrial policy for the reasons already discussed. But they will probably need at a minimum, a reactive firm-specific industrial policy whether they like it or not and whether they choose to call it that or not.

Is A New Technology-Industry Policy Culture Emerging In ISTC?

The second question to be posed about the ISTC mandate in action is whether the old MOSST-DRIE cultures can be merged to yield a better marriage between science and technology and Canada's industrial competitiveness. Along this dimension there are some glimmers of desirable change in evidence. But they are the types of change that, if they bear fruit, are unlikely to do so in the short run. There are other policy changes, however, where only good old-fashioned hard dollars will supply evidence of some policy action and success. An example of the first policy change is found in efforts to produce a new awareness and expanded use of advanced materials. An example of the second is the failed effort to secure new resources for meeting the goal of increasing R&D spending in the economy to achieve the often sought goal of 2.5 per cent of GNP. Both examples will be looked at briefly for illustrative purposes.

One of the three strategic technologies emphasized in the strategic technologies program was advanced industrial materials, referred to earlier. Advanced materials are generally defined as metals, alloys, ceramics, polymers and composites that exhibit markedly superior properties and performance characteristics over those materials that are more commonly in use.[22] The field also encompasses related processing and testing technologies. Such materials are used in a wide variety of industries including aircraft, sporting goods, automotive, mining equipment, computers, construction, packaging and communications. Traditional materials such as wood, copper, zinc, and steel are being rapidly supplanted by these advanced substitutes.

The impetus for technological change is coming increasingly from engineers and designers at the user end of the product cycle. In this process, integration and networking are the watchwords as links among product designers, manufacturers, materials experts and others concerned with product performance grow stronger.

From a policy perspective, however, the notion of advanced materials was problematical. They were more a concept than an identifiable policy category. They did not represent a discrete industrial sector but rather a generic family of processes and products that underlie the performance of most or all industrial sectors. But there were individuals in MOSST and DRIE who were concerned about their vital central importance to the competitiveness of the Canadian economy. Moreover, they were both a benefit to the Canadian economy and a threat to the traditional Canadian materials industry including minerals and metals such as nickel, copper, and steel.

In the past, Canada's industrial policy could in some sense be said to focus on materials as **outputs** for the traditional materials industry. The demand side was not entirely ignored but it was secondary. The new realities were forcing a focus on materials as **inputs** for manufacturing. This was already being recognized in the 1980s in other countries such as Japan and West Germany which had mounted strategic development programs in advanced materials.

How then does this case reflect the need for merged MOSST and DRIE cultures in policy thinking and organization? First, the need arises because neither of the previous organizations was structurally geared to think and make policy in ways that conformed to the practical realities of the advanced materials phenomenon. MOSST was organized primarily by institutional sector, namely, business, government, and universities. It also tended to think routinely in terms of the basic research, applied research and development continuum. DRIE, at its core, was organized by producer or vertical industrial sector rather than horizontally by users or cross-sector categories. Both these historic ways of thinking made overall sense in terms of past developments. But they did not coincide with the policy serendipity compelled by the advanced materials issue.

A second reason for a new policy culture arose from the need for greater actual technical knowledge. Initial thinking about the materials issue began with a small group of officials in MOSST but with some allies in DRIE as well. But the MOSST "system" was, relatively speaking, much more accustomed to dealing with aggregate R&D budgets and the like rather than with decisions in specific technical areas. The materials case, however, was technically specific. It required technical understanding. But at the same time, because it addressed a few general materials which were little understood and even exotic, it also sounded very much to those at the top that its advocates were arguing for a "picking winners" approach. In short, in Tory eyes, they were arguing for a now discredited "industrial policy", even though it was the exact opposite of a sector-specific policy.

A third feature illustrated by the case is the need for new approaches to the basic question of how to develop and deal with a suitable interest group clientele. It was not easy to obtain even a rough profile of this constituency. At one point about 400 to 500 conventional and 50 "new" material suppliers were identified. So were about 30 firms engaged in fabrication and another 50 user corporations or entities. In addition, eight associations, 12 universities, and nine provincial bodies were approached. As a strategy for materials was attempted, ISTC officials found themselves in the business of virtually forging new interest group associations to bridge the new producer-user melange of interests. Many corporate executives had to be educated about the new materials. Others were aware of them. But networks had to be painstakingly built.

While this type of technology and industry initiative was "bubbling up" from below, with both MOSST-types and DRIE-types involved in their own alliance building, initiatives also were launched higher up. A diffused high technology package of about $3.2 billion was proposed. It eventually produced a $1.3 billion program that the Prime Minister announced in 1987 along with the establishment of ISTC and NABST. Eventually, those pressing for an advanced materials strategy were able to garner about $60 million for this initiative.

At present it is still difficult to say exactly what the advanced materials strategy is. It does involve a great deal of networking and talking and hence is illustrative of part of the new ISTC mandate. It does involve some money but not for the old-style grants purposes. It is not sector-specific but some sectors may well benefit far more than others. If it works, it will yield quiet imperceptible benefits across sectors. If it fails, Canadians may not notice or will apportion blame elsewhere. This is without doubt one part of the new slogging world of thankless but necessary "industry, science and technology" policy making and implementation. More activities like it are underway in the ISTC but they will be difficult to evaluate.

Contrast this realm of the mandate with the second example of Tory hopes for ISTC, namely the Mulroney target of 2.5 per cent of GNP for R&D spending. Mulroney is not the first to succumb to the rhetorically seductive allure of R&D dollar targets. But juxtaposed against the Tories' battle against the budget deficit, this promise of the new ISTC mandate in action was doomed from the beginning. In any event, it is not one whose success or failure could ever be accurately attributed to ISTC only.

With respect to science and technology budgets, the Tories have both "given at the office" and exacted blood money from others. Some new money was found for a space agency but largely at the expense of other government labs. The research budgets of the National Research Council (NRC) and Environment Canada were cut but the aforementioned $1.3 billion (to be spent over five years) was found in the nooks and crannies of the federal budgetary mattress. The infamous Liberal SRTC tax break was leached from the system to be replaced by a much smaller and more carefully audited refundable scientific research and development tax credit.

Some of the above could be seen as good evidence of a more concerted science budget review role being played, especially since the "A Base" of the R&D budget was under attack, arguably for the first time. But this would be far too generous an interpretation, given the serendipitous nature of many of the actual dynamics behind these various gains and takeaways. The net result is that the needed increase in resources as a percentage of GNP, whether supplied by government or induced from the private sector is nowhere in evidence. In this case whether ISTC's new melded culture is forming does not matter much. The key is more direct spending and/or tax breaks but the Conservatives are reluctant, in this realm, to go beyond rhetorical policy making.

Data from 1987 are the latest available, and show that Canada spent 1.35 per cent of its gross domestic product on research and development. This compares with 2.69 per cent in the United States, 2.86 per cent in Japan, and 2.82 per cent in Sweden. Moreover, the federal share of R&D funded by the federal government has been reduced since 1984 from 35 per cent to 31 per cent.[23]

The Gap In ISTC Institutional Policy Capacity

In the evaluation of public policy there is usually far too little attention paid to the necessary institutional underpinnings. Too often, inherent institutional capacity is viewed as something separate from policy. Whatever one makes of the ISTC mandate in the 1990s era of free trade and globalization, some gaps in ISTC's inherent capacity seem quite evident. This is true whether or not one believes that an active or reactive industrial policy will be or should be a necessary complement to the FTA. How to characterize these gaps is not easy but at least two gaps seem evident to this author, especially in light of the difficult knowledge-based role to which ISTC must increasingly hitch its political star. These include Cabinet-level continuity and the problem of how to deal with key firms.

As Benoit Bouchard, the current ISTC Minister, contemplates the 1990s, the daunting mandate under his charge must be carried out in the light of three restrictions on Cabinet level continuity and capacity. First, he is Ottawa's ninth industry minister since 1982. The game of ministerial musical chairs has resulted in there being, on average, one minister per year. This is hardly conducive to "flagship" status. During this same period there have also been seven deputy ministers. Both of these positional issues take on new importance because the mandate implies that the ISTC Minister should have some permanence and staying power, much like Michael Wilson has had in

Finance. The new mandate implies the need to arrest the serious loss of prestige that the industry department suffered during the 1980s.

The second feature of Cabinet influence is that of determining how precisely ISTC can "spend less and talk more" and still have influence. How, in short, can it wean itself from its instinct for grantsmanship, become unambiguously a knowledge-based department and still have clout? This difficult task is not only essential for its internal advocacy role in Ottawa but also for how it builds its credibility with its industrial and scientific clientele. Since ISTC no longer brings as much money to the table, will anyone want to listen? The odds are stacked against this reliance on a non-money base of power.

A third closely related Cabinet reality is whether ISTC can in some practical sense shed some of its regional residues. With the formation of the Atlantic Canada Opportunities Agency (ACOA) and the Western Diversification Department (WD) in 1987, ISTC is, in theory, shorn of regional responsibilities.[24] If it has regional roles it is now as the "department for Ontario and Quebec." But ACOA and WD are agencies that do have more discretionary money than ISTC. Hence their strong regional pressures and demands on ISTC are not ended, but are merely relocated. Moreover, the Cabinet is still populated primarily by ministers whose instinct is overwhelmingly regional in nature. The majority of ministers tend not to think, let alone act, according to the dictates of criteria such as "international competitiveness."

For these reasons either the Mulroney government or a future prime minister elected in 1992 will have to ensure, at a minimum, that ISTC is given a minister of virtually equal continuity and clout to that of the Minister of Finance. The essence of the ISTC mandate, some of which is very sensible, requires dogged sustained political leadership by a minister and senior bureaucracy. Continuity is a precondition. The Canadian microeconomy, defined with primary attention to its international competitiveness, requires sustained ministerial attention over a full term of office (and preferably two terms). Little sustained "political intelligence," in the best sense of that phrase, will occur if the 1980s pattern of ministerial musical chairs is maintained in the 1990s.

It is of course not a sufficient condition for the realization of the aspirations inherent in the ISTC mandate. One is not looking here for the reappearance of some 1990s version of a C.D. Howe or for the quick emergence of a Canadian version of the Japanese Ministry of International Trade and Industry (MITI). Any serious student of the processes of economic development knows that no one or two factors ensure industrial progress and competitiveness.[25] But one can have little confidence that the problems facing the Canadian industrial and technology policy will be addressed if the ISTC portfolio is essentially viewed as being a short-term pit-stop for racing politicians. This assertion is not intended to discredit any particular incumbent in the ISTC portfolio. Rather it is intended to draw out the importance of continuity as one institutional precondition for a future chance at success.

The second gap in ISTC's inherent capacity is that of its ability to deal with key Canadian firms. This is in turn but one facet of its larger intermediation and consensus building role. ISTC certainly has an array of networks for dealing with groups and sectors important to its mandate but there appears to be an institutional blind-spot in the issue of how to build links with key firms in Canada.

Our discussion above of active and reactive industrial policy indicates how inherently controversial this element of institutional capacity is. If one eschews a positive industrial policy then it is logically a non-topic. But if, as we argue, there is substance to the notion of either an active industrial policy (including the desire to negotiate "product mandates" with foreign multinationals) or a defensive industrial policy, then the issue is important.

The logic of this chapter suggests that one way or another, the problem of how ISTC deals with key firms will arise. The most likely immediate impetus for it to emerge will be for reactive industrial policy reasons, as globalization takeovers proceed. This need not mean that Ottawa will get into new bouts of subsidizing activity. But it may well have to engage in forms of negotiation and jaw-boning regarding capital markets and indirect support for key firms in a far more concerted way than anyone is prepared to admit at present.

CONCLUSIONS

Three conclusions arise regarding the ISTC mandate and the early activities of Ottawa's aspiring department of the microeconomy. First, compared to the hodge-podge mandate of its immediate predecessor departments in the 1980s, the ISTC mandate has some sensible features. An effort to focus on international competitiveness and to meld at least some aspects of science and technology policy with industrial policy was long overdue at the federal level. There is some evidence to suggest that useful new ways of bridging the old cultures of MOSST and DRIE are beginning to occur. This kind of steady beavering away in the microeconomic underbrush is essential, no matter how un-glamorous it is for ministers who have been used to deriving their political credit from the announcement of grants. It is doubtful, how-ever, that this mandate is a sufficient complement to the free trade initiative or to other framework policies emphasized by the Tories to secure Canada's future competitiveness in international markets.

The Mulroney Conservatives are likely to be politically pres-sured into forging a reactive industrial policy. Though they are probab-ly right on practical grounds in believing that active industrial policies are unlikely to be satisfactorily devised in the current Canadian institu-tional setting, they are still likely to have to fashion some active in-dustrial policies to prevent Canada from losing out in the globalization process.

Thus, third and finally, ISTC and the government, even to carry out its current tasks, will at a minimum have to move to fill two institutional gaps. These include the need to secure a greater continuity of leadership in ISTC over the life of an entire political mandate. They also include the need to find mechanisms for ISTC to deal with key firms in an increasingly globalized world.

Notes

Special thanks are owed to Allan Maslove and Fred Bienefeld for constructive comments on an earlier draft. I am also grateful to several ISTC officials for agreeing to interviews. None of the above bears any responsibility for any remaining weaknesses in the analysis.

1   Government of Canada, *Meeting the Challenge: Industry, Science and Technology in Canada* (Ottawa, 1988), p. 1.

2   *Ibid.*, pp. 1-2.

3   See Harry G. Rogers, "Opening Remarks," Statement to House of Commons Committee on Regional Industrial Expansion, May 6, 1988.

4   *Ibid.*, p. 4.

5   Government of Canada, News Release, "New Industry, Science and Technology Programs," October 28, 1988, p. 1.

6   *Ibid.*, p. 2.

7   *Op. cit.*

8   For assessments of its early years see, Peter Aucoin and Richard French, *Knowledge, Power and Public Policy* (Ottawa: Science Council of Canada, 1974).

9   See *The Globe and Mail* [Toronto], January 30, 1990, p. B3.

10   See *Task Force on Federal Policies and Programs For Technological Development*, A Report to Minister of Regional, Industrial Expansion (Ottawa: Minister of Supply and Services, 1984).

11   For an analysis of why this happened see G. Bruce Doern, "The Political-Administration of Government Reorganization: The Merger of DRIE and ITC," *Canadian Public Administration*, Vol. 30, No. 1, 1987, pp. 34-56.

12   For an analysis of the FTA and how and why the decision was made see G. Bruce Doern and Brian W. Tomlin, *Leap of Faith, Leap of Fear: Politics and The Free Trade Agreement* (in press, 1990), chapters 1 and 2.

13   See Jean-Francois Bence and Murray G. Smith, "Subsidies and the Trade Laws: The Canada-U.S. Dimension," *International Economic Issues* (April-May, 1989), pp. 1-36.

14   See G. Bruce Doern, "The Tories, Free Trade and Industrial Adjustment Policy: Expanding the State Now to Reduce the State Later?" in Michael Prince, (ed.), *How Ottawa Spends 1986-87* (Toronto: Methuen Press, 1986), pp. 61-94.

15   See R. Harris, *Trade, Industrial Policy and International Competition* (Toronto: University of Toronto Press, 1985).

16   For a good review of this "shaping comparative advantage-industrial policy" debate, see Richard Lipsey and Wendy Dobson, (eds.), *Shaping Comparative Advantage* (Toronto: C.D. Howe Institute, 1987) and Graham Thompson, "The American Industrial Policy Debate: Any Lessons For the U.K.?" *Economy and Society*, Volume 16, No. 1 (February 1987), pp. 1-74.

17   See Donald G. McFetridge, (ed.), *Canadian Industrial Policy In Action* (Toronto: University of Toronto Press, 1985).

18   See Andre Blais, (ed.), *Industrial Policy* (Toronto: University of Toronto Press, 1986) and G. Bruce Doern, (ed.), *The Politics of Economic Policy* (Toronto: University of Toronto Press, 1986).

19   See Government of Canada, *1989-90 Estimates*, Part III, Regional Industrial Expansion and Ministry of State for Science and Technology (Ottawa: Minister of Supply and Services, 1989), pp. 1-1 to 1-10.

20   See Michael Atkinson and William Coleman, *The State, Business and Industrial Change in Canada* (Toronto: University of Toronto Press, 1989).

21   On the Connaught decision, see *Financial Post* [Toronto], December 14, 1989, p. 5, and *The Globe and Mail* [Toronto], December 14, 1989, p. B1.

22   See Ministry of State for Science and Technology, *Advanced Materials Technologies: Underpinnings of Industrial Competitiveness* (Ottawa: Ministry of State for Science and Technology, 1986) and Department of Industry, Science and Technology, *Advanced Industrial Materials* (Ottawa: Industry, Science and Technology Canada, 1989).

23   Statistics Canada data quoted in *The Ottawa Citizen*, September 1, 1989, p. E6.

24   See Donald Savoie, "ACOA: Something Old, Something New, Something Borrowed, Something Blue," in Katherine A. Graham, (ed.), *How Ottawa Spends 1989-90* (Ottawa: Carleton University Press, 1989), pp. 107-130.

25   See Daniel I. Okimoto, *Between MITI and the Market* (Stanford: Stanford University Press, 1989), pp. 107-130.

CHAPTER 4

ADJUSTING TO WIN?

THE NEW TORY TRAINING INITIATIVE

Rianne Mahon

Résumé

Pendant les élections de 1988, Mulroney a promis un ensemble de politiques généreuses pour soulager la douleur de l'adaptation à l'accord sur le libre-échange. Peu après les élections, cependant, il est devenu évident que la grande priorité des conservateurs était la réduction du déficit fédéral. La Stratégie de la mise en valeur de la main-d'oeuvre, la nouvelle initiative des conservateurs dans le domaine de la formation professionnelle, représente une tentative de s'occuper du problème de l'adaptation à l'intérieur des limites fixées par la priorité qu'est la réduction du déficit. Il s'agit de financer le transfert de priorités dans le domaine de la politique du marché du travail, qui passeraient de "l'équité" à "l'efficacité" en enlevant 775 millions de dollars à l'assurance-chômage. Il y a un danger très grave que cette politique ne fasse qu'exacerber la tendance à la polarisation des emplois et des revenus identifiée dans *L'Emploi du futur* publié par le Conseil économique.

The Labour Force Development Strategy (LFDS), the new Tory training initiative announced in April 1989, needs to be situated in relation to the Tories' commitment to two potentially contradictory objectives: to help the work force adapt to the new conditions of international competition **and** to wage war on the deficit. In the heat of the hard-fought "free trade" election, the Tories promised a new adjustment package once their Advisory Council on Adjustment had submitted its report.[1] With the Canadian Labour Congress (CLC) and other elements of the Pro-Canada Network keeping a watchful eye on the restructuring process, such an adjustment package was one election promise that could not easily be forgotten – despite the fact that, by the time the Advisory Council had submitted its report, *Adjusting to Win*, the Tories' number one priority had become the war on the deficit.

The LFDS does represent a shift in federal labour market policy. The new emphases – on active programs like training (relative to "passive" measures like Unemployment Insurance), and on efficiency (programs that focus on skill shortages and skills upgrading) rather than equity (focussed on the "employment disadvantaged") – accord with the general thrust of the Advisory Council's recommendations. Yet LFDS does so in a rather different way than the Council envisaged. The changed balance between active and passive measures comes via the appropriation of $775 million from Unemployment Insurance (a substantial component of the existing safety net).[2] The funds thus released will not increase the net resources available for federal training programs. Rather the money is to be used to shift the emphasis within the Canadian Jobs Strategy (CJS) from equity to efficiency. The government, in other words, was not prepared to put new money into its adjustment package; given its primary goal of cutting the deficit, it was only prepared to alter its priorities **within** the labour market policy envelope.

The money appropriated from Unemployment Insurance (UI) represents only part, however, of the total initiative envisaged by the Tories. In fact, the LFDS has a broader, if less visible aim: to lever more training expenditure out of the private sector via a restructuring of state-economy relations. In other words, the LFDS also attempts to reconcile the government's contradictory aims by "reprivatization", an attempt to shift a formerly public responsibility (training) to "private or quasi-public (self-administering) forms of organization of the decision-making process."[3] Privatization was also one of the objectives of the CJS but the means selected – e.g. various wage subsidy programs, – proved too meager to elicit the desired response. Thus, in addition to the program changes spelled out in *Success in the Works* (the two-volume background document to the LFDS), the government has initiated a round of task force consultations, organized by the Canadian Labour Market and Productivity Centre (CLMPC)[4] designed to obtain the commitment of the main labour market parties to taking on responsibility for active labour market policy. Once considered as a possible alternative to the Free Trade Agreement (FTA),[5] "corporatism" – the direct involvement of major producer groups in policy development and implementation – now seems to once again be on the agenda.

This paper will provide a preliminary assessment of the new training initiative. The first section focusses on the conception of economic restructuring which informs both *Adjusting to Win* and *Success in the Works*, arguing that both documents present too rosy a view of future labour market demand. By assuming that in the future all workers will need broader and higher skills (and, presumably, will be able to claim rising real wages in return) they overlook the trend toward skill and income polarization that set in during the 80s. Thus neither considers the kind of policies required to improve the terms of the equity-efficiency trade off. As a consequence the new training policy does little to counteract the emergence of a split level economy. In fact, the LFDS is likely to exacerbate the already visible polarization of the Canadian economy into good and bad jobs.

ECONOMIC RESTRUCTURING: GOOD JOBS FOR ALL?

Adjusting to Win and *Success in the Works* share a set of assumptions about the challenges facing the Canadian economy. Both recognize that Canada can no longer rely on its traditional strategy which focussed on resource exports as the engine of domestic growth. Future success depends on our capacity to make creative use of new techniques associated with information technology (microelectronics and telecommunications). As *Success in the Works* argued, "What counts for Canada now are not natural advantages, but the 'engineered' advantages we can create through technology, innovation and a skilled work force. The growth industries today are those which develop the people with skills to harness technology, create a high value-added product, and improve productivity."[6] It does seem that high value-added production is the most promising direction to take if Canada is to remain a high-wage economy, and active labour market policy has a contribution to make to setting the Canadian economy on that path. The high value-added economy, however, may yield good jobs for only one part of the population—an all too real possibility which both documents ignore.

More specifically, both documents share the view that Canada faces major labour market challenges on both the supply and demand sides. On the supply side, they share a concern with one set of developments—the aging of the work force[7] and a slowing both in immigration (a traditional source of skilled labour) and in the rise of female labour force. This will mean that employers will no longer be able to rely on new recruits to meet changing skill needs but will need to look to the existing work force. These points are generally accepted by most analysts.[8] Both reports also express concern over the relatively high level of school drop-outs[9] and the problem of adult illiteracy, issues which touch on the broader education debate. It is their demand side projections, however, which are the most problematic.

Both documents project a rising skill level, citing the projection that the percentage of jobs requiring more than secondary school education will rise from 44 per cent in 1986 to 64.1 per cent in the year 2000. Both stress the general rise in required levels of numeracy, literacy (regular and "technological") and analytical/problem-solving skills. These projections are based on an assessment of the implications associated with the diffusion of information technology and new organizational forms throughout the economy—a process which is transforming the goods-producing and service sectors alike. This wave of technological and organizational innovation is opening up a new economic option—the switch from mass production of standardized goods (and services) to high value-added activity—for Canada and other OECD countries.

In a high value-added economy, new technology and modes of organization are deployed to produce high quality goods and services. Competition is thus focussed on areas of activity where quality, not low costs, is the main concern. In manufacturing, high value-added production involves the adoption of programmable automation, new methods of work organization (from statistical process control to teamwork) and new relations with suppliers (co-operation on new product development and the creation of supply processes essential to the functioning of new "just in time" agreements). These innovations lower inventory costs and, more importantly, make it possible to combine economies of scope (exploitation of the flexibility inherent in the new techniques to produce a range of more "custom-designed" goods) and scale. Such developments will affect both large and small businesses, old and new industries. In those parts of the service sector closely bound to goods production, similar developments are taking place. Simultaneously, it is argued the traditional retail and personal service sectors will be forced to improve the quality of jobs (and pay levels) if they are to attract and keep the workers they require.

In occupational terms, the managerial/professional/technical strata are expected to show the greatest growth but all occupations are expected to require higher, broader and newer skills. More fundamentally, given the continuing pace of projected change, all members of the work force will need to be prepared for "lifelong learning." These changes, in turn, are seen to require a new emphasis on human resource development policy.

In general terms, the above analysis accords with the optimistic version of scenarios found elsewhere in the literature.[10] The high value-added route, moreover is attractive in that it promises both more interesting jobs and a way to maintain/restore the high-wage economies which Canada and other OECD countries established during the postwar boom. In other words, a high quality work force, rather than a dizzying spiral of wage cuts, can be the way to respond to the competitive challenge posed by the newly industrialized countries and those seeking to follow in their path. What is ignored, however, is the actual trend toward a more unequal pattern of development.

As the recent Economic Council of Canada study found, "two quite distinct growth poles account for virtually all of the employment expansion in the 1980s: one includes highly skilled, well-compensated, stable jobs while the other consists of non-standard jobs with relatively low levels of compensation and stability."[11] The Economic Council's findings generally support the conclusions of an earlier study done for Statistics Canada that found a trend toward income polarization in all parts of the economy.[12] Employment and Immigration's own Strategic Policy and Planning Unit had also warned in 1988 that high-skill, high-wage jobs were growing at a slower pace than low-wage jobs.[13]

The tendency toward polarization may reflect the impact of a number of diverse developments. Within the goods-producing sector, some firms are creating a two-tier work force, much like that of Japan's, in which a core of secure workers, possessing the polyvalent skills required to ensure "functional flexibility" (the ability to do a number of different jobs) is separated from the numerically flexible pool of "just-in-time" workers — the tragic human face of the kanban system.[14] Contracting-out to small, non-unionized firms also contributes to polarization as the latter are forced to bear the cost of fluctuations in demand. The uneven diffusion of new technology and organizational practices across industrial sectors also can contribute to polarization. For instance Kern and Schumann's study of the adoption of new production concepts in West German industry indicates that polarization is likely to occur as long as the high value-added model, with all its promise of good, well-paid jobs, is largely confined to certain industries.[15]

The real threat of polarization, however, is associated with developments in the service sector. As the Economic Council's study showed, throughout the 80s, it was this sector which was the the major source of new jobs — including the "non-standard" part-time, short-term and temporary-help agency jobs which alone contributed nearly one half of the new jobs created between 1980 and 1988, and now account for 30 per cent of total employment. This trend is expected to continue, albeit at a less dramatic pace. In addition to the Economic Council, a variety of sources have, in fact, explicitly linked their projections of skill and income polarization with the expansion of the service sector.[16] Others have cautioned against too simple an equation of service sector growth and polarization.[17]

Such caveats are important to bear in mind. The service sector is, moreover, not monolithic; it has yielded a mixed pattern of good and bad jobs.[18] The producer service sector — which includes transportation, communications and utilities; wholesale trade; finance, insurance and real estate; and services to business management — has really expanded in part as large firms contract out services previously performed in-house. From the standpoint of the kind of jobs provided, the producer service sector is divided. In the older transport, communications, and utilities division, where rationalization is leading to job loss, the wage and skill profile is similar to that in manufacturing.[19] New growth is concentrated in finance and services to business management where there is greater income polarization, especially in the latter which includes high-wage jobs in design and engineering, advertising and accounting and low-wage jobs in data processing, security services and catering.

In general, the producer services do make a significant contribution to economic growth and they can be organized to do this in ways that contribute to a more equitable distribution of income. It is the pattern of development within and between the other two branches — personal and social services — that displays the greatest potential for variation.

The personal and social services were by far the main sources of job creation in Canada during the 1980s and Employment and Immigration's strategic policy unit projects that it is occupations in these sectors, especially personal services, that will continue to show the most rapid growth.[20] Retail trade, food and accommodation made the biggest contribution, followed by health, social services and education. Yet there is a substantial difference in the wage profiles of the two divisions. Two-thirds of retail workers and 85 per cent of those employed in the food and accommodation sector had average hourly incomes in the bottom two-fifths — as opposed to slightly over one-quarter in health and welfare and less than one-quarter in education. Conversely, 40 per cent of those in education and over 20 per cent of those in services to business management had incomes in the top fifth as compared to 6.3 per cent in retail and 2.7 per cent in food and accommodation.[21] The social service sector, in other words, generally offers much more in the way of relatively high-wage jobs than does the consumer service sector. The latter is also the area of the economy which has generated the most "non-standard" jobs, according to the Economic Council.

The proliferation of low-wage service sector jobs has a particularly marked impact on women. Although there has been an increase in men taking non-standard jobs, women clearly outnumber men in such jobs, especially in the area of temporary-help agency work, where they account for 70 per cent of these" just-in-time" workers.[22] As Employment and Immigration's strategic policy unit noted, "although their numbers in the labour force are increasing, women still remain in the minority in all sectors of the economy except community, business and personal services."[23] Some service sector jobs offer relatively high wages and demand high skill levels. This is particularly so in the social services supplied by the public sector. Many, however, form part of the burgeoning low-wage, low-employment security segment of the labour market. Employers have traditionally looked to women to fill part-time jobs and they are doing so again as a means of increasing "numerical flexibility" rather than the more costly "functional flexibility" which requires an investment in training. In this context, pay equity remains little more than a pious sentiment.

There is also a regional dimension to the growing job polarization. The *Good Jobs, Bad Jobs* showed that the good private service sector jobs are more highly concentrated in large metropolitan areas like Toronto, Vancouver and Montreal. Dynamic producer services tend to cluster in areas which offer "access to highly skilled labour, to complementary activities (such as office functions, financial institutions, and other services), and to a market (other businesses in the goods and service sectors)."[24] These exacerbating disparities within and across provincial economies increase the need for effective regional development policies at the national and provincial levels.

Neither *Adjusting to Win* nor *Success in the Works* recognizes that the economic restructuring that occurred in the 1980s generated a pattern of polarized growth. As we shall see, this neglect is reflected in their vision of the kind of labour market policy required to help Canada make the transition to a high value-added economy. Before we review these recommendations, however, it seems useful to consider the kind of policy mix required to produce good jobs for all.

EQUITY AND EFFICIENCY IN A HIGH VALUE-ADDED ECONOMY

The split level economy is not the only possible outcome of the restructuring process. Policies designed to encourage the shift toward high value-added activity — including the development of an effective training system capable of delivering the kind of skills required — can help to counteract the trend. The development of effective "human resource" policy, however, will not be enough to arrest the trend to polarization. In fact, there is a real danger of policy bifurcation whereby quality training will be provided to core workers while another set of measures teaches the new poor to accept their lot in the unstable, low-wage sector. New initiatives, designed to improve the terms of the equity-efficiency trade-off, are required if the restructuring process is to yield good jobs for all.

A proactive labour market policy, if combined with an appropriate industrial strategy, can help to counteract polarization tendencies in the goods-producing sector. In contrast to a "rationalization" strategy which tries to lower costs by automating production, high value-added production requires workers who possess the polyvalent skills needed if the new production concepts are to work. According to two German experts, in the high value-added economy, work

> ...no longer involves more or less direct contact with material and production. Instead it encompasses activities such as planning, regulating and controlling in which humans handle technical systems rather than make commodities. This work resists division. It is most efficient if it is combined with functions such as planning and preparing the work, upkeep and repair of the machinery and inspection of the finished product. The traditional logic of rationalization holds that these functions should be separated from the manufacturing process. This new, more synthetic approach redefines factory jobs making them less fragmented and more complex.[25]

Such functional flexibility — the antithesis of numerical flexibility or "just-in-time" workers — depends, *inter alia*, on the existence of a training system capable of providing the skills required to not only perform current, but future tasks. Workers need a combination of theoretical and practical training — i.e. a combination of "institutional" and "on-site" training more akin to the apprenticeship model, which currently applies to only a small section of the work force. In North America, the norm for most has been informal, on-the-job training. High value-added production also requires more than the newer "competency-based" training systems which systematically skimp on the theoretical side.[26]

The market cannot be relied on to deliver such skills in adequate quantity as the latter constitute a kind of collective good. The threat of poaching—to say nothing of the inhibiting effect of the North American tradition of "managerial prerogatives" on the flow of information to those on the shop floor—operates as a strong disincentive for private firms to initiate such broad-based training. In Japan, the problem is solved by a rigid division between the publicly-funded school system which provides the basic theoretical foundations for future learning, and private training arranged by the large firms themselves. Basic standards for the latter are maintained by government certification of industry-based instructors. This system works because the large firms do not fear that competitors will benefit from their training investment: core workers are guaranteed "lifetime employment" with their firm.

The Japanese model, which depends on "lifelong" ties between core workers and their firm, goes against the grain in Western societies. The Japanese system, moreover, systematically recreates a division between core workers, whom companies are prepared to train, and "temporary" workers in whom companies are not prepared to invest. German experts like Wolfgang Streeck have argued that democratic corporatist self-regulation constitutes a more appropriate model for Western societies:

> ...democratic, since it is embedded in a parliamentary democracy and since it includes strong and independent trade unions on, in principle, a co-equal basis. While market motives and processes play a significant and recognized part in the system, they are controlled by, and embedded in, what are essentially collective agreements between monopolistic employers associations and trade unions exercising, under state licence, delegated public responsibility which enables them to impose effectively binding obligations upon their memberships.[27]

Streeck's democratic corporatist model represents a form of "reprivatization" in that bipartite bodies at the industry and plant level take over primary responsibility for co-ordinating the training system. It differs from simple privatization in one important respect. While the latter operates on the "laissez faire" principle, the former requires the state to maintain ultimate responsibility for ensuring that training meets the standards required. Thus in addition to its traditional role in delivering the necessary classroom training, the state has an important role to play in establishing strong national standards and the rules of the game which require firms to negotiate with the unions. It is through such rules that the state attempts to ensure that on-site training is able to deliver the kind of portable, polyvalent skills required for high value-added production. For such a system to work in Canada, of course, certain historic barriers would have to be overcome. Nevertheless, such regulatory mechanisms, located neither in the state nor in the market but rather cutting across the two, offer some promise. Through such a system, labour and the state might be able to both "force and enable" business to organize the kind of training required to make the transition to a high value-added economy.

Corporatist regulation of training for those currently employed, operating within a state-sanctioned framework designed to uphold clear national standards, is one mechanism for counteracting polarization, but it is not enough. Appropriate industrial policy initiatives, strong employment standards legislation, and the extension of collective bargaining rights to employees of small firms are also needed just to ensure the diffusion of the high value-added strategy throughout the goods-producing sector.[28] In addition, if all Canadians are to benefit from the restructuring of the economy, new initiatives are needed on the social policy front.

As the National Advisory Board for Science and Technology (NABST) recognized, "how we prepare people for roles in the personal and social service sector and the mechanisms for financing these services will have a significant impact on both the quality of the jobs and the capacity of individuals to take up new careers in this sector."[29] In other words, the kind of job creation-cum-training program recommended by the Senate's Sub-Committee on Training and Employment — one focussed, *inter alia*, on day-care, home care for the elderly, the eradication of illiteracy, environmental restoration and low cost housing — seems a logical complement to policies focussed on making the switch to high value-added production.[30] Such programs should not, however, be seen simply as job creation programs for the disadvantaged.[31] In fact, an even stronger case can be made for new social policy initiatives that would involve the creation of permanent public sector jobs: the renewal of the welfare state can be seen as an integral component of Canada's high value-added economy in that it generates a distinctive pattern of demand for innovation. (For example, policies designed to strengthen our existing public health care system in turn generate a pattern of demand for technical innovation which differs

significantly from that found in more bifurcated systems like the U.S.')
Certain Scandinavian researchers[32] have made this argument and,
while Canada's welfare state is not as well-developed as its Scandinavian counterpart, policies designed to foster the renewal of a
universalistic welfare state can contribute to developing our competitive advantage in the North American trading bloc.

Active labour market policy can thus be but one component of
the larger policy package designed to counteract the trend toward
polarization identified in the first section. Industrial relations, social
and industrial policy initiatives are also required. Nevertheless, the
way labour market policy is structured will affect the outcome. If the
private sector is merely exhorted to provide the skills that core workers
need while the public sector focusses on "the disadvantaged," then
neither equity nor efficiency will be served. If training policies aim only
at those to be employed in the production of high value-added goods
and services, efficiency will come at the expense of equity. If the terms
of the equity-efficiency trade offs are to be improved, programs need
to be devised which not only upgrade the basic skill levels of all, but
which also provide the range of intermediate skills required to produce
high value-added goods and services **and** quality social services.

THE LABOUR FORCE DEVELOPMENT STRATEGY: SUCCESS PERHAPS, BUT FOR WHOM?

By the end of the '80s, the Advisory Council on Adjustment was but
one of many voices calling for realignment of Canada's labour market
policy.[33] The main thrust of the criticism was that too much emphasis
was placed on passive measures (like UI) rather than on training.
Moreover, the CJS came under fire for its preoccupation with the
problems of disadvantaged members of the labour force while little was
being done to upgrade and enhance the skills of those currently
employed. In this section it will be argued that the criticisms of past
policy were only partly right. Indeed, more needs to be done in the
area of human resource planning if Canada is to make the transition to
the high value-added economy. Yet the Advisory Council, whose
recommendations inform the LFDS, overlooked the weaknesses of the
CJS as a means of promoting greater equity. The LFDS not only fails
to correct the old weakness on this front, it is likely to exacerbate the
polarization tendency.

It is true that the CJS focussed on those considered to be at a
disadvantage in the labour market. As Prince and Rice noted in last
year's *How Ottawa Spends*, "with its emphasis on promoting employ-

ment opportunities for a number of disadvantaged groups in Canadian society, the CJS is in the social policy business."[34] Nearly 60 per cent of CJS expenditures in 1988-89 were devoted to Job Entry (and Re-Entry) and Job Development. These programs focussed on youth, women re-entering the labour market, social assistance recipients, and the long-term unemployed.[35] A mere 13 per cent went to apprenticeships (Skill Shortages) and an even smaller amount (5.2 per cent) to Skill Investment and the Industrial Adjustment Service (IAS), programs which focus on retraining current members of the labour force whose jobs are at risk as a result of restructuring.

While the emphasis which the CJS placed on helping those who need it most may seem appealing in times of restraint, it left the policy vulnerable to charges of ignoring the rest. The Advisory Council thus argued for a greater emphasis on the efficiency side. What the Council failed to see is that the CJS not did not meet the objective of improving labour market efficiency; it fell far short of its stated concern to promote greater equity. Eligibility restrictions, such as those pertaining to UI recipients who wished to follow a training program (six months on UI), seemed designed more to lower wage expectations than to help displaced workers acquire the skills needed to obtain good jobs. Low level training allowances for CJS beneficiaries and inadequate support services (day-care, housing subsidies, transport, etc.) constituted a strong disincentive to participation. For those who persevered despite these disincentives, the main means of delivering training — wage subsidies to employers — offered no guarantee that the skills thus imparted would provide them with a way out of the low wage segment of the labour market. In fact, the Canada Employment and Immigration Commission (CEIC) explicitly rejected the House Committee on Labour, Employment and Immigration's suggestion that the provision of portable skills become a condition for receiving a subsidy under Skill Investment, arguing that job retention, not the acquisition of portable skills, was the program's main objective.[36] Stimulating private sector job creation (of any kind) seems to have been the CJS's main goal, not training which would help the "employment disadvantaged" to gain access to good jobs. As Wolfe and Yalnizyan have argued,

> Most public sector programs concentrated on preparing people for jobs with low skill levels and...low wages. Where publicly funded training is aimed at a higher technical level, the content is often defined by employer needs which...tend to limit the range and portability of skills. These programs may also put participants at a disadvantage because they rarely provide in-depth train-

ing experiences. Graduates from six-month training courses purchased through the Canadian Jobs Strategy find themselves competing with those who have two- or three-year diplomas in the same subject...The short duration of training becomes of questionable benefit, since there is little or no opportunity to reach skill levels offering more stable, higher paying employment.[37]

In other words, the CJS not only failed to place enough emphasis on "efficiency," as the Advisory Council argued, it also failed to deliver on the equity front because it lacked the means to ensure that target groups were not simply being catapulted into the booming low-wage sector. In fact, its chosen instrument — wage subsidies — can be seen as a means for propping up low-wage employers.

If the CJS failed to counteract growing inequalities in the labour market, the LFDS is likely to exacerbate the problem. The LFDS attempts to shift priorities within the existing program structure from equity to efficiency. First, the federal government intends to withdraw its contribution to UI, making UI a purely contributory scheme, as it is in the U.S. This weakens the fund's capacity to contribute to the stabilization of aggregate demand. Second, the program changes are to be funded by appropriating at least $775 million from UI,[38] money made available at the expense of those stuck in the low-wage segment of the labour market. Thus Bill C-21 aims to raise minimum entrance requirements and reduce the maximum duration of benefits for all recipients. The minimum qualifying period has been raised from 10 to 20 weeks, depending on regional unemployment rates. This change will have a particularly adverse impact on holders of "non-standard" jobs in areas of lower unemployment like Toronto and other large cities where the bad jobs as well as the good tend to cluster. In all areas but those with the highest unemployment levels, maximum benefit periods will be reduced. Penalties will be raised for those who quit their jobs without "just cause,"[39] or are fired for misconduct or who refuse to take a new job on offer. Under the old system, benefits for people in these categories were delayed by one to six weeks on top of the two-week waiting period, and the benefit rate was the same as for other claimants. They will now have to wait for seven to twelve weeks on top of the norm and their benefit rate will be lowered a full 10 per cent (to 50 per cent of previous earnings). The fine for knowingly submitting false information will be raised from three to nine times the maximum weekly benefit rate.

The LFDS is thus to be funded via a tightening of the safety net much as the Advisory Council recommended, although the Council stopped short of recommending such cuts. To some it may seem appropriate that the money for the new training initiative will come from a "passive" program like UI, at a time when we need to reduce the deficit even while we prepare for the brave new world opened up by increased international competition. Yet, what this Bill is asking us to do is to accept the further erosion of one of the cornerstones of postwar economic stabilization policy. And it is those who are in the most vulnerable position who are being asked to bear the greatest cost. As the Senate Committee studying the UI reform bill argued,

> The motivation behind these changes appears to be not simply to divert funds to new training programs, but to promote what one witness euphemistically described as the "adhesion" of workers to their jobs. The government would seem to believe that many of the unemployed are in a position of their own making, and that, with proper "incentives," they would find work or remain in their jobs longer.[40]

This approach, in other words, puts pressure on those caught in low-wage job ghettos where working conditions and lack of opportunities for career advancement constitute strong disincentives to long-term employee commitment. It is likely to be even more disastrous for workers who have been forced to take the growing number of unstable jobs highlighted in the Economic Council's study as they are likely to fill the ranks of "repeaters," albeit not by choice. In this respect alone, the LFDS moves sharply away from equity considerations.

In addition, the LFDS envisions no change in program composition,[41] only a reshuffling of expenditure priorities within the CJS. Thus the funds available to support unemployed workers enrolled in training programs (UI section 26, formerly section 39) are to be doubled, much as the Advisory Council recommended. "Displaced older workers" – a group singled out by the House Standing Committee on Labour, Employment and Immigration, IAS and others – are to receive $100 million, probably under Skills Investment which can fund basic skills upgrading in addition to subsidizing employers who hire older workers. An additional $50 million is to go toward the participation of social assistance recipients in CJS programs. All of these changes are consistent with the Advisory Council's emphasis on programs which have a "trampoline effect", in that they ostensibly help various categories of unemployed workers get back into the labour market. In this sense, they are consistent with the basic thrust of the CJS. The only changes are that the problems faced by older workers are now specifically referred to – a point on which CEIC had refused to budge when requested to do so by the House Standing Committee—and more money will be available to social assistance recipients and the long-term unemployed. Nothing has been done to ensure that these beneficiaries get the kind of training required to enter (or re-enter) the labour market core nor have the rules been changed to enable UI recipients to enroll in basic literacy and numeracy programs while on UI.

The LFDS appears to place more emphasis on proactive measures. The budget of the IAS, a program to help industry develop its own adjustment measures, has been doubled, as the Advisory Council recommended. Job Entry will receive $100 million, some of which is targeted at quadrupling federal support for co-operative education, especially at the high school level. The government also hopes to make some progress on the apprenticeship question.[42] Yet on the critical question of human resource planning, the LFDS falls well short of the Council's recommendations, let alone Streeck's "democratic corporatist regulation."

Even the Advisory Council recognized that something had to be done to force business to improve its training performance. Firms in Canada spend too little on training—less than half, on a per-employee basis, than is spent in the United States, itself a laggard in this area. Moreover, when training is provided, firms frequently favour those possessing above-average skill levels like managers, professionals and technicians. The majority of workers tend to get short-term job-specific training which leaves them ill-equipped to deliver the kind of work demanded in high value-added production. In its critique of private sector practices, the Council supported the findings of studies done by the unions.[43] The Canadian Auto Workers' (CAWs) studies of technological change at Northern Telecom and in the auto and aerospace industries indicate that even in the industries where the new production concepts have made the most headway, serious problems remained concerning the quantity and the quality of training provided.

Thus from the Advisory Council's standpoint, the CJS was right to place more emphasis on the private sector[44] and, through programs like the IAS and Innovations, had begun to encourage the kind of sectoral initiatives needed. Nevertheless, the government has not gone far enough:

> The Council believes that the private sector will not increase its training efforts simply because it is exhorted

> to do so...The government should act immediately to
> ensure that companies begin offering basic training.[45]

In other words, the CJS, which sought to privatize job creation and training, suffered from the traditional weakness of Canadian economic policy. In Canada, policy-makers too frequently have shared the business community's "firm-centred" managerial culture — a culture which "emphasizes the self-sufficiency of the firm, the independence of management in making decisions on investment and workplace organization, and the reliance, whenever possible, on markets for the allocation of capital and labour."[46] This approach is a long way from the kind of "democratic corporatist regulation" of training required in a high value-added economy. Perceiving this, the Council recommended that the federal government consider requiring all firms applying for government assistance to submit human resource plans. More importantly, it actually supported a mandatory training tax, not too dissimilar to the grant/levy system long demanded by the unions.

The LFDS, however, again appears to rely on moderate financial incentives while avoiding the stick of mandatory contributions. Thus $65 million is to be allocated to support:

° building networks of organizations (industry associations, unions, and/or training institutes) that share human resource concerns;

° providing financial and technical assistance in the analysis of human resource issues facing sectors, industries, and firms, particularly small firms;

° helping with the development and implementation of employment equity plans as required under the Federal Contractors Program and the *Employment Equity Act*; and

° providing seed funding for select initiatives resulting from these plans, such as assisting with the capital or equipment costs in establishing national occupational training centres.[47]

The government's stated aim is to convince business to spend an additional $1.5 billion by 1994, which would take Canadian private sector spending on training and related matters up to the U.S. level. Yet even if the funds targeted for entry-level training are added to the IAS and Community Futures[48] programs (which are explicitly designed to promote a "training culture" in the private sector) the amount — $230 million — is too small to elicit the desired response.

There are signs that the government is beginning to face up to the need for more direct action. For instance, the Deputy Minister of Employment and Immigration told the Canadian Manufacturers' Association that if business does not double its volume of spending over the next five years, it will face the possibility of imposed measures such as the levy/grant system.[49] Yet the government is clearly reluctant to accept the Advisory Council's advice that such action is needed now. The only real sign that it is prepared to go beyond the "firm-centred" culture that has inhibited effective action in the past, is the consultative exercise established in conjunction with the LFDS. It is this exercise to which we now turn.

RESTRUCTURING STATE-ECONOMY RELATIONS?

The LFDS seems to pin its hopes for reprivatizing labour market policy as it concerns the core, on the consultative exercise involving business, labour and other groups and organized by the Canadian Labour Market Productivity Centre (CLMPC). The carrot offered is a small one in financial terms: if the task forces organized by the CLMPC can come to an agreement on how to spend the $775 million appropriated from UI, then the government will follow their recommendations. The need for market-induced restructuring constitutes the stick: failure to co-operate means that business and labour will have to meet the new competitive pressures without the kind of assistance that each party is coming to see as necessary. At first glance, these seem rather inadequate incentives to overcoming the historic barriers to corporatism in Canada.

The federal government has, of course, shown occasional interest in tripartite consultation in the past, notably in the 70s when a series of sectoral task forces were organized under the old Department of Industry, Trade and Commerce. Such exercises, however, foundered on the barrier posed by the relatively decentralized character of the labour movement and employer associations. In the early 80s, another attempt was made, this time led by the Business Council on National Issues (BCNI) — an association which brings together most of the leading firms in Canada — and the Canadian Labour Congress (CLC) which was specifically concerned with reorienting federal labour market policy. While this initiative did result in the creation of the CLMPC, the latter languished in benign neglect for several years, in large part because the poor economic conditions of the time reduced employer interest in corporatist experiments. In the field of labour market policy, these difficulties have been exacerbated by joint federal-provincial responsibility for education/training.

Nevertheless, as business began to recognize that future competitiveness depended on its ability to respond to the new wave of technological and organizational innovations — a recognition aided by the "Japanese challenge" — new, largely bipartite initiatives were launched at the firm and sectoral levels. The unions and their co-ordinating bodies also recognize that training is an issue of growing importance on which they cannot afford to leave business unilaterally to decide. In fact, a recent poll of corporate and union officials indicated that both groups ranked education/training high on the agenda and both felt that improvement in the private sector's record would require joint business-labour involvement.[50] Finally, it would seem that provincial governments have been overhauling their education/training systems especially in the industrial heartland of Ontario and Quebec.

There were signs, then, that the labour market parties — and the provinces and territories — were ready for a new federal initiative. Certainly business, labour and representatives of other groups accepted the invitation, despite labour's strong objections to the appropriation of funds from UI. During the summer of 1989, seven task forces were organized under the aegis of the CLMPC. While it is too early to draw firm conclusions about the work of the CLMPC task forces, it is nevertheless possible to provide some indication of where the process seems to be headed.

Around the end of January, a preliminary summary of the results of the task force meetings was presented to federal and provincial representatives in Quebec.[51] The report supported *Working Together to Manage Change* (the earlier CLMPC study) in calling for the establishment of a permanent federal-provincial council of labour market ministers who would be responsible for setting national standards. Policy implementation would be in the hands of local labour market boards, composed of business, labour, education and community representatives. The new local boards would supervise the activity of Canada Employment Centres, which would be required to devote more of their resources to counselling. The supposed target groups would include the less educated, older workers, women and people living in depressed areas. The six month rule, limiting access to UI funds while training, would be abolished and UI claimants could enroll in basic literacy and numeracy classes. A Canadian Apprenticeship Board, bringing together representatives of both levels of

government as well as business and labour, would be created with
occupation-specific committees to advise the board.

These recommendations might result in some improvements,
although they lack the vision found in certain task force reports,
especially the one dealing with social assistance recipients. Missing
too, is the recognition expressed in numerous reports that, on its own,
labour market policy cannot provide the necessary solutions. The most
glaring silence, however, is on the critical question of human resource
planning—the critical area from the standpoint of promoting the
transition to a high value-added economy. This is not by accident
because it was on this human resources planning task force that the
business and labour representatives ultimately failed to reach agreement. The business and labour representatives on this task force
diverged sharply on three key issues: the delivery and financing of
training and the regulatory mechanism governing both.[52] These
divisions, in turn, reflect more fundamental differences.

According to business, training should be provided by public
institutions (especially when it involves basic training) and by
employers themselves. The financial burden should be shared by
business, labour and government, especially when basic and portable,
higher-level skills are involved. In adopting this view, business, in
effect, has conceded that the kinds of skills required do possess the
characteristics of a non-private good. On the question of mandatory
employer contributions, business was not prepared to go as far as the
Advisory Council.[53] Business representatives rejected the notion of a
training tax in favour of a **voluntary** approach, using tax credits to
induce employers to move toward the goal of spending one per cent of
payroll on training over the next five years. Business was not opposed
in principle to bipartite organizations whose task it would be to determine the kinds of training required at the sectoral level. Such organizations could, moreover, administer finances associated with programs
agreed to for that sector. Nevertheless, the establishment and the
operating principles of such organizations should be entirely of a
voluntary character. At the national level, only modest changes were
proposed: the creation of a National Advisory Council on Training,
bipartite in character, with research support from the CLMPC (or a
similar, bipartite organization).

This position reflects only a marginal departure from the classic
"firm-centred" culture so deeply embedded in the Canadian business
community. Essentially, market signals are considered to work quite
well, enabling firms to recognize what is required to remain competitive and when new initiatives are needed. For firms in sectors most

exposed to the winds of international competition, the need for co-operative (business-labour and inter-firm) solutions will be apparent — when such solutions are indeed necessary. Individual workers will also come to see that their survival in the labour market of the future depends on new investment in their human capital. In addition to helping the unemployed make it back into the labour market, the state's role, then, is to facilitate such co-operative measures when the demand arises.

If business took a more voluntaristic approach than the Advisory Council's, then the unions' position was bolder. The unions placed particular emphasis on public institutions as the most appropriate site for generating the kind of broad, developmental skills required.[54] Their position, however, was not that the state should bear primary responsibility. Although training for the unemployed should be financed by government, employers should foot the bill for retraining their current work force.[55] However, employers cannot always be relied upon to supply the right quantity and quality of training nor can they be expected to guarantee equitable access to all of their employees. Thus a new system of joint regulation is needed in which state authority would be used to compel corporations (above a certain size) to contribute to training and to give labour a veto power over the use of these funds at firm, sectoral and provincial levels.[56]

The position taken by the union representatives on the task force is consistent with the kind of principles outlined in union documents such as the Ontario Federation of Labour's statement on education and training.[57] Training is a right and a tool for equity. It should be available to all, not just the youngest and best-educated. It should be broadly-based and developmental, not job- or company-specific, and its aim should be to enhance workers' capacity for control over the labour process. Neither market-signals nor corporate planning can be relied upon to provide broad access or to deliver the quality and quantity of training needed if the Canadian economy is to make the shift to high value-added production.

The unions' demand for a central role in training decisions also takes aim at the state. While the unions strongly support public institutions as mechanisms of delivery, their argument for bipartite control of the decision-making process at all levels suggests that the state is too removed from the real site of action to be involved in detailed planning. It cannot be expected to develop a training plan flexible enough to meet the varied needs of local and/or sectoral labour markets. Nor can it oversee the implementation process without incurring heavy administrative costs. Unions are already present in the workplace and, as organizations whose function it is to advance the interests of all their members (in good working conditions and methods of work organization, stable employment and the like) they have an interest in pushing employers to provide such training opportunities.

Clearly, the gap between the two positions is large, so it is not surprising that the two sides have not been able to come to an agreement. It would be easy to end the analysis here, noting that once again, Canada's "adversarial industrial relations system" has proved an impenetrable barrier to corporatist initiatives. Yet this would be to ignore signals coming from those other sites of labour market policy formation: the provinces.

At one level, the response to the LFDS by the provinces and territories was predictable. There were complaints that the provinces had been left out of the consultative process; a demand that public training institutions (under provincial jurisdiction) regain their central role in training and, in particular, that the latter obtain the "multi-year financial stability" required to be effective;[58] and an expression of concern over the federal government's termination of its financial contribution to UI as a move which threatens to increase the burden on provincial/territorial governments. Yet, the provinces, too, recognize that "innovative approaches...will be required to deal with the structural changes resulting from the advent of new technologies and the globalization of markets."[59] They also seem to be taking steps toward a restructuring of state-economy relations via new forms of co-operation with the labour market parties. Thus, British Columbia has established a task force on employment and training, while Manitoba has set up a Skills Training Advisory Committee. New initiatives have also been taken in Quebec and Ontario.[60]

It is not possible to discuss these initiatives in detail here but it may be useful to consider the direction in which the Ontario government seems to be headed as it intersects in a rather interesting way with the views articulated by business and labour during the consultative exercise. The Ontario government appears to lean in the direction of the unions' position and in this respect, to hold the possibility of providing a more effective means to promote the growth of high value-added activity by pushing the companies to expand training for **core** workers. Unfortunately, the measures thus far envisaged do little to counteract the polarization tendency.

In December the Toronto newspapers carried stories signalling the government's intention to pare down the role of the Ministry of Skills Development (responsible for developing labour market policy).

The Ministry would now focus primarily on those currently employed.[61] Responsibility for other programs would be shifted to the Ministries of Labour, Education and Industry, Trade and Technology. *The Toronto Star* clearly recognized that this was part of the general reorientation in economic policy associated with the activities of the Ontario Premier's Council. While the Council's earlier reports had focussed on industrial policy (for high value-added production), the importance of an appropriate "people policy" had been recognized and a new report, focussed specifically on this dimension, was in the making.

The federal government was not unaware of these developments. At the meeting of first ministers in November, Ontario tabled a report indicating its intention to create a new training board, with equal representation from business and labour. The proposed Ontario Training Board, would not merely be an advisory agency: its mandate would be "to provide strategic direction and assume **direct** responsibility for worker training and related activities."[62] Its guiding principles indicate that its primary concern is to promote restructuring in the direction of high value-added activity:

° the level of training activity in industry must be increased;

° training is a shared responsibility of the workers, the company and the government: **fundamental skills** — government responsibility; **portable skills** — shared responsibility; **company specific skills** — company responsibility.

° training should be considered as an integral part of competitiveness strategy;

° training needs to be of high quality;

° those that train should not have to subsidize those that do not;

° effective training can be carried out only in the context of good labour relations.[63]

The board's main task would be to see to the establishment of bipartite sectoral groups which will focus on developing sectoral training standards and needs; securing training places to meet these needs; and negotiating " funding and cost sharing arrangements" to support these activities. The document does not go into detail on the latter, but informed sources indicate that some form of compulsory training tax is a concrete possibility. In this and other respects, the Ontario proposal envisions more in the way of restructuring state-economy relations than either the business representatives on the CLMPC human resource planning task force or the federal government were prepared to accept. If the new board is given real teeth (via the imposition of some form of training tax or levy/grant system), Ontario may indeed possess the kind of mechanism needed to supply the broad, polyvalent skills required in a high value-added economy.

Unfortunately, however, the Ontario proposal is much weaker on the "equity" side. It does take up the issue of "downside adjustment" which is to be handled primarily by regional committees. These committees, made up of business, labour and community representatives, are to deal with training needs (and possibly, job creation)[64] not met by the sectoral committees, with a particular emphasis on small business. The latter, presumably, is expected to absorb those thrown out of the high value-added core by the restructuring process. The regional committees may well assist them not to find good jobs but rather to join the swelling ranks of those condemned to the low-wage, low-security sector. The fact that the second part of the new Ontario strategy fails to address the problem of growing polarization in the labour market is, in a sense, not surprising. The Premier's Council — the moving force behind the policy shift — has embraced a dichotomous view of the economy (tradable and non-tradable) and has consistently argued that resources be shifted away from the non-traded sector in order to give the tradable sector the resources required to move into high value-added activity. In its training policy document, the Premier's Council has been prepared to soften its stance a little (viz. the regional committees) for political reasons but the basic thrust is the same as that articulated in *Competing in the New Global Economy*. It may be pushed into making even further concessions, because the first draft of the training report ran into some difficulties which opened the way to a second round of negotiations in which the unions are attempting to widen the underlying vision and thus the scope for action. This second round might lead the Ontario government to recognize the need for the kind of active social policy measures discussed earlier in this chapter. If it does not, the best we can expect is improved policies for workers lucky enough to hold on to "good" jobs.

CONCLUSION

The Tories' new training initiative has not settled the question of what kind of labour market policy Canada needs for the 1990s and beyond. The thinking behind the LFDS, however, does indicate the direction in which this government wishes to go — a direction which will exacerbate the already marked tendency toward polarization in the job market. Tightening the safety net (UI) to produce a "trampoline" effect will simply serve to bounce the unemployed into the booming low-wage segment of the labour market. Equity is to be sacrificed to efficiency — although the government is still hesitant about intervening to ensure that the latter objective is, indeed, met.

The government may, however, be forced to bite the bullet. The CLMPC task forces have joined the Senate and others in rejecting the government's proposal to raid UI in the name of active labour market policy. If the growing chorus of opposition manages to torpedo Bill C-21, and the Tories persist in their battle against the deficit, the only way out will be the imposition of some form of training tax. This would move federal policy closer to the new Ontario approach, centred on establishing the preconditions for growth of a high value-added economy. While this would constitute a step in the right direction, it is hardly sufficient to reverse the tendency to income polarization that set in during the 80s. If nothing is done to force both levels of government to adopt an integrated social and economic strategy designed to improve the terms of the equity-efficiency trade off, then gender, racial and regional inequalities will widen. The slogan "adjusting to win" will only apply to a small part of the work force, primarily those located in large urban settings.

Appendix 4.1
Membership of CLMPC Task Forces

1. Human Resource Planning:

Bob White, president of the CAW;

Michael Blondin, assistant director of the United Steelworkers of America;

Austin Thorne, secretary-treasurer of the Canadian Federation of Labour;

Ron Evason, president of the Society of the Plastics Industry of Canada;

Peggy Hilmer, president, Maggi-O Ltd.;

Dr. Ed Luterbach, president, Red Deer College;

Ken Georgetti, president, B.C. Federation of Labour;

Colin Pattison, Communications and Electrical Workers of Canada;

Tom D'Aquino, president, Business Council on National Issues;

Victor Harris, vice-president, Stelco Inc.;

Robert B. Strother, vice-president human resources, Noranda Inc.;

Barry Foster, vice-president human resources, RCA Inc.

2. Unemployment Insurance Recipients

David Adams, assistant director of education, CUPE;

Andre Chartrand, vice-president international, International Association of Heat, Frost, Insulators and Asbestos Workers;

Alphonse Finn, plant manager, Pecheries F.S. Fisheries of New Brunswick;

Douglas Fowlow, president, Western Community College of Newfoundland;

William Mann, senior vice-president human resources, Southam Inc.;

Jack Pearpoint, president, Frontier College;

Gerard Docquier, national director for Canada, USWA;

Cliff Evans, international vice-president, U.F.C.W.;

Jean Dube, vice-president human resources, Rolland Inc.;

Kam Gajdosik, director, Construction Labour Relations Association of Manitoba;

Hubert Saint Onge, human resources manager, Shell Canada.

3. Apprenticeship

Jim McCambly, president, Canadian Federation of Labour;

Guy Dumoulin, Building and Trades Dept. AFL/CIO

Gerry Stoney, vice-president, International Woodworkers of America;

John Halliwel, vice-president, Canadian Construction Association;

Michael Parker, vice-president operations, Procor Ltd.;

Marica Braundy, co-ordinator, Kootenay Women in Trades and Technology Association;

Bruce Ashton, co-ordinator of apprenticeship, International Brotherhood of Boilermakers, Iron Ship Builders, Blacksmiths, Forgers and Helpers;

Bob Biggar, administrative assistant, International Association of Machinists;

Don Exner, operations manager, Degelman Industries Ltd. Regina;

Michael McGrath, executive director, Canadian Automotive Repair and Service Council (CARSC);

John Thygesen, vice-president, Fuller and Knowles Co. Ltd., Alta.

4. Entry-Level Training

Jim Turk, director of education, Ontario Federation of Labour;

Stu Sullivan, Energy and Chemical Workers Union;

John Fleck, regional personnel superintendent, Sears Canada;

Douglas Light, president, George Brown College;

William Beckel, Carleton University;

Alex Dagg, International Ladies' Garment Workers' Union;

Al Hatten, national director employment initiative, YMCA Canada;

Tom Savage, chair and president, ITT Canada Ltd.;

Carolyn Clarke, C.P. Hotels.

5. Social Assistance Recipients

Daryl Bean, president, Public Service Alliance of Canada;

Marcy Cohen, Canadian Congress for Learning Opportunities for Women;

Peter Vivien, vice-president, Business Council on National Issues;

Linda Torney, president, Labour Council of Metro Toronto and York Region;

Ken Murdoch, director of programs, Northwest Child and Family Services Agency - Winnipeg;

Peter Woolford, vice-president, Retail Council of Canada.

6. Older Workers

Nancy Riche, executive vice-president, Canadian Labour Congress;

Marcel-Guy Pepin, conseiller syndical, Confederation des Syndicats Nationaux;

Tim McCarthy, president, New Brunswick Federation of Labour;

Tom Norton, executive director, Associations of Canadian Community Colleges;

Bob Colosimo, vice-president industrial relations, C.P. Rail;

Gaston Lafleur, president, Conseil Quebecois du Commerce de Detail;

Joanne Delaurentis, vice-president and director of public affairs, Canadian Bankers' Association.

7. Co-Operation Education*

John Fryer, president, NUPGE;

Ken Page, co-ordinator, co-op education, Scarborough Board of Education;

Bob Phillip, executive director, Industry-Education Council of the Region of Hamilton-Wentworth;

William Frank, vice-president of operations, Edwards Fine Foods, N.S.

Susan Hart-Kulbaba, president, Manitoba Federation of Labour;

Efre Giocobbo, research director, ACTWU;

Dale Landry, president and chief executive officer, Holland College, P.E.I.

* Note that there were **seven** task forces. The co-op education and entry-level training were, however, to combine their reports.

Notes

I would like to thank Greg Albo, Donald Swartz, Katherine Graham, Armine Yalnizyan and one of my anonymous sources for their insightful comments on the first draft of this chapter. I would also like to thank those who made available useful information on developments at the federal and provincial levels.

1   In January, Mulroney set up an advisory council to look into the kind of adjustment measures needed to complement the Canada-U.S. Free Trade Agreement (FTA). The council was headed by J. de Grandpre, chair of the board of Bell Canada. The other members were: J. Bennett, vice-president of The Manufacturers Life Insurance Co.; G. Cummings, president of National Sea Products; J. McCambly, president of the Canadian Federation of Labour; and N. Wagner, chair of the board of Alberta Natural Gas Company. Its report, *Adjusting to Win: Report of the Advisory Council on Adjustment* (Ottawa: Supply and Services Canada) was submitted in January of 1989. *Success in the works* (Ottawa: Supply and Services Canada, 1989), (two volumes) appeared in March.

2   Bill C-21 is designed to "save" nearly $1.3 billion in Unemployment Insurance expenditures by tightening conditions of access and the imposition of stiff penalties on certain groups. The Bill would also cut the federal contribution to UI (reportedly worth $3 billion in 1989), making the program exclusively self-financing. On Valentine's Day, the Senate threw the bill back to the House, voicing a strongly-worded critique of a package that seems designed to harmonize Canada's social security system with its weaker American counterpart.

3   Claus Offe, "Social policy and the theory of the state," in *Contradictions of the Welfare State*, J. Keane, (ed.) (Boston: MIT Press, 1984), p. 112.

4   The CLMPC was founded in 1984 after several years of discussions involving the CLC, the Business Council on National Issues (BCNI) and the federal government. The CLC and the BCNI were both interested in taking over the direction of federal labour market policy but could not agree on the mode of private sector financing—an issue which continues to divide the two parties. The resolution of the earlier conflict was to set up a bipartite consultative body on labour market and produc-

tivity issues which the government agreed to help finance. See Appendix A for a list of the task forces and their members.

5   For an argument in this vein, see L. Panitch's excellent study for the Macdonald Commission, "The Tripartite Experience" in K. Banting, (ed.), *The State and Economic Interests* (Toronto: University of Toronto Press, 1986).

6   *Success in the Works: A Profile of Canada's Emerging Workforce* (Supply and Services Canada, 1989), p. 2.

7   By the year 2000, 48.8 per cent of the labour force will be between the ages 35-54, as opposed to 38.5 per cent in 1986. The growth in this age group takes place at the expense of young labour force entrants, which is expected to fall from 51.0 to 40.7 per cent.

8   Issue could be taken with the assumption that immigration will drop, largely because immigration flows are partly a reflection of immigration policy.

9   In February 1990, the Minister of Employment and Immigration, Barbara McDougall, announced that $300 million will be spent over the next five years to encourage young people to stay in school. Like the LFDS, however, the new program does **not** involve new money. The funds have been taken from existing programs like the Summer Employment/Experience Development program (designed to stimulate the creation of summer jobs for students). See *The Globe and Mail* [Toronto], February 10, 1990, for more details.

10   In the United States, M.J. Piore and C. Sabel's *The Second Industrial Divide* (New York: Basic Books, 1985) and S. Cohen and J. Zysman's *Manufacturing Matters* (New York: Basic Books, 1987), among others, have drawn attention to this alternative. In Germany, the work of Wolfgang Streeck (now at the University of Wisconsin) and others at the Wissenschaftszentrum in Berlin explore this line while the group centred around Chris Freeman (Science Policy Research Unit, University of Sussex) has made a central contribution to understanding the possibilities opened up by the new wave of innovation. French "regulation theorists" like A. Lipietz and R. Boyer, have also made an important theoretical contribution to this debate.

11   *Good Jobs, Bad Jobs: Employment in the Service Economy*, Economic Council of Canada (Ottawa: Supply and Services Canada, 1990), p. 17.

12   J. Myles, G. Picot and T. Wannell, "Wages and Jobs in the 1980s: Youth Wages and the Declining Middle," Statistics Canada Research Paper No. 17, July 1988.

13   *Planning Environment Assessment Document* (Ottawa: Supply and Services Canada, 1988).

14   The CAW's study, *Computer Automation and Technological Change: Northern Telecom* (Toronto: CAW, 1988) suggests that this is what is happening in one of Canada's leading "high tech" firms.

15   "New Concepts of Production in West German Plants," H. Kern and M. Schumann in *Industry and Politics in West Germany*, P.J. Katzenstein, (ed.) (Ithaca: Cornell University Press, 1989). In Ontario, the leading industries in this regard seem to be auto, aerospace, steel and office equipment. See D. Pecaut, "A new approach to building a competitive Canadian workforce," in *Discussion Papers for the World Forum on International Competitiveness*, jointly sponsored by the Ontario Premier's Council and the Canadian Manufacturers' Association, undated.

16   See, for example, R. Kuttner, "The Declining Middle," in *The Atlantic Monthly*, 1983; M. David, "The Political Economy of Late Imperial America," *New Left Review* 143, 1984; E. Rothschild, "The Reagan Economic Legacy," *New York Review of Books*, July 21, 1981; C. Freeman and C. Perez, "Long waves and changes in employment patterns," a paper presented at the ALC conference on Structural Change and Labour Markets, Saltsjobaden, Sweden, June 1988; and A. Jackson, "The Rise of the Service Sector and the Quality of Jobs: A Labour Perspective," CLMPC *Labour Issue Papers*, December 3, 1988. Robert Reich has also pointed to a connection between service sector growth - particularly in the area of "routine personal services." Cited in Valpy's column, *The Globe and Mail* [Toronto], May 5, 1989.

17   See B. Bluestone and B. Harrison, "The Great U-Turn: An Inquiry into Recent U.S. Trends in Employment, Earnings and Family Income," presented at the ALC conference, June 1988, and J. Myles, G. Picot and T. Wannell, "Wages and jobs in the

1980s: Changing youth wages and the declining middle," Statistics Canada Research Papers Series, no. 17, 1988.

18   See G. Esping-Andersen, *The Three Worlds of Welfare Capitalism* (London: Polity Press, 1990); J. Myles, "Decline or impasse: The current state of the welfare state," in *Studies in Political Economy* 26, 1988; *The Report of the Industry Committee* to the National Advisory Board on Science and Technology (Ottawa, 1988) - henceforth NABST report; A. Jackson, "The rise of the service sector and the quality of jobs: A labour perspective," CLMPC Labour Issue Papers, December 3, 1988; and Economic Council of Canada, *Good Jobs, Bad Jobs* (February 1990). The latter uses a distinction — dynamic versus traditional — which is similar in important respects to that developed by Esping-Andersen.

19   See Jackson, *op. cit.,* for the data to support the argument here and in the next few paragraphs.

20   The top ten occupations are: salespersons; food services; bookkeepers; secretaries and stenographers; chefs and cooks; cashiers and tellers; janitors and cleaners; truck drivers; sales management occupations; and barbers and hairdressers. Most of these, as the report notes, require low to medium skill levels. Of the higher skill occupations expected to grow in the next decade, health diagnosis and treatment and leisure (coaches and instructors) fall within these two branches. *PEAD*, pp. 4-5.

21   *PEAD* notes that just over half the full time/full year jobs created in the period 1980-1985 were below the low income cutoff for a family of four in an urban area. It also suggests that some of these low income jobs were in occupational groups (management and administration) usually considered high wage. The data on income cited above suggest that it is reasonable to assume that a good proportion of these low paid managers work in the retail, food and accommodation sector.

22   *Good Jobs, Bad Jobs, op. cit.,*, p. 12.

23   *PEAD, op. cit.*, p. 11.

24   *Good Jobs, Bad Jobs, op. cit.*, p. 11.

25   Kern and Schumann, *op. cit.*, p. 93.

26   See Dorothy Smith and George Smith's studies of the develop-
      ment of competency-based training programs for the plastics
      industry. (The Nexus Project, Toronto: Ontario Institute for
      Studies in Education, 1987-1988) which report on what looks to
      be a new form of "Taylorism": the competency-based system was
      designed by interviewing workers about the performance re-
      quirements of their particular job classifications. This informa-
      tion was then used to design training packages that teach
      workers only what they need to know. This system is the direct
      opposite to the kind of forward-looking training system
      described by Streeck and others.

27   W. Streeck, "Skills and the limits of neo-liberalism: The
      enterprise of the future as a place of learning," in *Work, Employ-
      ment and Society*, 3:1 1989, p. 103.

28   As the Economic Council noted, "part-time and short-term
      work is particularly prevalent in small firms and non-union
      settings. And both small-firms and non-union jobs, which are
      typical in both traditional and dynamic services, have repre-
      sented major sources of employment growth during the 1980s,"
      quoted in *Good Jobs, Bad Jobs*, p. 13. The Ontario Federation
      of Labour was thus quite right to argue that new initiatives in
      the area of industrial relations policy are a necessary component
      of any restructuring strategy which aims to counteract the
      polarization tendency. See "The unequal bargain," Document
      Four, produced for the OFL's 33rd Annual Convention, Novem-
      ber 1989.

29   NABST, *op. cit.*, p. 44.

30   *In Training, Only Work Works*, Report of the Senate Sub-Com-
      mittee on Training and Employment (Ottawa: December
      1987). *Good Jobs, Bad Jobs* doesn't spell out the kind of social
      policy initiatives required but its analysis strongly suggests that
      an efficient and effective "non-market" service sector is a vital
      component of the high value-added economy.

31   The Americans adopted such a policy (New Careers) during the
      war on poverty. It was designed to train low-salaried or un-
      employed people for paraprofessional jobs in fields like medical
      care, education and neighbourhood redevelopment and thus
      offered a way of simultaneously creating good jobs (and the
      qualification of workers who staff them) and expanding social
      services in a cost-efficient way. The program, however, like

others justified in terms of aid to disadvantaged groups, was vulnerable to backlash in times of restraint because it was not seen as serving the interests of the majority. See J. Wegner Johnston, "An overview of U.S. federal employment and training programs," in *Unemployment: Policy Responses in Western Democracies*, J. Richardson and R. Henning, (eds.), (Beverley Hills: Sage, 1984).

32   Cf. E.S. Anderson and B.A. Lundvall, "Small national systems of innovation facing technological revolutions: An analytical framework," in *Small Countries Facing Technological Revolution* (London: Frances Pinter, 1988) and J.O. Anderson and L. Mjoset, "The transformation of the Nordic models," in *Cooperation and Conflict* 22, 1987.

33   These include such diverse sources as the House Standing Committee on Labour, Employment and Immigration, *A Review of the Canada Jobs Strategy* (Ottawa, 1988); the report of the CLMPC task force on adjustment, *Working Together to Manage Change* (Ottawa: January 1989); *Competing in the New Global Economy*, Volume III (Toronto: Ontario Premier's Council, 1989); the Canadian Federation of Independent Business, *Skills for the Future* (Toronto, 1989); and D. Wolfe and A. Yalnizyan, *Target on Training* (Toronto: Social Planning Council of Metropolitan Toronto, February 1989).

34   "The Canadian jobs strategy: Supply side social policy," M.J. Prince and J.J. Rice in Katherine A. Graham (ed.), *How Ottawa Spends, 1989-90: The Buck Stops Where?* (Ottawa: Carleton University Press, 1989). In addition to the program focus on the groups noted here, the equity objective was to be served by attempting to increase the labour force participation rates of four target groups: women, Native Peoples, the disabled and visible minorities.

35   Calculated from the data provided in *Adjusting to Win*, Figure 2.12, p. 50. In addition to the programs mentioned here, CJS funds were spent on Community Futures (seven per cent), the program which focusses on designated communities; Innovations (2.6 per cent), designed to support novel approaches to labour market problems; and operations and maintenance (10 per cent).

36   *Response of the Government to the Second Report of the Standing Committee on Labour, Employment and Immigration* (Ottawa: Supply and Services Canada, 1988), p. 11.

37   Wolfe and Yalnizyan, *op. cit.,* p. 50.

38   In fact, Bill C-21 would enable the government to use up to 15 per cent of UI monies for "active labour market" purposes. On the basis of the fund's current size, the money appropriated could be as high as $2 billion. The Senate was particularly enraged with what it called the "Henry VIII" clause, section 26(3), which attempts to give the government "extraordinary latitude on the details of the developmental assistance programs" (Senate, *op. cit.,*p. 29). The bill, in other words, authorizes the government to do what it will with the monies thus liberated from UI.

39   "Just cause" would include things like being forced to work in hazardous conditions and sexual harassment.

40   Final Report of the Senate Committee on Bill C-21, *op. cit.,* p. 14.

41   There is one possible exception to this statement in the form of a brief note that some of the money to be devoted to the apprenticeship program might go to a new program "to be based on industry-defined requirements and geared to growing occupations such as those in the services sector (e.g. financial and business management occupations, computer programming, child care, hospitality and home care of the elderly)." *Success in the Works, op. cit.,* p. 7. Informed sources, however, indicate that CEIC's new plans really entail just another form of wage subsidy for employers in the booming "bad jobs" business.

42   The problems with the current system are defined in terms of "persistent shortages of skilled workers in some apprenticed trades, high withdrawal rates, slow progress in the area of national standards and certification, and the low participation rate of women in the Apprenticeship Program." *Success in the Works, op. cit.,* p. 7. Meltz, however, argues that the main problem can be traced to the private sector which is reluctant to abandon its historic reliance on immigration to supply skilled workers. When it does bother to train apprentices, it shows a disturbing tendency to let these go during economic downturns. Moreover, some firms complain of shortages when the real

problem is the relatively poor wages and/or working conditions
that they offer. See N. Meltz, "Approaches to human resources
planning," prepared for the CLMPC consultations, July 10,
1989.

43   Such studies have often been funded by Labour Canada's Technology Impact Research Program and its successor, Technology
Impact Program (TIP). These programs have made a significant contribution to union capacity to handle these issues.
One hopes that TIP will not fall victim to the Tories' deficit-cut-
ting axe.

44   The CJS sought to increase the private sector's role in part by
offering wage subsidies to employers who provided on-the-job
training for various categories of employment disadvantaged
workers. In addition, it sought to subject provincial educational
bureaucracies to the whip of competition by allowing project
managers, under the indirect purchase option, to choose between public and private training establishments.

45   *Adjusting to Win, op. cit.,* p. 43.

46   Atkinson and W. Coleman, *The State, Business and Industrial
Change in Canada* (Toronto: University of Toronto Press, 1989),
p. 33.

47   *State, Business and Industrial Change*, p. 6.

48   The funds allocated to Community Futures have also been
doubled by the addition of $50 million — a move consistent with
the CLMPC task force's recommendations. It should also be
noted that $45 million will go to measures to stimulate self-
employment and entrepreneurship as well as geographical
mobility among the unemployed.

49   *The Globe and Mail* [Toronto], June 15, 1989.

50   *The Globe and Mail* [Toronto], January 18, 1990.

51   The following points are largely drawn from *The Financial Post*
[Toronto], February 3-5, 1990. Conversations with some of the
participants have generally confirmed the *Post's* report and
have helped to fill in the gaps.

52   The same issues divided the corporate and union officials sur-
      veyed by Environics for the CLMPC, which suggest that the
      failure to reach agreement cannot simply be attributed to the
      particular views held by the business and labour representatives
      on that task force. *The Globe and Mail* [Toronto], January 18,
      1990.

53   Business favoured more market-oriented means such as
      Registered Education Savings Plans (business' counter to the
      unions' long-standing demand for paid educational leave); in-
      dividual training accounts to which both employers and workers
      could voluntarily decide to contribute tax deductible sums; and
      corporate tax credits.

54   The "institutional" emphasis did not preclude on-site training.
      In fact, one of the unions' recommendations was that public
      institutions develop the capacity to provide training in the work-
      place during working hours.   Nor did it exclude non-profit
      organizations in the private sector, although the latter tend to
      specialize in the needs of those currently outside the labour
      market facing difficulty in gaining a new foothold therein. See
      "A labour perspective on training: A submission by the labour
      group to the CLMPC task force on human resource develop-
      ment," (Ottawa: September 1989).

55   The rationale here was that the state does enough to reduce
      employer costs by providing pre-employment education and by
      preparing the unemployed to re-enter the labour market.

56   More specifically, the unions recommended the establishment
      of Worker Education and Training Councils (bipartite in char-
      acter) at the national and provincial levels. The role of the
      national council would be limited to overseeing the implemen-
      tation of a new national training act which would specify the
      employers' obligation to train their employees (specifying that
      a certain percentage of payroll had to be devoted to employee
      training; employee rights to adult basic and higher-level train-
      ing; joint labour control over the content and delivery of such
      programs). The provincial councils would have the main role,
      administering the payroll tax in a manner consistent with
      regional economic needs but also compatible with the broad
      standards set out in the national act. The main mechanism,
      however, would be mandatory joint training committees at the
      level of the firm. The latter would have to come to agreement

as to what constituted approved expenditures in a manner consistent with national and provincial standards.

57   *Education and Training*, Document Five. Prepared for the OFL's 33rd convention, November 20-24, 1989.

58   Here the provinces are clearly rejecting the federal government's turn to funding private sector course purchases, allowing the latter to choose from private sector training vendors as well as from provincial institutions. See "Partners for people: A human resource adjustment and development strategy for the 1990s," the mutual position of the provinces and territories, November 1989.

It should be noted that Mulroney agreed to establish a federal-provincial task force on education in order to prepare Canadians to meet the competitive challenges of the future. The federal government finally announced that it had chosen Douglas Wright, president and vice-chancellor of the University of Waterloo. Wright is a member of NABST and is well known as a champion of closer ties between business and the universities. *The Globe and Mail* [Toronto], February 6, 1990.

59   *Partners for People*, p. 5.

60   For example, in Quebec, the Conseil consultatif du travail et de la main-d'oeuvre and the commissions de formation professionelle; in Ontario, Vision 2000, a major consultative and research exercise organized by the body responsible for the community colleges, the Regents Council of Ontario, and the soon-to-be-released Ontario Premier's Council report on training.

61   *The Toronto Star*, December 16, 1989; *The Globe and Mail* [Toronto], December 15 and 26, 1989.

62   "*Training and the labour market: A challenge*," prepared for the annual conference of first ministers, November 9-10, 1989.

63   *Training and the labour market*, pp. 7-8.

64   There may be some kind of tax incentive to encourage firms to save part of their profits in a special account. Such funds could be drawn on to create new jobs in high unemployment areas and taxes would not have to be paid on them under these circumstances.

CHAPTER 5

DEFINING THE AGENDA FOR

ENVIRONMENTAL PROTECTION

Douglas A. Smith

Résumé

Ce chapitre traite de la renaissance des questions relatives à l'environnement et de la façon dont Environnement Canada y répond sous le gouvernement conservateur. On démontre que l'appui politique accordé à l'environnement a fluctué au cours du passé et que ces fluctuations ont limité la capacité d'Environnement Canada de fournir un cadre efficace à ses politiques.

Le degré élevé auquel le public s'intéresse actuellement à l'environnement fournit une occasion importante pour le développement de nouvelles approches plus efficaces en matière de politique environnementale. Si la question a été embrassée par le gouvernement conservateur, la nature précise du nouveau programme du gouvernement en matière d'environnement reste à être dévoilée.

Dans ce chapitre on soutient que le contrôle de la pollution répond d'autant mieux à des critères de coût-efficacité qu'il est orienté vers le marché. Si l'accent est mis sur le coût et l'efficacité en politique environnementale, il ne s'agit pourtant pas de priver nos efforts de ressources, Au contraire, il faut reconnaître que les ressources dont nous disposons sont limitées, ici comme ailleurs. Penser en termes de coût et d'efficacité assure tout simplement que chaque dollar dépensé pour un meilleur environnement favorise celui-ci au maximum.

Un aspect intéressant du nouveau programme en matière d'environnement qui sous-tendra l'approche du gouvernement conservateur, c'est que les diverses définitions, souvent contradictoires, du développement durable risquent de rendre impossibles des liens directs entre le concept de développement durable et des initiatives politiques précises. Du point de vue économique, l'essentiel est de veiller à ce que toutes les décisions quant à l'allocation des ressources tiennent compte des coûts environnementaux de diverses actions. Cela semble raisonnable en principe, mais il sera difficile d'y parvenir de façon à satisfaire tous les groupes qui appuient maintenant en général le mouvement vers le développement durable.

INTRODUCTION

The resurgence of interest in environmental issues has been both rapid and dramatic. Discussions of soft technologies, non-polluting lifestyles and fundamental changes in consumer values have re-emerged. These and related issues characterized the first phase of the environmental movement during the 1960s and 1970s. What factors explain this rapid return to a heightened concern with the environment? What policy responses are likely and what will be their implications? These questions define the focus of this examination of environmental policy in Canada.

Initially, policy concerns in this area focussed almost exclusively on local air and water pollution. The concerns about energy policy in the 1970s added a conservation dimension to environmental concerns but market responses to higher energy prices led to this issue receiving less attention. Currently, however, environmental concerns go far beyond the traditional pollution problems of air and water. The most important additions to the list of environmental policy concerns are the global environmental problems, namely acid rain, the ozone layer and the greenhouse effect. In addition, issues of solid waste disposal and toxic chemicals play an important role in the current policy debate.

It is possible to point to some successes in earlier initiatives to improve the environment. Residents of Sudbury, for example, have a far more attractive and presumably healthier community than was the case before the introduction of controls for emissions from smelters. In this case, a local success had the unintended effect of contributing to the acid rain problem. However, reduced particulate emissions can be documented in other localities where the same solution did not have this unintended effect.

In the case of water pollution, our policies have focussed on controlling large-scale emissions of wastes that are not extremely harmful in small quantities but reduce water quality when large quantities are emitted. Examples include waste emissions from breweries, refineries and other private sector emitters of industrial wastes. These problems are not confined to the private sector. Municipal incineration and sewage disposal created many of the problems that were addressed in the first round of concern over pollution problems. Currently, this focus has shifted to much smaller quantities of toxic chemical wastes that often are the source of longer term health problems than the pollutants that we already control.

This chapter documents the changing popularity of environmental issues. The role of cyclical factors in shifting attention away from environmental issues in the early 1980s is assessed along with secular factors, like income levels, that explain the differing environmental perspectives of developed and less-developed countries. As a policy issue, environmentalism crosses standard political boundaries. Strong environmentalists can be found in all Canadian political parties. Even if this were not the case, the political process would push all parties into pro-active policies in the current atmosphere of public opinion. The differences among the parties lie in the specific form of action they propose on environmental issues. In particular, the current government may be more receptive than the other parties to some of the market-oriented control policies discussed in this chapter.

In the initial section of this chapter, the recent history of expenditures by Environment Canada is reviewed. This is followed by an assessment of the sources of demand for pollution control expenditures and the nature of the costs that are involved in various environmental improvement efforts. These points are illustrated with reference to specific environmental problems like acid rain and policies to reduce destruction of the ozone layer. The policy section of the chapter considers a series of possible methods of implementing our concerns about environmental issues. Many programs of environmental improvement are extremely expensive so that effective environmental policy requires the use of efficient policy instruments. At a time when public sector resources continue to be constrained, there may be important benefits from developing control policies that rely more on market incentives and less on the control powers of a large bureaucratic apparatus.

TRENDS IN FEDERAL ENVIRONMENTAL EXPENDITURES

This section reviews the history of recent expenditures by Environment Canada. It should be made clear at the outset that this is an imperfect measure of the impact of the federal government on the environment. Departments such as Agriculture Canada have responsibilities that relate to the environment. In addition, the regulatory powers of Environment Canada lead the private sector to incur compliance costs that are many times greater than the costs attributed to the government. Responsibility for environmental issues is shared with both provincial and municipal governments and their contributions must be assessed to put the federal role in proper perspective. These elements of the overall allocation of resources to the environment are also considered in this section. The possibility that future environmental problems will cause the federal role to expand due to the global nature of these problems is also discussed.

Environment Canada was established in 1970 to incorporate all of the environmental agencies of the federal government into one department. This followed the initial phase of widespread public concern over the environment. The department has grown but until recently, as an earlier commentator pointed out,[1] the department has not had a specific constituency to promote its interests relative to other demands on the federal treasury and relative to the concerns of those most directly affected by the often substantial costs of pollution control.

The record of expenditures by Environment Canada since its inception is documented in Table 5.1. This table shows expenditures from 1970 to 1988 in absolute terms and as a fraction of total federal government program expenditures. It is important to note the impact of a number of government reorganizations on the relative size of Environment Canada. In 1980, some of the department's responsibilities were transferred to the Department of Fisheries and Oceans, the department gained some resources from the Department of Regional Expansion in 1983 and lost some responsibilities to Agriculture Canada in 1985.

The data in Table 5.1 show that federal expenditures on the environment have not changed significantly as a fraction of total federal program expenditure since 1970. The ratio increased somewhat immediately after the establishment of the department, but has varied only slightly since that time. Relative expenditures in 1987-88 are quite comparable to those of 1979-80 and 1980-81. There has been neither a dramatic increase nor a significant decline in federal environmental expenditures when reviewed relative to total program expenditures.

Data on projected spending for Environment Canada have been provided recently in the 1990-91 *Estimates*. Expenditures will increase approximately 11 per cent in contrast to overall government of Canada expenditures that will grow more slowly than the rate of inflation. No major new spending commitments or program initiatives are contained in these spending plans. However, Environment Canada is committed to the introduction of a new environmental agenda during 1990 and most observers expect that information on new initiatives and their financing will appear in that document.

Table 5.1
Environment Canada Expenditures as a Proportion of Total Federal Program Expenditures[1]
(Millions of Dollars)

Year	Environment Canada	Total Federal Program Expenditures	Share of Total (%)
87-88	774	96,507	0.84
86-87	751	89,730	0.84
85-86	701	85,793	0.82
84-85[2]	754	77,703	0.97
83-84	698	70,469	0.99
82-83[3]	634	61,305	1.03
81-82	526	52,790	1.00
80-81	450	51,690	0.87
79-80	382	43,840	0.87
78-79[4]	395	39,864	0.99
77-78	358	37,352	0.96
76-77	316	34,209	0.92
75-76	295	29,226	1.01
74-75	250	22,847	1.09
73-74	206	17,447	1.18
72-73	168	13,800	1.22
71-72	131	12,704	1.03
70-71	102	11,357	0.90

1   All data from Public Accounts of Canada.
2   In 1984-85, parts of the Administration and of the Environmental Services Program were transferred to Forestry and to Agriculture.
3   In 1982-83, some responsibilities of Regional Economic Expansion were transferred to the department.
4   In 1979-80, a number of department activities were transferred to Fisheries and Oceans, and Parks Canada was transferred to the department from Indian Affairs and Northern Development.

A related perspective on the activities of the department is shown in Table 5.2. This table shows relative employment levels for Environment Canada from 1980-81 to 1989-90. These data show a relative decline in employment in the department but the change is not large. The absolute employment numbers have declined in parallel with the overall decline in public service employment since 1985. Together with the data in Table 5.1, this table suggests that environmental issues have had only average priority at the federal level over the last decade.

Table 5.2
Relative Employment of Environment Canada
(Person Years)

Year	Environment Canada[1]	Total Public Service[2]	Share (%)
89-90	9,964	228,196	4.4
88-89	9,897	231,164	4.3
87-88	10,217	233,125	4.4
86-87	10,323	236,230	4.4
85-86	10,294	242,086	4.2
84-85	11,616	241,539	4.8
83-84	11,735	238,935	4.9
82-83[3]	11,771	236,467	5.0
81-82[3]	11,602	234,409	4.9
80-81[3]	11,570	232,118	5.0

1   Figures for Environment Canada from Treasury Board Estimates until 1985; figures after 1985 from Part II of the Main Estimates.
2   Treasury Board Estimates.
3   Data estimated by applying the percentage changes of unadjusted figures to the adjusted Treasury Board data for 1983-84.

In a later section of this chapter, the data requirements for better environmental policy making by Environment Canada are discussed. Although the focus of this discussion will be on a better method of measuring the results of environmental policy, there are also significant gaps in our information on the resources that we expend on the environment. The data in Tables 5.1 and 5.2 can be compiled annually from the Public Accounts but there is no regularly published and accessible source of data on the environmental expenditures of other levels of government. Tracking the resources devoted to environmental improvement by the private sector is an even more difficult task.

The absence of these data makes it difficult to describe our current environmental efforts accurately because a complete resource allocation picture requires data on expenditures by other levels of government and by the private sector. Table 5.3 shows the importance of this point in comparing the environmental expenditures of the federal government with those of local and provincial governments. These data were compiled jointly by Environment Canada and by Statistics Canada for the years shown in the table.

Table 5.3
Environmental Expenditures by Level of Government
($000)

Year	Local	Provincial	Federal	Total	Federal Share(%)
1972-73	762,717	476,230	391,898	1,600,935	22.6
1977-78	1,848,283	1,167,521	783,431	3,799,235	20.6
1981-82	2,533,807	2,254,600	1,510,472	6,298,879	24.0

Source: Environment Canada, State of the Environment Report for Canada, p. 238.

In Table 5.3, it is clear that local governments have the major responsibility for environmental expenditures although the relative shares of the federal and provincial governments increased in 1981-82. As global problems grow and replace traditional issues such as sewage emissions, this shift away from local governments will almost certainly continue. It should be noted that many local government expenditures involve shared costs with other levels of government.

The data to assess the pollution control expenditures of the private sector on a comparable basis with the three levels of government in Table 5.3 simply do not exist. In a survey conducted by Statistics Canada for the report referred to in Table 5.3, expenditures by the forest industries, the mining industry and the petroleum industry were estimated. These data show that expenditures by these three industries alone in 1982 were nearly 70 per cent of the expenditures of the federal government.

A more precise perspective on the relationship between the expenditures of the public and private sectors can be provided by considering the case of the Montreal Protocol to reduce the consumption of substances that harm the ozone layer. This agreement requires Canada to reduce its consumption of chlorofluorocarbons (CFCs) and halons in a series of steps that began in 1989 and that will reduce consumption to 50 per cent of 1986 levels by 1998.[2] Signatories of the Montreal Protocol account for most of the world consumption of ozone-depleting substances.

Implementing the Montreal Protocol is the responsibility of Environment Canada and this will require resources that will change the distribution of expenditures among the three levels of government and, presumably, increase the financial and human resources of Environment Canada. Any change that might be evident in future versions of the three tables shown above will still very substantially understate the total resource commitment of the Canadian economy to reducing emissions of these harmful chemicals. An assessment of the regulatory impact of the costs and benefits of Canadian participation in the Protocol showed that the costs to Canadian consumers and firms of meeting these requirements exceed the regulatory costs of the federal government by a factor that ranged from 65 to nearly 90. This implies that in this case public sector costs were substantially less than five per cent of total costs. This ratio cannot be applied to all public sector environmental initiatives but the example underscores the importance of focussing on resource allocation to pollution control by all sectors, not only the public sector.

The review of expenditures on environmental improvement in this section shows that there has been an increase over time in these expenditures but little overall change in the extent to which environmental issues have been accorded any kind of priority status. There are a variety of explanations for this situation. The fundamental factor is that attention to the environment, for reasons discussed below, is an issue that is driven by the political process. Environmental groups have been active throughout this period but this is not enough to galvanize the political process into action. Until recently, the Canadian public has not made the environment an important issue and the political process has simply reflected this.

A related factor is the inability of Environment Canada to build a constituency beyond environmental groups. In addition, there is some indication that Environment Canada has not been particularly successful in dealing with the Department of Finance and Treasury Board in advancing its case relative to other claimants on the overall expenditure priorities of the government. These central agencies have traditionally required strong benefit-cost results to support expenditure allocations and Environment Canada, until recently, has not always approached its issues from this perspective. In the future, Environment Canada must be prepared to use this kind of analysis to substantiate its claim for more resources. Recent changes in the organization of the department indicate a movement in this direction.

Environment Canada is now at a critical point in its role as the agency primarily responsible for environmental policy in Canada. Its success to date has been limited but this reflects as much the state of public opinion as it does the performance of the department. Public opinion is now strongly behind devoting more resources to environmental improvement. The opportunity to establish an effective policy framework has been created. The following sections of this chapter explore alternative policy approaches available to Environment Canada with particular emphasis on policies offering the greatest potential to generate substantial improvements in the environment in the most cost-effective manner.

THE POLICY MANDATE FOR ENVIRONMENT CANADA

The rationale for environmental policy is derived primarily from the economic analysis of open access resources. Open access resources frequently generate policy problems because, by definition, these are resources for which property rights are either undefined or incompletely defined.[3] The primary result of this absence of ownership rights is that damage to such resources can occur without penalty or payment. The solution to this problem requires that the government must either act to establish enforceable private property rights or create rights that it can enforce itself.

This approach to environmental problems is illustrated most clearly by the types of pollution that private property rights can deal with effectively and those for which the costs of a private system mean that some form of collective action will be desirable. In the simplest case, property rights prevent me from using my neighbour's property to dump refuse, thus controlling one form of pollution. Private lakes or trout streams offer a further example of how ownership backed up by a legal system can limit the extent to which environmental resources are misused. In the case of acid rain, however, the limitations of a purely private system are illustrated. Even with complete ownership rights, distant sources of pollution are difficult to deal with, particularly when the lake owner must bear the burden of proof that a specific polluter should be required to pay some form of compensation for the damages resulting from his actions. The ozone layer and the greenhouse effect are further examples of policy problems in which action through the legal system is not technically impossible but would be prohibitively expensive.

These perspectives on environmental policy define the role for Environment Canada in cases in which private actions to control pollution are expensive relative to using government. This role is to define and enforce property rights for environmental resources for which the private market is unable to respond because of the high costs involved. For global environmental problems, the actions of individual governments will have limitations that are similar to those of individuals in the examples above.

In the jargon of economists, open access resources allow consumers and producers to use these resources without paying the full social cost of their use. The result is a divergence between the social cost of using an environmental resource and the private cost paid by the user. This gap is referred to as an externality and pollution is a classic example of a negative externality. If there are effective ways of defining property rights for either private individuals or the government acting on behalf of individuals, then there can be a social gain as a result of this form of government intervention.[4]

This approach to environmental problems is widely accepted among economists and is the cornerstone of the economic analysis of environmental problems. As a result, the critical comments of some noted ecologists or environmentalists are particularly hard to understand. Contrary to the statements of some members of this group, economists are not obsessed with the benefits of narrowly defined economic growth. In fact, the opposite is closer to the truth. Using the framework described above, any economist would insist that all the costs of growth should be measured, not just those for which there are explicit market payments. Environmental resources are regarded as valuable and their destruction has costs that should be charged against the production of the goods that use these resources as inputs. Pollution as an economic problem results from using the environment as an unpriced input because of the absence of property rights.

The economists' message about the misuse of environmental resources due to inappropriate pricing has been discovered recently in the literature on sustainable development.[5] As outlined above, environmental problems are fundamentally the result of market pricing mechanisms that are flawed because they are incomplete. Environmental assets such as air, water or the ozone layer have been used without cost in the production of goods and services because they are open access resources. The closer environment-economy linkages of the sustainable development literature can be viewed in terms of putting proper values on environmental resources.

Effective environmental policy must ensure that all costs related to economic growth are incorporated in economic decision making. Private decision-makers will take into account only those costs that they incur directly. Costs associated with the use of open access environmental resources are external to these decision-makers. These negative effects will be taken into account only if harmed parties are provided effective access to the courts or if public environmental policies are introduced. In addition, it is necessary that the pricing of non-renewable resources should take into account the demands of future as well as current demanders. However, it is most likely that this will be the case when allocation of these resources is through traditional market mechanisms.

In this approach to environmental analysis, the social costs of all activities must be assessed where social costs are the sum of private and external costs and these assessments must be reflected in the overall process of economic decision-making. In this chapter, appropriate pricing of environmental assets in economic decisions is taken as a working definition of sustainable economic development.[6] A misguided approach, in which the costs of using environmental resources do not affect economic decisions, is equivalent to the obviously false assumption that environmental resources have no social value.

The implementation of the concept of sustainable development requires a commitment to conduct more detailed environmental impact assessments in a variety of policy areas affecting the environment. The linkage between ecology and economic activity is in the externalities associated with environmental resources not being priced appropriately. Effective environmental policy will require detailed assessments of the costs and benefits from a social perspective of different policy options. Thus, benefit-cost studies demonstrating the overall social benefits of control policies to deal with externalities can be an important part of the process of environmental improvement. From an economic perspective, at least, this approach should define the policy direction of the department.

THE DEMAND FOR ENVIRONMENTAL IMPROVEMENT

The environment has become a political issue that crosses traditional party lines. In particular, as we move from general support for the environment to specific policy issues, it becomes more difficult to label individuals except to the extent that they will be affected directly by proposed restrictions.

Crandall[7] describes how a coalition of environmentalists, firms and unions representing midwestern coal producers in the U.S. was able to convince the Environmental Protection Agency (EPA) to require U.S. utilities to install the best available technologies to reduce sulphur emissions at all thermal generating plants. The alternative of directly controlling the quantity of emissions would have been cheaper and would have achieved the same environmental objective. However, it also would have increased the demand for low sulphur western coal and reduced the demand for the high sulphur coal of the midwest substantially. Emissions were reduced but at a higher than necessary cost thereby depriving the economy of more resources to use for environmental improvement and other purposes.

In spite of the problems that arise when particular policies are proposed that imply costs for identifiable groups, there can be no doubt about the existence of a dramatic increase in the demand for pollution control. In Canada, poll results from leading research organizations like CROP, Canadian Facts or Gallup all confirm a widespread public concern with environmental issues.

This upsurge in public concern is relatively recent. It is difficult to identify a specific date for this shift in public opinion but most polls suggest the mid 1980s. It is noteworthy that increased support for environmental policies appears to be widespread among developed countries. A recent survey cited in the U.K.-based publication, *The Economist*, shows recent dramatic increases in both the United Kingdom and the United States in environmental concerns. Respondents have increasingly answered that they consider environmental issues to be pressing or feel that greater expenditures must be devoted to environmental improvement.

The breadth of public support for environmental improvement reflects in part the transition from local environmental problems to global problems. There are widespread concerns about ozone depletion, acid rain and the greenhouse effect that cross both income levels and general political preferences in the population. This is in contrast with the environmental causes of the 1960s and 1970s. At that time, works such as *The Limits to Growth* had the strongest appeal to owners of Volvos.

Misinformation and misperceptions about the severity of different environmental problems undoubtedly exist and this may mean that the true and lasting depth of environmental concern is overstated at least in certain segments of the population. For example, a series of CROP survey reports cited in a joint publication of Statistics Canada and Environment Canada,[8] show that from 1981 to 1984, between 70 and 80 per cent of survey respondents identified acid rain as the most serious environmental problem facing Canada. More recent polls show high levels of concern over PCBs. Although acid rain and PCBs are by no means unimportant, it is hard to believe that a fully informed public would rank either ahead of ozone depletion, global warming or the disposal of more commonly used toxic chemicals other than PCBs.

The actions of the Conservative government on environmental policy track the attitudes of the Canadian population quite closely. At the beginning of their first mandate in 1984, the environment was not a crucial issue and small cuts were made in the budget of Environment Canada. Their overall environmental policies were broadly similar to those of the previous Liberal government.

More recently, the Conservative government has acted to adopt the environment as their issue or at least to prevent other parties from securing it. Evidence of increased government concern can be found in the passage of the Canadian Environmental Protection Act (CEPA), the enhanced role of the Minister of the Environment within Cabinet, the heightened profile and resourcing of Environment Canada and the announcement of new Environment Canada priorities scheduled for release during 1990.[9]

In the future, growing real incomes in Canada and throughout the world should increase the demand for environmental improvement. However, in the short run, income differences among countries will explain some of the policy differences between the developed world and the less-developed countries (LDCs). This will be the case particularly for the greenhouse effect in which the long run solution will have to be an international agreement in which the developed countries assist the LDCs to introduce policies that benefit both.

Cyclical fluctuations may also play an important role in determining future demands for pollution control within Canada. This has been the clear pattern in the case of local pollution problems in the past. Solutions are costly and when the unemployment of specific individuals can be linked to environmental policies during a recession, they are often modified. Some pollution control regulations require the use of the best feasible technologies to reduce pollution where feasibility is defined in terms of the ability of individual firms to pay for such technologies. This is probably an inevitable aspect of the environmental policy process but is certain to become more of a factor during any cyclical downturn.

DON'T WORRY - IT'S GETTING WORSE

This is a well-known saying, the humour of which tends to be appreciated almost exclusively by economists. It is, however, particularly relevant for understanding the current degree of environmental concern and the implications of this concern for Environment Canada. The significance of the proposition is illustrated using as examples actual and prospective Canadian environmental policies to deal with acid rain, global warming and the ozone layer.

Environmental policy can take the form of creating privately enforceable legal rights or more visible approaches enforced by government. The model of the political process used by economists views political parties as sellers of packages of policies designed to further the probability of election or re-election. These political markets are reasonably competitive and work, albeit imperfectly, to translate public demand into policies. If public demand is strong, the response will be rapid as evidenced by the rapid transformation to environmentalism of most political leaders in North America and Europe. The standard lament that politicians are excessively devoted to opinion polls is curious in this context since it simply describes the process through which the political system generates information about what voter-demanders want. Recently, the public demand as revealed in virtually all polls has been for more attention to environmental issues. The political marketplace in this case has responded quickly to this shift in opinion.

For "hard-core" environmentalists, an intensified government concern for the environment but one which weighs competing interests and assesses both costs and benefits will never be enough. Of course, environmentalists are an important interest group and without the continuing stimulus of such groups, overall resistance to environmental improvement would be stronger. Ironically, it is the committed environmentalist who can worry less as a specific environmental problem worsens. Correcting environmental problems always involves costs, but as a problem becomes worse, the benefits of doing something about it increase proportionally. The environmentalist who always wants these costs incurred is joined by other taxpayers as the severity of a problem increases. As a result, the probability of an effective policy response increases.

The most frustrating issues for environmentalists are those problems that impose only moderate environmental costs. Environmental problems with limited costs fail to generate political support of sufficient magnitude to prompt a policy response. In many ways, acid rain is a classic example of a problem that has not been sufficiently severe or costly. It can be regarded as the ironic misfortune of environmentalists or anyone concerned about this problem that acid rain generally has the effect of making lakes clearer. The increased acidity is extremely harmful to aquatic life, imposes costs on the sport fishery, promotes the oxidization of many structures and reduces the rate of timber growth.

In terms of policy analysis, the clearest benefits of policies to reduce acid rain are associated with the sport fishery. Increased lake acidity due to acid rain has eliminated fishing in many lakes and threatens it in others. How do we measure the importance of this? How should we value the damage to lakes as a result of acidification? Economists argue that we should try to measure what affected individuals would be willing to pay to prevent or offset the damage due to acid precipitation. The addition of these values across different members of the community would tell us the value attached to this form of environmental damage and the amount that should be spent to prevent it. In fact, the Ontario Ministry of the Environment has conducted surveys in an attempt to develop this type of data. They have also measured the impact on tourist facilities and other individuals who may bear costs resulting from acid rain. The central point of this example is that government can measure the benefits of policies to reduce pollution only if the damages from forms of pollution like acid rain can be measured. This should be straightforward, in principle, but the practical problems of such measurements are substantial. This means that the absence of data on damages from acid rain makes it hard to know how much should be spent to reduce the emissions that cause it.

In the political process, acid rain has been dealt with less effectively precisely because many of its costs are not immediately visible. Reductions in the growth rates of forests occur over many years as does the oxidization of structures. For recreationists, acid rain is without odour. In lakes in which fishing is harmed, swimmers and boaters may feel better off because the acidity has eliminated some aquatic vegetation. The achievement of reductions in acid precipitation has been slowed considerably by our current lack of information on the dollar magnitude of damages. In the ironic sense referred to above, evidence that the problem was worse would have generated a speedier policy response.

In this context, it is interesting to observe that acid rain is not simply the result of a conflict between private firms and the public interest as is sometimes alleged. Privately-owned INCO is the largest single emitter of sulphur oxide in Canada but the thermal generating plants of Ontario Hydro contribute as well. In the United States, the most important contributors to the acid rain that reaches Canada are the thermal generating plants in the Ohio Valley. However, the largest single source of emissions of sulphur oxide in North America is the publicly-owned Tennessee Valley Authority which runs 14 coal-burning thermal generating plants.

As a policy problem, acid rain has been difficult because its costs are diffuse and not highly visible while the costs of preventing it are clear and substantial. This takes on added significance because the prevailing winds move the emissions between Canada and the United States necessitating international co-operation.

In the long run, lower levels of acid precipitation will be achieved through substantially reduced sulphur emissions. There seems little doubt that by somewhere around the year 2000, most thermal generating plants will use low sulphur coal and will be equipped with technologically advanced scrubber units to remove the remaining sulphur. The transition will be very costly, primarily for producers and consumers of electricity in the U.S., while the benefits will disproportionately favour Canada. One interpretation of U.S. policy since 1980 is simply that it has been intended to delay the inevitable transformation. This delay allows existing plants to wear down instead of being replaced immediately with new low emission plants. This somewhat pessimistic interpretation is the result of the combination of diffused and uncertain benefits from controlling acid rain and high and concentrated costs associated with immediate improvements.

The lack of effective progress on acid rain stands in marked contrast to the development of policies to preserve the ozone layer. The success of the international policy framework to deal with ozone depletion can be attributed to a combination of the high costs of inaction and the relatively low costs of restricting the use of ozone-depleting chemicals. The response in the form of an international agreement to reduce the use of substances that deplete the ozone layer followed the development of a scientific consensus on this subject with only a short delay. Officials at Environment Canada played a key role in promoting and implementing this international agreement.

The first concrete step in the international policy process to protect the ozone layer was taken in 1987 in the form of the Montreal Protocol on substances that deplete the ozone layer. This international agreement to reduce the use of CFCs and halons came into force and began the reduction process in July of 1989.[10] The signatories of the Protocol account for more than 85 per cent of world consumption of ozone depleting chemicals. These countries are committed to reducing their consumption to 50 per cent of 1986 levels by 1998. In fact, negotiations involving Environment Canada and other Protocol signatories are underway to accelerate this schedule with a view to completely eliminating the use of CFCs by the year 2000. Some signatory countries including Canada are already publicly committed to exceeding the required reductions of the Protocol.

The ozone example is instructive about potential future policy directions for Environment Canada for a number of reasons. As noted above, if current and expected future harm from an environmental problem like ozone destruction is large, the benefits of effective control measures are also large. In the case of ozone, this was clearly the case. Estimates of the human health impacts of ozone depletion indicated that without the Montreal Protocol, there could be an extra 760 annual deaths due to skin cancer in Canada plus as many as 10,000 annual cases of cataracts.

The published benefit-cost results of implementing the Protocol estimated that it would produce benefits of $3.2 billion in 1989 dollars measured from 1990 to 2075. This amount is a present discounted value that weights benefits according to when they occur using an interest rate. On the cost side, the present discounted value of costs to industry and consumers from reducing our uses of these substances were estimated to be $194 million in 1989 dollars over the same time interval as the benefits. These estimates require the use of a statistical value for the willingness to pay for reducing the risk of contracting these effects and an appropriate discount rate to convert the stream of benefits and costs over time to a single number. In the study in which these estimates are reported, the ratio of benefits to costs is always high and is in excess of 15 in the case in which the most plausible values of these variables are used. The benefit-cost results supported this policy initiative strongly and contributed to generating a consensus for it and for subsequent control measures to go beyond the reduction requirements of the Montreal Protocol.

Like acid rain, ozone depletion is a global environmental problem. As a result, an effective policy required international co-operation and the Montreal Protocol is instructive about useful future roles for Canada. In the development of the Protocol, Canada played an important role in pushing for reductions within the framework of an international agreement.

The fundamental policy problem that was faced is what economists call the "free rider problem." Since the stratosphere is common to all countries, any individual country that did not sign the Protocol and bear the costs of meeting its requirements would nevertheless receive the same kinds of benefits as participants. This reduces the incentives for both unilateral action and joining in the collective efforts of other countries if it is possible to share the benefits without incurring any of the related costs. In fact, this implies that unilateral action by major polluting countries may be a poor global policy if this reduces the propensity of other countries to join in this policy approach.

The Montreal Protocol dealt with the potential free rider problem through a combination of trade sanctions for non-participating developed countries and a set of requirements that took into account the fact that less-developed countries now use only small quantities of these substances. In this regard, the policy process leading up to the Protocol can serve as a model for future policies to deal with global problems and of the effective role that can be played by a small country.[11]

The other relevant aspect of the Montreal Protocol is the method of implementation chosen by Environment Canada. Historically, the high degree of enthusiasm of economists for market-oriented procedures has been matched by a correspondingly low degree of enthusiasm among environmentalists and policy-makers. Economists favour this approach because it maximizes the productivity of resources devoted to environmental improvement.

In the case of the Montreal Protocol, the normal expectation would have been that Environment Canada would use the standard command and control approach that generally characterizes its policies. Under such an approach, the 20 per cent reduction in CFC consumption mandated in the Protocol for 1992 would have been achieved by requiring all users to reduce their consumption in this proportion. Such an approach would be inefficient because the costs of reducing consumption differ substantially among users and these differences are not taken into account.

For a variety of reasons, Environment Canada chose instead to use marketable permits to reduce consumption, the rights to which were allocated to producers.[12] Producers are not constrained in terms of whom they can sell to and as a result, the system makes the right to use CFCs fully transferable. In 1992, for example, when CFC consumption must be cut to 80 per cent of 1986 levels, producers will simply be allocated the right to sell 80 per cent of their 1986 outputs.[13] Market forces will allocate this reduced supply to those users for whom CFC reduction costs are highest. Relative to traditional command and control policies that would require uniform reductions across all users, this approach achieves the same overall cut but at a lower cost to the economy. The potential to use this approach on a more widespread basis is considered in a later section of this chapter.

The other global environmental problem for which the ozone experience is relevant is the greenhouse effect.[14] The analysis above indicates that the preferred policy approach would involve an international agreement since countries that do not act to cut emissions of carbon dioxide would benefit from the actions of those that do. In part because the scientific consensus on the likely extent of and impacts of global warming is substantially less complete than in the case of ozone, an international agreement is not imminent. From a Canadian policy perspective, this suggests that the benefits of working for such an agreement are likely to be greater than the gains from proceeding unilaterally. In fact, recent statements of policy intentions suggest that Environment Canada is prepared to act to reduce Canadian emissions that contribute to global warming prior to the attainment of an international agreement. The expected costs of such a policy have not been articulated.

THE COSTS OF POLLUTION CONTROL

The goods and services consumed by Canadians can be characterized for the purposes of this discussion as either consumption goods or environmental goods. Consumption goods consist of automobiles, VCRs and fast food but they also consist of higher education, health care and the arts. Environmental goods consist of clean air, clean water and an ozone layer that maintains the existing probability of contracting skin cancer.

Effective environmental policy must reflect the relatively obvious fact that if we want a cleaner and more healthy environment, we must pay for it. This is at least somewhat in contrast to the frequently expressed views of environmentalists, many of whom seem to believe that the entire burden can fall on polluting firms. The principle of "the polluter should pay" is generally correct, but it is important to be clear about the true identity of the polluter. The ultimate polluter is the consumer of products, the prices of which do not cover the environmental costs of producing them.

This chapter has argued that on the grounds of both good economics and a better environment that we should devote more resources to environmental goods in the future. There are already indications that Environment Canada will be provided with more funding and this trend seems reasonably likely to continue for some time. However, this expansion at Environment Canada will not be without limit or scrutiny. The federal government still faces important budgetary constraints implying that we should not expect to observe a massive expansion in the Environment Canada bureaucracy. Indeed, as noted above, since Environment Canada is a regulatory department, it can expand substantially its central role of developing objectives and frameworks without a large increase in its size.

There may be an unintended positive aspect of the growth constraints that Environment Canada is likely to face. Its spending and regulatory initiatives will be scrutinized by the central agencies responsible for the deficit and for efficiency in spending and regulating. Are there implications here for the kinds of policy approaches Environment Canada should choose to implement its policy agenda? This issue is assessed in the following section.

NEW APPROACHES TO ENVIRONMENTAL POLICY?

Effective environmental policy should provide the maximum benefit in terms of environmental improvement for the resources expended. The general position of economists is that environmentalists should be supporters of market-oriented approaches to pollution control because these policies are frequently the most effective. Overall electoral support for environmental spending is currently high but this support is not without limit even for the environment. A few examples of wasteful or ineffective environmental policy could reduce considerably the existing degree of enthusiasm for such initiatives. Many factors explain the decline in the earlier phase of support for the environmentalism of the 1960s and 1970s but some responsibility must be attributed to failures of this type in policy formation. As a result, the implementation of an environmental policy framework in which the benefits and costs of policy alternatives are weighed carefully should be a high priority for environmentalists as well as for economists.

At this point, it is worth noting the pressures that inevitably face any democratic government in this regard. In an adversarial parliamentary system, it is necessary not only to implement effective policies but to make those policies visible. In the area of environmental policy, there may be a trade-off between the effectiveness and visibility of some policies to control pollution. Product bans, for example, are visible indicators of good intentions. Almost always, however, they are an inefficient method for attaining a specific pollution control objective. The same is true for government edicts that pollution should be reduced through the use of specific control technologies.

Much of this political trade-off is inevitable and will lead to poor policy. However, by articulating clearly its objectives for the control of specific pollutants, Environment Canada can do much to deflect demands for more interventionist approaches. The frequently encountered difficulty with market-oriented solutions is that it is difficult to point to specific actions being taken by government. Often, this is desirable because government does not have sufficient information to regulate effectively in a detailed way. Market-oriented approaches are designed so that decisions about trade-offs in reducing pollution are made by market participants who have the most information on comparative control costs.

Governments that choose market-oriented approaches will be unable to specify the control process in advance and as a result must try to ensure that the focus is on results. In the case of ozone, for example, the Montreal Protocol specified a series of reductions in the consumption of CFCs. Since Environment Canada chose to use marketable permits to achieve the required consumption reductions, it is not involved actively in how these reductions are achieved. The department can, however, describe the aggregate reductions that are taking place with great precision. It must do so effectively if it is to convince others of the environmental validity of this approach.

The successful experience of Canada and other countries in using marketable permits to protect the ozone layer may promote the use of such policies on a more widespread basis. Hahn[15] reviews a series of initiatives in the United States, France, Germany and the Netherlands and describes both the strengths and the limitations of policy approaches in which marketable permits served as the vehicle for reducing pollution.

An approach based on marketable permits begins by defining a target for pollution control. Firms emitting a specific pollutant must achieve this target in the aggregate. The government does not specify how firms should reach this target but ensures that the aggregate target is met. Firms are allowed to trade emission quantities subject to the overall target. This transferability of emissions among firms is the feature of marketable permits that makes them such an effective method for reducing pollution in the most cost-effective manner.

The experience of Environment Canada with marketable permits allocated to producers in the case of the Montreal Protocol has been positive. As environmental regulations become more stringent, control costs rise at an increasing rate implying increasing benefits of more efficient control policies. The department is scheduled to announce a new agenda for environmental improvement in 1990. Its specification in this announcement of control approaches will likely indicate the extent of its commitment to the market-oriented policies discussed in this chapter.

The other necessary component of an improved environmental policy is better information on the environmental effects of various activities of the private sector and also the government. Activities generating negative environmental externalities must be assessed in a cost-benefit framework. Current reports about the new environmental legislation to be introduced by the Minister of the Environment indicate that this will be a priority area. The suggestion is that all major projects of the federal government would require a detailed environmental impact assessment prior to consideration by Cabinet. This would apply as well to activities in which the government is providing assistance to the private sector as in the case of energy or pulp and paper development projects. Developing a strategy for compiling comparable information for purely private sector activities is one of the more difficult responsibilities of the department under the new *Canadian Environmental Protection Act* (CEPA). The provision of such information is a necessary first step for implementing the type of environmental policy framework discussed in this chapter.

Notes

I am indebted to Katherine Graham, David Hoffman and Donald McFetridge for helpful comments.

1   M. Whittington, "Department of the Environment," in G.B. Doern (ed.), *Spending Tax Dollars: Federal Expenditures, 1980-81* (Ottawa: Carleton University, 1980), pp. 99-118.

2   See Douglas Smith and Keith Vodden, "Global Environmental Policy: The Case of Ozone Depletion," *Canadian Public Policy*, Vol. 15, no. 4, December 1989, pp. 413-423.

3   For a discussion of open access resources, see John H. Dales, *Pollution, Property and Prices* (Toronto: University of Toronto Press, 1968).

4   The classic reference is Ronald Coase, "The Problem of Social Cost," *Journal of Law and Economics*, Vol. 3, October 1960, pp. 1-44.

5   Sustainable development is the key contribution of the Brundtland Report. See *World Commission on Environment and Development: Our Common Future* (New York: Oxford University Press, 1987).

6   This chapter focuses on externalities as the central problem in dealing with sustainable development. Many other commentators would also include resource pricing. For a discussion of resource pricing, see John F. Chant, Donald G. McFetridge and Douglas A. Smith, "The Economics of the Conserver Society," in W. Block (ed.), *Economics and the Environment: A Reconciliation* (Vancouver: Fraser Institute, 1989), pp. 1-93.

7   R.W. Crandall, "Curbing the Costs of Social Regulation," *Brookings Bulletin*, 15, Winter 1979, pp. 1-5.

8   Environment Canada, *State of the Environment Report for Canada* (Ottawa: Supply and Services Canada, 1986).

9   Lithwick and Maslove discuss the impacts of free trade and Meech Lake on the federal environmental role. Fragmented responsibility for environmental issues preceded Meech Lake but the terms of the *Canadian Environmental Protection Act* allow for provincial devolution only if their standards meet or

exceed the federal standard. The growth of global environmental problems not referred to directly by Lithwick and Maslove increases the federal role and blunts at least some of their concerns about the possible reluctance of some provinces to pursue environmental issues aggressively. See N.H. Lithwick and A.M. Maslove, "The Sum of the Parts: Free Trade and Meech Lake," in Katherine A. Graham (ed.) *How Ottawa Spends: 1989-90* (Ottawa: Carleton University Press, 1989), pp. 25-31.

10   The reduction requirements for CFCs and halons of the Montreal Protocol are discussed in Smith and Vodden, "Global Environmental Problems." References below to impacts and benefit-cost results are also found in this paper.

11   It is important to note that the U.S. Environmental Protection Agency also played a crucial role in putting together the consensus that led to the adoption of the Montreal Protocol.

12   In implementing the Montreal Protocol, Environment Canada chose to allocate the marketable permits to producers in the form of production authorizations. This decision was made on the basis of a consideration of the transaction costs of allocating these rights to producers or users. More detail is provided in Smith and Vodden, "Global Environmental Policy."

13   In fact, all of the existing evidence suggests that the reduction requirements of the Montreal Protocol will be exceeded.

14   The range of uncertainty about potential greenhouse impacts is very large. At one extreme, some scientists argue that we should already be taking actions to reduce carbon dioxide emissions. Other apparently noted and respectable scientists hold opposing views. The costs of reducing emissions may be so high that solid evidence of benefits will be required to generate specific policy responses.

15   R.W. Hahn, "Economic Prescriptions for Environmental Problems: How the Patient Followed the Doctor's Orders," *Journal of Economic Perspectives*, vol. 3, No. 2, Spring 1989, pp. 95-114.

CHAPTER 6

LITTLE HELP ON THE PRAIRIE:
CANADIAN FARM INCOME PROGRAMS
AND THE WESTERN GRAIN ECONOMY

Michael J. Prince

Résumé

Au cours de la période 1984-89, les transferts fédéraux vers l'agriculture de l'Ouest ont atteint des niveaux sans précédent. Dans ce chapitre on examine l'impact qu'ont les programmes fédéraux d'appui au revenu des agriculteurs sur les producteurs de grain des Prairies. On soutient que si ces initiatives en matière de politique agricole étaient nécessaires pour l'économie del'Ouest, basée sur le grain, elles auront éventuellement des effets graves. Parmi ceux-ci, le plus inquiétant c'est que les programmes créés pour stabiliser et augmenter les revenus des agriculteurs à court terme risquent de faire baisser à long terme les prix et les revenus en encourageant un excès de production. On discute l'examen de la politique agricole lancé par le gouvernment Mulroney en novembre 1989 et ses rapports avec les mesures de protection conçues pour les agriculteurs. Des réformes graduelles et fondamentales sont à l'étude, dont la notion de "découplage", c'est-à-dire l'idée que les programmes de transfert de revenus aux agriculteurs ne devraient plus être liés à la production de denrées particulières. Les retombées de la politique de 1984-88 ainsi que de ce nouvel examen rendent beaucoup plus probables des conflits fédéraux-provinciaux et interrégionaux au sujet de la politique canadienne en matière d'agriculture, au cours de ce deuxième mandat des conservateurs.

During the past five years, federal transfers to Western agriculture reached record levels. Canadian government assistance to the Prairie grain sector exceeded $11 billion, representing about 80 per cent of total net grain cash income over the 1984-89 period. In 1987 for example, in response to a sharp decline in world grain prices caused by the international grain subsidy war, the Mulroney government provided additional support, above existing stabilization programs, of approximately $17,000 per Prairie farmer.

In a very real sense, as Conservatives have emphasized, the federal government stood by grain producers as they faced difficult circumstances, offering them substantial financial assistance. Consequently, the phrase "little help" in the title of this chapter may seem odd or inaccurate. Yet public spending of this magnitude has both immediate and longer-term impacts, and costs as well as benefits. Our interest in this chapter, therefore, is to consider a fuller range of effects that federal farm income programs have on Western grain producers and the Canadian agri-food industry.

The main argument of this chapter is that while recent federal agriculture policy initiatives for the Prairie grain sector were welcomed and needed, these initiatives have many potentially serious effects. These policy effects include:

°   farmers becoming too reliant on transfer payments;

°   the discouragement of crop diversification and innovation;

°   a retreat from sound financing principles;

°   frustration of the federal deficit reduction plan;

°   the creation of an unpredictable policy environment and raising expectations of future "bail outs"; and,

°   failure to relieve serious farm debt problems.

The most disturbing aspect of the existing agriculture income support system is the cruel paradox that programs instituted to stabilize and raise farm incomes in the short term may end up depressing prices and incomes over the long term by encouraging excess production. The Canadian agriculture policy review initiated by the Mulroney government in November 1989 must address these flaws if it is to improve the workings of the farm safety net system and enhance the viability of the farm community.

In the first section, we outline and assess the Mulroney government's agriculture policy agenda and record for the 1984-88 period. The results of this agenda are considered in the context of the Prairie farm crisis of the 1980s. In the second, we describe the Canadian farm income security system — the agricultural safety nets — and examine the main federal policy responses to the Prairie crisis, including the quantum leap in federal expenditures. The third section analyzes the effects of safety net programs on Prairie farm income and notes the strengths and shortcomings of the farm income security system. In the fourth section, in keeping with the theme of this edition, we discuss the Conservatives' agricultural policy approach for the 1990s. We conclude with a comment on Ottawa's 1990-91 agriculture spending plans. Agriculture Canada's spending is to decline $823 million or 30 per cent in 1990-91, and most of that decline is in Western grain programs.

The analysis shows that over the 1984-88 period, the Mulroney government achieved only modest progress in implementing their agriculture policy agenda. Existing federal (and provincial) farm stabilization programs were inadequate in providing income protection to Western farmers facing severe financial stress. This prompted the government to introduce several measures of special assistance. The effects of these policy actions have been mixed. While helping to stabilize and even augment Prairie farm incomes, safety net programs have not solved the farm debt problems, and they have distributional effects which raise the issue of equity among farmers. Under the recently launched agriculture policy review, farm income support programs are being examined. Both incremental and more fundamental policy reforms are under discussion, including the notion of "decoupling", that is, the idea that farm income transfer programs no longer be tied to the production of specific commodities. The legacy of the 1984-88 record combined with this new policy review and the 1990 Budget and Estimates suggest a much greater likelihood for federal-provincial and inter-regional conflict over Canadian agriculture policy in the Tories second mandate.

FEDERAL AGRICULTURAL POLICY, 1984-88: GOALS AND RESULTS

Table 6.1 presents the Conservatives' approach to agriculture policy in terms of intended goals and actual results over the 1984-88 period. The Tories expressed a broad strategy toward agriculture policy early in their first mandate, a strategy closely linked to their overarching agenda of economic renewal through government restraint. At various times and in different documents, the Mulroney government expressed six main goals in agriculture policy. Overall, these goals called for a reduced and modified role for Ottawa in the agri-food industry.

Table 6.1
The Conservatives' Agriculture Policy Agenda and Record, 1984-88

Intended Goals*	Actual Results*
1. Reduce federal spending.	Federal spending increased dramatically.
2. Have provinces and producers share more of the financial responsibility.	Mixed success overall. National Tripartite Stabilization Plan established yet unresolved on Crop Insurance.
3. Pursue federal-provincial co-operation.	Continuance of historical pattern of harmony. National Agriculture Strategy, 1986.
4. A more market-sensitive industry.	Partial results (e.g. Canadian Rural Transition Program, 1986.)
5. Streamlined regulatory interventions.	Modest outcomes.
6. International competitiveness and trade liberalization.	Some action and ongoing advocacy. A founding member of the Cairns Group.**

Notes: * Based on various documents. See text and Appendix 6.1 in this chapter for details and references.

** Established in Cairns, Australia, in 1986, to promote agriculture trade reform through GATT negotiations. Besides Canada, the Cairns Group includes Argentina, Australia, Brazil, Chile, Columbia, Hungary, Indonesia, Malaysia, New Zealand, the Philippines, Thailand, and Uruguay.

In general the Conservatives achieved only minimal to modest progress in realizing their agriculture policy goals in their first mandate. Arguably, they failed to implement the most fundamental shifts in policy they had intended. First, the federal financial role in agriculture was not reduced in either absolute terms or vis-à-vis the provincial governments. Federal agriculture spending grew from $3.2 billion in 1984-85 to over $6 billion in 1988-89. Over the 1984-88 period, Ottawa spent about $17 billion on agriculture — double the federal expenditure for this sector in the previous four year period. This also represented a fourfold increase in income support for farmers over that four year period.[1]

As the 1989 Budget papers explained, these large, unintended expenditures in the agriculture sector were due to four factors:

° **First,** the federal government...intervened to assist grain farmers caught in the price collapse resulting from the international grain trade war. The trade war had its roots in the farm policies of certain countries, which encouraged uneconomic grain production and eroded the market share of traditional producers (like Canada).

° **Second,** confronted with three major droughts within five years, which particularly hurt the Prairies, the federal and provincial governments introduced special measures to supplement the crop insurance program.

° **Third,** although agriculture is a shared responsibility, the federal government has borne the brunt of the costs associated with these difficulties.

° **Fourth,** concurrent with declining market incomes, particularly in the grains and oilseed sectors, the value of farm assets declined by 25 per cent relative to 1981 levels and some farmers found themselves with neither the cash flow nor the security needed to cover their debts. The government introduced a number of measures to help restore the financial viability of the Farm Credit Corporation and, through the Farm Debt Review Boards and various transition programs, to provide assistance to farmers in difficulties.[2]

Thus, many key initiatives in Ottawa's actual agriculture policy agenda, especially pertaining to farm income protection, developed in response to unexpected events. While some of these initiatives are consistent with specific elements of the initial agenda, such as promoting national reconciliation, perhaps most policy responses over the 1984-88 period deviated and even detracted from the intended goals of government restraint and a "depoliticized" agri-food industry. Instead, Agriculture Canada has an increased presence in the sector, not less, and government transfers now account for a larger share of farm income in Canada.

Table 6.2
Distribution of Farm Borrowers and Farms
by Financial Status, Prairie Provinces

Estimate*	Manitoba	Sask.	Alberta
Farm Credit Corporation (1987)			
Stable	76.3	60.3	67.9
Cash-flow difficulty	18.3	28.3	22.2
Insolvent	5.4	11.4	9.9
Total	100.0	100.0	100.0
Agriculture Canada (1986)			
Stable	87.3	86.0	85.7
Financially vulnerable	6.5	6.3	6.6
Deteriorating	3.8	5.3	4.7
Nonviable	2.4	2.4	3.0
Total	100.0	100.0	100.0
Economic Council			
All farms (1985)			
Stable	73	75	81
Vulnerable	12	10	8
Deteriorating	10	10	8
Nonviable	5	5	3
Total	100	100	100
All farms (1987)			
Stable	67	72	74
Vulnerable	12	11	9
Deteriorating	8	8	7
Nonviable	13	9	10
Total	100	100	100

Source: Estimates by the Farm Credit Corporation and Agriculture Canada were reported in Canada, House of Commons Standing Committee on Agriculture, *Farm Input Costs*, June 1987, pp. 10-11. The Economic Council of Canada estimates are from L. Auer, *Canadian Prairie Farming, 1960-2000*, (Ottawa: Economic Council of Canada, 1989), p. 26.

Note: Estimates by the Farm Credit Corporation and Agriculture Canada focus on the debt-servicing capacity of farm borrowers, and those by the Economic Council are based on census data and taxation statistics of all Prairie farms.

Table 6.2 presents information on the magnitude of the financial crisis of Prairie farms in the mid- to late-1980s. The results vary somewhat, in part because of differences in survey methods and definitions. While all three surveys show that most Prairie farmers were financially stable (family income was sufficient to cover basic living expenses), a range of about 15 to 40 per cent were under some financial stress, that is, about 20,000 to 50,000 farmers. As the Economic Council estimates show, the financial stress in 1985 became a crisis in 1987.

Although grain prices were already down in 1985, they dropped to disastrous levels in 1987. Measured in real terms, they fell to their lowest point in over 50 years. As a result, the number of farms in financial difficulty increased sharply — from 23 per cent in 1985 to 28 per cent in 1987; the proportion of nonviable operations jumped from four to 10 per cent. Despite the important contribution of non-farm and off-farm sources of income, in 1987 farm cash expenditures exceeded total farm-family income on one out of every 10 Prairie farms.[3]

THE CANADIAN FARM INCOME SECURITY SYSTEM

What may be called Canada's agriculture safety net or farm income security system comprises institutions and policies that directly affect the flow and level of incomes to farmers. The farm income support system is certainly a subsystem of the larger agri-food policy sector and may, depending on the direction reforms take, become more closely integrated with the traditional income security system. Like other components of social security, the agriculture safety net programs, in providing cash benefits and augmenting the incomes of farmers, address states of dependencies and risks associated with the market economy.

Agriculture Canada's strategic objectives are to promote the growth, stability and competitiveness of the agri-food sector. Canadian farm income policy can be seen as resting on three basic farmer-oriented goals. One is income adequacy ensuring that farmers and their families have an adequate standard of living. "Frequently, the objective is stated as that of ensuring adequate levels of income for the operators of small family farms."[4] The intent of this goal is to alleviate low or poverty income levels among farmers. A second goal concerns equity or income comparability. The aim here is to provide farmers with income-earning opportunities and living standards comparable to those enjoyed by other Canadians. Thus, on average and over time, the rates of return for resources devoted to primary agricultural production should be close to the rate earned by comparable resources in other occupations. The third goal is income stability. The aim is to protect farmers against wide income fluctuations from one year to another due to market volatility and natural hazards such as droughts.

In Canada, the national system of financial support programs for farmers represents a five-level structure of income transfers. Level one consists of income stabilization programs such as Crop Insurance, the *Agricultural Stabilization Act* (ASA), and the *Western Grain Stabilization Act* (WGSA). Level two includes credit assistance programs provided by the Farm Credit Corporation and other agencies. Level three entails tax assistance policies such as the Fuel Tax Rebate Program. Level four includes transition or adjustment assistance initiatives like the Canadian Rural Transition Program. Finally, level five consists of disaster or special assistance measures such as the Canadian Crop Drought Assistance Program and the Special Canadian Grains Program (SCGP).

An overview of Canada's agriculture safety net system is given in Table 6.3. Among the oldest safety net programs are income stabilization programs such as Crop Insurance. In many respects these programs are similar to social insurance programs like Unemployment Insurance and the Canada/Quebec Pension Plans. They involve a collective pooling of risks and resources in order to provide at least a partial replacement of income. Financed by producer levies and government contributions, a relationship between premiums and coverage is maintained which, in turn, confers a sense of entitlement to benefits. Unlike social insurance programs, however, farm income stabilization programs are voluntary, not compulsory. Moreover, these stabilization programs provide benefits to participating active members of the farm labour force. In this sense, level one programs are earnings supplementation measures.

Table 6.3
Canada's Agriculture Safety Net System

Level	Policy Type	Objectives	Illustrative Federal Programs
1	Income Stabilization	Moderate short term price or yield fluctuations and production risks.	Crop Insurance, 1959; Western Grain Stabilization, 1976; Agricultural Stabilization, 1958/1985
2	Credit Assistance	Reduce farmer's risk of fluctuating interest risks and to assist farmers in temporary financial stress.	Farm Credit Corporation, 1959; Farm Debt Review Boards, 1986
3	Tax Assistance	Help farmers to finance and operate their farms by reducing costs of inputs.	Fuel Tax Rebate Program, 1984
4	Transition Assistance	Support farmers leaving agriculture to non-farming activities and jobs.	Canadian Rural Transition Program, 1986
5	Special Assistance	Maintain farm incomes in periods of crisis or disaster.	Special Canadian Grains Program, 1986 and 1987; Canadian Crop Drought Assistance Program, 1988

Note: Under broader conceptions of the agriculture safety net system could be added one or more of: Farmers' own responsibility for managing risk, national supply management programs, certain transportation programs for agriculture such as the *Western Grain Transportation Act*, animal disease and pest control legislation, and counterpart provincial programs.

Appendix 6.1 provides a chronological summary of major federal agriculture policy developments from 1984 to 1990. This period is characterized by considerable policy activity, most of which is reactive to climatic or economic crises. Read together, Tables 6.3 and Appendix 6.1 indicate that the Mulroney Tories have introduced legislative reforms and/or new policy initiatives at all five levels of the safety net system. These interventions have added to the complexity of the system, raised its political visibility both domestically and internationally, and generated concerns over equity between various agriculture sectors and different producing regions. Many of these reforms and initiatives were in direct response to the financial problems in the Prairie region.

When compared with the Trudeau Liberal record, notable features of Conservative government policy and spending on agriculture are underlined. Grace Skogstad has pointed out that, "Agriculture Canada undertook no new major expenditure programs after the passage of the *Western Grain Stabilization Act* in 1976."[5] Moreover, the department's level of spending declined in real terms from then into the early 1980s. New agriculture policy initiatives by the Liberals were few and emphasized a marketing orientation.

By contrast, under the Tories, Agriculture Canada has experienced an active legislative and programming record of major changes to established policies and the introduction of several new policies. The Tories endeavoured to show strong leadership and sensitivity to the severe financial problems facing the farm sector while, at the same time, pursuing their fiscal plan of government restraint and deficit reduction.

The real politick behind the Tories' 1984-88 record in agriculture, however, was essentially a policy of giving priority to the financial needs of producers over other agenda goals. It would be a mistake to interpret this outcome as a simple case of the Mulroney government capitulating to special interests or running away from deficit reduction. Rather, the factors which help explain the Tories' agriculture policy record are a complex mix of domestic and international politics, economic and climatic conditions and farm policy dynamics. These factors include the severe financial stress in the Prairie farm community symbolized by falling grain prices since 1980, reaching their lowest level ever in 1987, and aggravated by droughts in 1984, 1985 and 1988. The result, as noted earlier, has been that Agriculture Canada's spending did not decline as planned but rather skyrocketed over the 1984-88 period. This spending pattern was also due to the statutory obligations under the major farm stabilization programs to protect producers' incomes and the introduction of special assistance programs prompted by inherent limitations in the statutory programs to compensate for weak prices over a prolonged period. During this period, actual expenditures of several agriculture programs exceeded the Main Estimates in certain fiscal years because of the serious financial problems facing farmers. The difference between actual expenditures and the Main Estimates was obtained through various ways: supplementary estimates, funds being "resourced" from future years in a program's budget, and Special Governor General's Warrants.

Behind the political imperative to respond to these real problems were the following elements: The Prairie provinces were well represented in the government caucus and the inner circle of the Cabinet, the Prime Minister's personal attention to agriculture policy issues, the shared partisanship between the Mulroney Conservative government and two of the three Prairie premiers (who, at that time, called for special assistance for grain farmers), and the farm trade subsidy war between the United States and Europe with Canadian farmers caught in the crossfire. On this last factor, the 1987 and 1988 SCGP initiatives were aimed at relieving financial stress in the grain sector, preventing inappropriate resource withdrawals out of the sector, and maintaining Canada's export market share. Associated with this has been a strong willingness to value Canadian farming as both an important business sector and a valuable way of life.

In both absolute and real terms, federal spending on agriculture grew dramatically over the 1984-89 period. Table 6.4 provides a specific illustration of this, showing federal support to Prairie farmers in 1987. Total support in terms of direct payments, rebates and liabilities represented just over $4 billion or $31,000 per self-employed farmer in the Prairie provinces. Of this, Ottawa directly provided net benefits of $2,539 million to approximately 130,000 self-employed Prairie farmers.

In the context of Canada's income security system, this level of support is quite substantial in expenditure terms and fairly concentrated in relation to the target groups.[6] Prairie farm income support in 1987 greatly exceeded federal expenditures in the region under the Canada Assistance Plan ($469 million and 180,000 recipients) and children's benefit programs (Family Allowances $486 million and the Child Tax Credit $322 million for 660,000 and 437,000 beneficiaries respectively).

Table 6.4
Federal Support to Farmers in the Prairie Provinces, 1987

	Manitoba	Sask.	Alberta	Total
		(Millions of dollars)		
Direct payments[1]				
Western Grain Stabiliz. Act (net)	255	743	360	1,358
Agricultural Stabiliz. Act (net)	--	-3	-6	-9
Crop insurance (net)	17	41	54	112
Dairy subsidy	11	7	19	37
Other direct payments[2]	1	7	23	31
Rebates	26	53	116	195
Special Canadian Grains Program	155	408	252	815
Total (net)	465	1,256	818	2,539
Other major liabilities				
Farm Credit Corporation (cumulative deficit)[3]	107	340	153	600
Payments to railways[4] under *Western Grain Transportation Act*	136	483	251	870
Total direct payments, rebates and liabilities	708	2,079	1,222	4,009
		(Thousands of dollars)		
Payment per farmer (self-employed)	28	36	26	31

1   Net payments are total payments less farmers' contributions.
2   Includes such payments as compensation for animal losses and damage to waterfowl.
3   The cumulative deficit is attributed to the Prairie provinces on the basis of their respective shares of FCC loan arrears during 1987/88.
4   Net of the $71.7 million that was to be refunded to the federal government in 1987/88.

Source: L. Auer, *Canadian Prairie Farming, 1960-2000* (Ottawa: Economic Council of Canada, 1989), p. 61.

It surpassed Unemployment Insurance benefits ($1,676 million to 186,000 claimants), and even rivalled spending under the federal elderly benefit programs (Old Age Security, Guaranteed Income Supplement, and Spouse's Allowance, $2,228 million and 478,000 beneficiaries) in the Prairie provinces. In fact, direct federal support to Prairie farmers in 1987 equalled federal Family Allowances payments ($2,534 million) to over 3.6 million families across the country.

True, this level of support to Prairie farmers is exceptional and historically atypical, while these other federal social transfers are regular and ongoing expenditure commitments under Canada's social policy contract. Our intent in making these agriculture and social program comparisons is to underscore the importance of farm support expenditures for the Prairie economy (a fact commonly noted by economists and agriculture policy analysts) as well as for the Canadian income security system (a point curiously missed by social policy analysts). Viewing agriculture safety net programs as part of, or likened to the income security system raises important administrative and political questions about how these farm programs should and in fact do interact with other social programs, the extent to which various needs and risks are addressed adequately and fairly, and how farm family income compares with the average Canadian family income.

The Mulroney government has introduced about a dozen major initiatives in agriculture - initiatives which are about equally divided between substantive amendments to existing policies such as the ASA and WGSA, and new policies such as the SCGP and those on rural transition and farm debt review. Their focus has largely centred on Prairie farm income stabilization, credit problems of producers, and the deficit position of certain safety net programs. Many of these new program initiatives have been in the form of special assistance (level five in the safety net system) and stopgap measures. When the major safety net programs (primarily level one stabilization policies) did not provide farmers with adequate income protection during extended periods of financial stress, the Tories filled the gaps with new programs like the SCGP, special drought assistance programs, Farm Debt Review Boards, special funds for the Farm Credit Corporation, and the Rural Transition Program. For example, over the 1984-85 to 1988-89 period, the federal government committed over $1 billion to address the credit problems of Canadian farmers.

EFFECTS OF SAFETY NET PROGRAMS ON PRAIRIE FARM INCOME

How effective are federal agricultural policies in stabilizing farm income and reducing farm-asset fluctuations? What has their impact been on the distribution of income within the Prairie agriculture sector? That is, who gets what and why? Table 6.5 summarizes the available evidence for addressing these issues.[7]

With respect to income stability and adequacy, federal programs have been relatively effective in both reducing major fluctuations in farm income and in augmenting low incomes. Up to the mid-1970s, income transfers from federal agricultural programs represented less than 10 per cent of realized net farm income. From the mid-1970s to the early 1980s, they represented on average between 20 to 25 per cent of farm income. Over the 1984-88 period, federal support to the grain sector constituted about 80 per cent of Prairie farm income, in excess of $11 billion of the $14.3 billion total net grain cash income for that period.[8]

The most substantial income support has come from the WGSA and the SCGP. In 1987-88, payments under these two programs provided $2.2 billion in direct support to Prairie farmers. Table 6.6 shows that WGSA and SCGP payments reduced the number of farmers in financial difficulty from 50 to 28 per cent across the Prairie region. According to the Economic Council's estimation:

> In the absence of these two programs, almost one-third of Prairie farmers would have been in a nonviable financial situation, with no cash income for living expenses. Payouts under the WGSA and the SCGP reduced that proportion to one-tenth. Income support enabled farmers to continue producing, and the Canadian Wheat Board to continue selling, Canadian wheat and coarse grains at competitive prices. Canada was therefore able to maintain its share of world markets.[9]

In terms of stabilizing the value of farm assets (land and buildings), "the events of the 1980s are a clear indication that the relationship between net farm income and asset values is not stable." Stabilizing and augmenting farm income to ensure a level of adequacy "does not automatically lead to a pre-determined asset-value level."[10]

Table 6.5
Effects of Selected Federal Agriculture Programs
on Prairie Farm Income and Wealth

Program	Income Adequacy	Asset Stability	Distributional Effects
Western Grain Transportation Act (WGTA)	Significant indirect income transfers, increasing since 1975.	No major impact on land price changes.	Large grain producers benefit most.
Western Grain Stabilization Act (WGSA)	Considerable stabilization and augmentation of total net farm income in the region since 1983.	Likely alleviated slide in land prices.	Larger grain farms benefit more than smaller farms.
Special Canadian Grains Program (SCGP)	Major impact in 1987 and 1988.	Slowed the decline in land values.	No impact.
Crop Insurance	Increased average level of net farm incomes, since 1983.	No real impact.	Program excludes livestock producers and forage and pasture farms.
Two-Price Wheat	Generally minimal effect. Only in 1987 did it raise farm income.	Slight impact.	Small effect within farm sector.
Farm Credit Corporation (FCC)	Stabilizes aggregate Prairie farm income. Uncertain whether it increases income.	Contributed to land-price inflation in late 1970s and early 1980s.	Intended to help new farmers, small farms, and less well-off farmers.

Note: Net farm income refers to total cash receipts from market sales and direct government farm transfer payments less total operating expenses and depreciation charges.

Source: As these effects are based on both theoretical and empirical analyses, they should not be taken as definitive conclusions but rather as likely policy outcomes. L. Auer, **Canadian Prairie Farming 1960-2000** (Ottawa: Economic Council of Canada, 1989); Economic Council of Canada, **Handling the Risks** (Ottawa: Economic Council of Canada, 1988); and, M. Fulton, K. Rosaasen and A. Schmitz, **Canadian Agricultural Policy and Prairie Agriculture** (Ottawa: Economic Council of Canada, 1989).

Table 6.6
Distribution of Farm Incomes in the Prairie Provinces,
With and Without WGSA and SCGP Payments,*
by Degree of Financial Stress, 1987

	Manitoba	Sask.	Alberta	All Three Provinces
		(Per cent)		
Without WGSA and SCGP:				
Stable	43	46	59	50
Vulnerable	12	11	10	11
Deteriorating	10	11	9	10
Nonviable	35	32	22	29
Total	100	100	100	100
With WGSA and SCGP:				
Stable	67	72	74	72
Vulnerable	12	11	9	10
Deteriorating	8	8	7	8
Nonviable	13	9	10	10
Total	100	100	100	100

Note: * Payments under the *Western Grain Stabilization Act* and the Special Canadian Grains Program.

Source: *Handling the Risks*, A Report on the Prairie Grain Economy (Ottawa: Economic Council of Canada, 1988), p. 70.

Referring again to Table 6.5, we see that federal agriculture safety net programs have at most slowed but not arrested the fall in farm land values and, in the case of the Farm Credit Corporation, may have contributed to the volatility of land values.

In terms of the distributional effects of federal farm income programs on the Prairie agriculture sector, benefits went disproportionately to large-scale and high-cost producers. Relatively little help was given to operators of small, marginal farms. Also, as Table 6.7 shows, benefits favoured grain and mixed types of farms over livestock and specialty farms by a wide margin, thus providing relatively more benefits to Saskatchewan than to Manitoba or Alberta. These distributional effects are largely the result of WGSA and SCGP payments being commodity-specific transfer programs.

Table 6.7

Average WGSA and SCGP Payment by Type of Farm and Distribution of Farm Types by Province, Prairie Region

	Grain	Livestock	Specialty	Mixed	All Types
			Type of Farm		
			(Thousands of dollars)		
Average WGSA and SCGP payment*	21,149	4,552	4,620	16,455	16,333
Distribution of Farm Types by Prairie Province**			(per cent)		
Alberta	42	30	8	20	100
Saskatchewan	71	8	2	19	100
Manitoba	54	17	9	20	100

Notes: *   Payments for 1987 under the *Western Grain Stabilization Act* and the Special Canadian Grains Program.

  **   For 1986

Source: Adapted from L. Auer, *Canadian Prairie Farming 1960-2000* (Ottawa: Economic Council of Canada, 1989), Table 4-5, p. 29 and Table 4-8, p. 32.

Spriggs and Van Kooten identify five problems that arise when commodity-based programs are used to provide income support to farm families on the grounds of social justice or to offset trade distortions. They argue that commodity-based farm income programs:

° tend to confer greater benefits on larger production units - benefits depend upon the size of output. However, it is difficult to justify why farm families with larger production units, and supposedly greater wealth and perhaps larger incomes, should receive greater income transfers than those with less wealth and smaller incomes.

○   may not translate into income support for the needy farm family. This would be the case if the particular producer did not grow the subsidized product.

○   convey a subsidy only on those farmers who choose to participate by paying levies and hence only to those who make a particular business decision. On social justice grounds, one could argue that the subsidy should be based on need.

○   are not tailored to satisfy the needs of the individual because programs like WGSA pay a subsidy on the basis of a five-year average.

○   may be part of a strategy for encouraging other countries to remove their trade distorting policies, but programs like SCGP provide a recipe for ever-increasing levies of domestic protection.[11]

According to Don Mazankowski, the Deputy Prime Minister and Minister of Agriculture, Ottawa as well as the provinces and producers learned several important lessons from the 1984-88 period of governance.[12] First, they learned that Canada's major safety net programs do not provide farmers with adequate protection during extended periods of financial stress. The need for special assistance like SCGP is closely linked to the nature of the payment formula in front line stabilization programs such as the ASA and WGSA. The payment formula of these programs is based on a moving five-year average of price. Unfortunately, when the industry moves down the price cycle and remains at the bottom for a prolonged period, the level of support erodes at a time when it is most needed. The agriculture policy community also learned "that when the delivery of federal support is divided along regional or commodity lines, equity becomes an issue. When different support programs are designed to meet the needs of specific regions and commodities, it is difficult to ensure all farmers are treated fairly."[13] Third, the Tories witnessed how the current farm safety net system can put a heavy financial claim on the federal public purse. Over the 1984-88 period, the Mulroney government spent about $17 billion on agriculture, double the amount in the previous four-year period. A fourth basic lesson is that if producers are not committed to the voluntary programs, such as crop insurance schemes, and do not participate in them, then the programs will be of limited effectiveness. Concerns continue over the number of unin-sured farmers and the lack of affordable insurance for the replacement value of lost yields. In 1988, for example, only about 50 per cent of farmers in Manitoba purchased crop insurance. In 1989, following a serious drought, the number increased to about 70 per cent. This leads to a final point which Mazankowski calls the most important lesson—

the interdependence of all the key participants in the Canadian agri-food system, namely federal and provincial governments, industry, individual farmers, suppliers, producer organizations and consumers. "One of the major challenges that we face is to share the responsibility [for agriculture] in a manner that is fair and equitable, and that best serves the interests of the industry as a whole, both in the short and the long term."[14] These lessons or interpretations of the 1980s, provide a context for the Conservatives' agriculture policy review and vision for the 1990s.

THE POLITICS OF REFORMING AGRICULTURAL POLICY IN THE 1990s: GROWING TOGETHER OR GROWING APART?

In November 1989, the three federal Agriculture Ministers released a policy review paper entitled, *Growing Together: A Vision for Canada's Agri-Food Industry.*[15] This policy document is likely to be dubbed the Green Paper, referring to the colour of its outside covers. In policy-making terms, this review can also be described as a "green paper,"[16] as *Growing Together* is not a definitive statement of federal government policy. Instead, it sets out some principles for choosing a new vision for Canada's agri-food industry, and identifies various directions for change on which to build a policy framework for the 1990s. This allows the Mulroney government to test and assess the political feasibility of a range of policy options. *Growing Together* serves several political and policy functions for Agriculture Canada and the Tories. It conveys Ottawa's thinking on the agri-food industry; provides information about the status of Canadian farmers and farm commodities; invites participation by and a working partnership of all the key players in the agricultural policy field; and, stimulates discussion and debate on reviewing and reforming agricultural policies and programs.

Earlier, in December 1988, the Minister of Agriculture stated that a new vision for the agri-food sector was needed in order to bring policy into line with the new realities facing agriculture. In April 1989, federal budget papers previewed the Conservatives' approach to agriculture for the 1990s. That approach:

> ...will be to foster a productive and **economically viable** industry that is able to become increasingly **self-reliant** in a stable and predictable policy environment which does not impede innovation, risk-taking or diversification. The farm sector will be encouraged to respond to new

market opportunities and changes will be made to
policies and programs that insulate farmers from market
signals. As well, federal policies will focus on **environmentally sustainable** development consistent with the
long-term conservation of Canada's soil and water base
and safety and health of Canadians.[17]

In Prince Albert in August 1989, the federal and provincial
governments called for a thorough review of agricultural policies with
a view to addressing the problems and opportunities facing Canada's
agri-food sector and developing a new policy framework, building on
the National Agriculture Strategy. The *Growing Together* Green Paper
is designed to launch this comprehensive review of current policies and
programs.

Growing Together identifies seven agriculture policy areas requiring re-examination and redirection for the 1990s. These are: (i)
marketing, trade development and value-added; (ii) financing and
managing the family farm business; (iii) safety nets; (iv) supply management; (v) agriculture transportation; (vi) food safety and quality; and,
(vii) sustainable agricultural development.

The Green Paper sets out four overall goals on which to develop
a new vision for the future of agriculture. These are: more market
responsiveness; greater self-reliance in the agri-food sector; a national
policy which recognizes regional diversity; and increased environmental sustainability. The first three of these goals are variations on ideas
embedded in the Tories' 1984-88 agenda and expressed by the 1985
Nielsen Task Force Report on Agriculture and the 1986 National
Agriculture Strategy statement agreed to by Ottawa and the provinces.
The fourth goal reflects the recent increased public concern and
political awareness of the need for sustainable economic development.
This is another sense in which *Growing Together* is a green (read:
environmentally sensitive) paper.

The goals of "greater self-reliance in the agri-food sector" and
"a national policy which recognizes regional diversity" especially raise
concerns and issues about the farm income support programs. On the
notion of greater self-reliance, the Green Paper states:

Greater self-reliance means that given the right tools ...
farmers are free to manage their own operations in
response to market signals. It does not mean eliminating
government support. Certainly, the federal government
has demonstrated, by unprecedented support in recent

years, a clear commitment to assist the industry...But it does mean that the nature of public support may need to be changed to ensure that government support does not mask market signals. Large federal government support in recent years has not solved all the problems facing the industry, and may have distorted market signals.[18]

On the goal of a national agriculture policy which recognizes regional diversity, the Green Paper emphasizes the "need for a more national agriculture policy which fosters greater equity between all commodities and regions. We must find ways to develop national policies which are flexible in the face of regional realities but encourage a more level playing field."[19] And on the issue of assistance to particular regions, it states:

> To ensure enhanced prosperity, disincentives to diversification within a region must be removed...The federal government fully recognizes that regionally specific programs are necessary from time to time if the agri-food sector is to successfully accommodate change...Transition assistance may also be required to enable those farmers leaving agriculture to move into more economically rewarding non-farm activities with dignity.[20]

The Green Paper summarizes in frank fashion the issues behind why the agriculture safety net programs are a major part of this policy review.

> The past few years have demonstrated that there are substantial gaps in our safety nets, denying the predictability that farmers need to remain efficient, competitive, and self-reliant. Trade wars, drought and floods have generated ad hoc government responses and have weakened the financial viability and responsiveness of many stabilization programs. We have also seen how difficult it is to treat farmers equitably when stabilization programs are designed along commodity and regional lines.[21]

Although the expression "decoupling" is not used in *Growing Together*, the idea of severing farm income transfers from the production of specific commodities is raised in relation to international trade negotiations and the notion of a farm-based stabilization plan. Thus,

> ... despite the progress with tripartite stabilization, recent countervail actions against Canadian hogs and pork have pointed to the need to assess whether a more generally available program might better serve the needs of the Canadian industry. An approach which allows governments and producers to share the costs of insuring against all risks which can affect the viability of the farm unit, and is available to all regions and commodities, might allow for better planning and less challenges internationally.[22]

To assist in addressing these immediate problems as well as in developing long-term program options, the Green Paper suggests seven principles for safety net reform. They are:

1   Producers should be provided with the tools or mechanisms to plan for their own long-term farm stability.

2   Stabilization programs should be designed to offer short-term support for producers as adjustments are made toward long-term market trends.

3   We must examine the feasibility of designing safety net programs which focus on the viability of the individual farm unit.

4   Safety net programs should encourage a level playing field within Canada, while recognizing regional differences. Regional differences can be taken into account through flexibility under a net benefit ceiling.

5   Funding of safety net programs should be cost-shared among producers, provincial governments and the federal government.

6   Objective criteria, and cost-sharing arrangements, should be established for determining the existence, extent and responses of any widespread or multi-year phenomena.

7   The implementation of all forms of safety nets — credit programs, tax policies, stabilization programs and disaster assistance — should be undertaken so that sound land use and animal farming practices are encouraged.[23]

The next step in this policy review process was a national conference on the agri-food industry held in Ottawa in December 1989. More than 1,600 people representing every segment of the industry and both levels of government participated in the conference. The aim of the conference was to "provide an opportunity for all partners to talk together, to better understand some of the issues facing them, to further develop the principles outlined in this paper, and to launch the process of turning them into concrete actions."[24]

In the area of farm safety net programs, federal-provincial working groups are already established and have begun to develop policy options which will be discussed with all partners in industry. The hard policy tasks and political risks associated with reforming the safety net were identified by the Minister of Agriculture in his keynote address to the conference.

> This policy review is our chance to agree on permanent criteria for dealing with short-term problems. To agree on how assistance should be targeted. To agree on an equitable sharing of costs. And to agree on how to deal with special circumstances in a manner consistent with our long-term plans. But — and this is important — let's not be so focussed on the short-term that we forget the long-term. We have to improve our safety net for the longer term. And it won't be easy. Regional and commodity differences will be tough to reconcile. There seems to be general agreement that we need to move forward on a faster track with reforming the safety net for grains and oilseeds. While moving faster, it should proceed within the overall framework for safety net improvement outlined in our policy paper.[25]

Under this recently launched agriculture policy review both incremental and more fundamental reforms are under discussion, including the idea of "decoupling" farm income support programs.[26] The legacy of the 1984-88 record combined with the politics of international farm trade liberalization and the comprehensiveness of this new review suggest a much greater likelihood for federal-provincial and interregional conflict over Canadian agriculture policy in the Conservatives' second mandate. From a political analysis perspective, it seems an open question whether Tory efforts at reforming agricultural policy in the early 1990s will result in the industry and country growing together or growing apart.

The 1990-91 Agriculture Spending Plan

For 1990-91, the government projects a decrease in Agriculture Canada's departmental expenditures of $823 million, almost a 30 per cent decline from the forecast expenditures for 1989-90. The Grain and Oilseeds Program area alone is estimated to decline by $763 million or 69.9 per cent to $328 million. This decrease is due almost entirely to the reduced resources under the Canadian Crop Drought Assistance Program.[27]

Despite calls for additional special assistance for Prairie grain farmers to compensate for poor weather and the recent re-escalation of the international grain subsidy war by the United States, the 1990 Federal Budget did not provide any relief or reassurance of help. In reaction, the Saskatchewan Finance Minister said, "There was not one word about agriculture in the budget speech. We view this with great dismay. It strikes at the engine of economic growth in this province."[28]

Expenditures for the agriculture safety net system will decline in 1990-91 by several hundred million dollars. In addition, there is a marked drop in Person Years (PYs) for the Income Protection activity in Agriculture Canada's domestic policy and programs area, falling from 122 PYs in 1989-90 to only 21 PYs for this year. Fiscal year 1990-91 sees the virtual disappearance of special assistance to individual Prairie farmers (level five programs in the safety net). The Two-Price Wheat Policy Compensation Program and the SCGP ended in 1989-90, and no new ad hoc initiatives were contained in this budget nor are any likely to be announced. In the Green Paper, Agriculture Canada notes that transition assistance (level four of the safety net) may be required to allow farmers leaving agriculture to move into non-farm activities effectively and with dignity. The department's spending on adjustment assistance to farmers, however, is expected to drop 40 per cent, from $66.5 million in 1989-90 to $39.4 million in 1990-91.

Spending under Fuel Tax Rebates and Refunds (level three of the safety net) is planned to drop 58 per cent, from $87 million to $36 million. While tax assistance is down, credit assistance (level two) is anticipated to increase 63 per cent, from $40.1 million to $65.4 million. In addition, the Farm Credit Corporation intends to request that Parliament increase the contributed capital for 1989-90 from $625 million to $825 million, then to $1,125 million for 1990-91. These changes will allow the FCC to raise its maximum allowable borrowing levels.[29]

Farm income stabilization programs (level one of the safety net) are projected in the aggregate to decline slightly in 1990-91. Federal payments under the WGS and ASA programs will increase while there is a decrease in federal contributions for Crop Insurance. Beyond the agriculture safety net system shown in Table 6.3, Western transportation subsidies will grow 17 per cent because of increased payments to the railways under the WGTA.

These expenditure and policy choices suggest that the Mulroney government has determined that the Western grain sector has improved, moving from a situation of exceptional crisis to one of more typical stress; and, that work is underway to develop a more effective and predictable grain safety net system by 1992 or 1993. Indeed, Agriculture Canada predicts a return to normal grain production and exports for 1990-91. However, because of lower government payments and higher costs, net market returns to grain producers this year are expected to be below the drought-reduced returns of 1988.[30] Moreover, the department's 1990-91 expenditure plan contains the cautionary line that, "the ability of farmers to withstand the 'boom and bust' shocks inherent in the agricultural sector is diminishing, primarily as a result of the trade war between the United States and the European community."[31]

The immediate outlook is not bright for many Prairie farmers. Agriculture Canada's farm income forecast for 1990 is that realized net farm income will be 32 per cent below the 1984-88 average. The 1990 total net farm income for Canada is estimated to be almost 43 per cent lower than 1989. This drop in farm income is expected to be most pronounced in the Prairie provinces due to continued low world grain prices and the sharp drop in federal government program payments, noted above. The projected declines in total net income in 1990 for the three Prairie provinces are: Alberta 65.9 per cent, Manitoba 78.1 per cent, and Saskatchewan 85.4 per cent.[32]

In Saskatchewan, farm income may well be less than zero this year, with grain farmers spending more to plant and harvest their crops than they earn from selling them. In the absence of federal special assistance and in response to federal budget cuts that will cost Saskatchewan $100 million annually, Premier Grant Devine announced on March 5, 1990 cuts of $250 million in provincial programs over the next two years, to be redirected to help farmers and to keep health, education and social service programs secure.[33] Farming in the Western grain economy remains in a state in which much is to be endured and little to be enjoyed. We shall have to await another budget at another time to see if the necessary international and domestic policy changes occur that will provide more than a little help on the Prairie.

Appendix 6.1
Chronology of Major Federal Agriculture Policy Developments,
1984-90

1984   °   Canadian Agricultural Export Corporation (Canagrex) is terminated by the new Conservative Government.

°   Fuel Tax Rebate Program is introduced as a "temporary measure."

1985   °   Study Team Report on Agriculture to the Ministerial (Nielsen) Task Force on Program Review. Recommended a more market-oriented policy approach.

°   Capital Gain Tax Exemption up to a $500,000 lifetime limit to assist farmers and businesses.

°   *Western Grain Stabilization Act* amended to allow an interim payment in which preliminary cash flow calculations indicate a substantial payment will be required.

°   *Agricultural Stabilization Act* amended to enable the introduction of cost sharing plans involving a producer, the federal government and/or the provinces.

°   *Farm Improvement Loan Act* extended from mid-1985 to end of 1986.

°   Farm Credit Corporation reduces interest rate to 12.75 per cent for a five-year term on loans made in 1981-82 at between 14 and 16.75 per cent. Foregone federal revenues estimated to be $80 million over the five years.

1986   °   Dairy policy statement giving a five-year commitment to continued stability for the industry.

°   Budget announces expenditure reductions in Agriculture Canada of about $260 million over three years.

°   Federal-Provincial Working Group on Farm Finance formed.

- A $111 million write-off of the deficit in the Canadian Wheat Board's barley accounts in 1986-87.

- Two-Price Wheat Program amended to allow the Canadian Wheat Board to set domestic prices at between $200 and $404 per tonne.

- Canadian Rural Transition Program announced to ease the adjustment for farmers seeking alternative employment.

- Farm Credit Corporation's $700 million Commodity-Based Loan Program introduced. It reduces interest rates and links them to commodity prices, producing a six to eight per cent range of interest rates, with the FCC carrying part of the cost.

- Farm Debt Review Boards being established to offer debt review and advisory services to farmers in financial stress.

- Fuel Tax Rebate Program revised and extended to 1988 at a cost to Ottawa of $120 million, primarily of benefit to farmers.

- Tobacco Diversification Plan of $33.5 million initiated to address economic adjustment in the tobacco industry.

- Crop Drought Assistance Program for producers in Western Canada implemented.

- *Prairie Grain Advance Payments Act* amended to streamline administrative procedures and allow the Canadian Wheat Board to quickly enact the act's emergency provisions.

- Under the *Agricultural Stabilization Act,* federal-provincial agreements signed establishing national tripartite stabilization schemes for hog, cattle, and lamb producers.

- A National Agriculture Strategy endorsed at First Ministers' conference. Agreed that there be improved protection against climatic and economic risks and that stabilization programs be self-sustaining and actuarially sound.

- Special Canadian Grains Program of $1 billion to assist grain farmers caught in the price collapse due to the international grain trade war.

1987
   ° Prime Minister Mulroney requests the Economic Council of Canada to undertake a study of "The Future of the Prairie Grain Economy."

   ° Agriculture Canada signed new agreements, under the *Agricultural Stabilization Act*, with provincial governments and producers for apples, sugar beets and beans.

   ° New Cabinet posts of Minister of State for Agriculture and Minister for Grains and Oilseeds created to support Minister of Agriculture.

   ° *Farm Improvement and Marketing Co-operatives Loans Act* passed.

   ° Farm Debt Review Boards, now at work in every province, received a $100 million cash infusion.

   ° A $750 million debt-write-down for the Western Grain Stabilization Fund announced.

   ° Special Canadian Grains Program of $1.1 billion to grain farmers.

   ° Canadian Rural Transition Program extended to end of 1990-91 with an additional $28 million.

   ° The Atlantic Livestock Feed Development Initiative designed to assist Maritime farmers to produce more of their own livestock feed commenced with a total budget of $35 million. The long-term goal is to make the region fully self-sufficient in livestock feed by the year 2000.

   ° Farm Credit Corporation bailed out and senior management changed. Federal refinancing package of a $100 million write-down, deferment of a $103 million loan payment, and $330 million to cover loan obligations for the next three years.

1988
   ° Fuel Tax Rebate Program amended to increase by one per cent per litre for farmers and other primary producers to offset corresponding increase in the excise tax on gasoline.

   ° Two-Price Wheat Program terminated perhaps in anticipation of the Canada-U.S. Free Trade Agreement.

    o   *Western Grain Stabilization Act* amended to encourage greater producer participation (by raising producer levy rates for one per cent to four per cent), broaden the scope of coverage, and put the program on a stronger financial basis.

    o   National Grains Bureau established in Winnipeg for co-ordinating policy development of the grains and oilseeds sector.

    o   Canadian Crop Drought Assistance Program, a $850 million federal-provincial cost-shared program, announced during the federal general election.

    o   *Canadian Grain Act* amended providing, *inter alia*, the authority to prescribe the length of time in which grain must be priced after delivery is given.

1989   o   Budget states government intention to save about $90 million in 1989-90 and $110 million in 1990-91 by re-negotiating existing Crop Insurance cost-sharing agreements.

    o   East of Buffalo Grain and Flour Freight Subsidy Program terminated for an annual savings of about $40 million.

    o   Branchline Rehabilitation Program terminated one year early, expected savings of $48 million in 1989-90 and $4 million in 1990-91, with $16 million redirected to the Grain Transportation Agency to assist in transportation system improvements.

    o   No new loans to be made under the Farm Credit Corporation's Commodity-Based Loan Program. Savings estimated at about $14.5 million over two years.

    o   Agreement reached on a negotiating framework for agriculture in the Uruguay Round of GATT Multilateral Trade Negotiations. The agreement provides for an immediate short-term freeze on domestic and export support and protection during the negotiations and sets out longer-term objectives.

    o   *Prairie Grain Advance Payments Act* and *Advance Payments for Crops Act* to be amended to remove the interest-free provision of government guaranteed loans at harvest time. Estimated savings of about $27 million in 1989-90 and 1990-91.

° Under the Fuel Tax Rebate Program, rebates to farmers and other primary producers on the federal sales tax on motor fuels extended to the end of 1990. Impact on federal revenues estimated to be $125 million for the 1990 tax year.

° Federal-Provincial Crop Insurance Review Discussion Paper released.

° Amendments to the *Crop Insurance Act* tabled in the House of Commons.

° *Growing Together*, a policy Green Paper, issued by Agriculture Canada.

° National Conference on the Agri-Food Industry held in Ottawa to launch policy review process.

1990 ° Federal budget contains no new initiatives for Prairie farmers or other producers. Agricultural programs are exempted from plan to convert business subsidies and grants to repayable loans.

° Agriculture Canada's 1990-91 *Estimates* project a $823 million decline, 30 per cent of departmental spending, due principally to reduction in the 1988 Canadian Crop Drought Assistance Program.

° A review of grain safety net programs to be undertaken by Agriculture Canada in fiscal year 1990-91.

° Farm Credit Corporation raises its five-year fixed interest rate from 12.25 per cent to 13 per cent, prompted by the recent rise in market interest rates.

Note: This chronology is a selective inventory of federal agricultural initiatives over the 1984-90 period, with an emphasis on those directly relevant to the Prairie grain sector.

Notes

1   Don Mazankowski, "Notes for an Address," Deputy Prime Minister of Canada and Minister of Agriculture, at the opening of the Canadian Agricultural Outlook Conference, (Ottawa: December 12, 1988), p. 4.

2   *The Budget Papers* (Ottawa: Department of Finance, April 27, 1989), pp. 63-65.

3   L. Auer, *Canadian Prairie Farming, 1960-2000: An Economic Analysis*. A study prepared for the Economic Council of Canada (Ottawa: Supply and Services, 1989).

4   George L. Brinkman, *Farm Incomes in Canada* (Ottawa: Economic Council of Canada and the Institute for Research on Public Policy, 1981), p. 2. These farm income goals of adequacy, equity and stability are expressed in Agriculture Canada, *1990-91 Estimates*, Part III, Expenditure Plan (Ottawa: Supply and Services, 1990), pp. 2-4 to 2-7, 4-16, 4-43, 4-53 and 5-27. For discussion on these goals and related issues, see also, J.D. Forbes, R.D. Hughes and T.K. Warley, *Economic Intervention and Regulation in Canadian Agriculture* (Ottawa: Economic Council of Canada and the Institute for Research on Public Policy, 1982), chapter 3.

5   Grace Skogstad, "Agriculture: Sharing the Responsibility," in Michael J. Prince (ed.), *How Ottawa Spends, 1987-88* (Toronto: Methuen Press, 1987), p. 274. For historical analyses of federal agriculture spending by policy and program orientation, see Brinkman, *Farm Incomes in Canada*, chapter 6; Richard Shaffner, *The Quest for Farm Income Stability in Canada* (Montreal: C.D. Howe Institute, 1977); and Forbes, Hughes and Warley, *Economic Intervention and Regulation in Canadian Agriculture*, chapters 2 and 5.

6   Calculations in this paragraph by the author are based on Minister of National Health and Welfare, *Inventory of Income Security Programs in Canada, January 1988* (Ottawa: Supply and Services, 1989), pp. 91, 95, 101, 179 and 182. These expenditure figures are for net benefits paid in Alberta, Saskatchewan and Manitoba for the 1986-87 fiscal year. The number of beneficiaries are for March 1987.

7   For a more thorough examination of the possible criteria with which to evaluate Canadian agricultural policy, see Murray Fulton, Ken Rosaasen, and Andrew Schmitz, *Canadian Agricultural Policy and Prairie Agriculture,* a study prepared for the Economic Council of Canada (Ottawa: Supply and Services, 1989), pp. 30-33. Also see Ray D. Bollman, "Who Receives Farm Government Payments?" *Canadian Journal of Agricultural Economics,* 37:3 (November 1989), pp. 351-78, for an analysis of how the benefits of selected programs are distributed among Canadian farmers.

8   See Auer, *Canadian Prairie Farming,* p. 10 and Fulton, Rosaasen and Schmitz, *Canadian Agricultural Policy and Prairie Agriculture*, p. 68.

9   Economic Council of Canada, *Handling the Risks: A Report on the Prairie Grain Economy* (Ottawa: Supply and Services, 1988), p. 70.

10   Fulton, Rosaasen and Schmitz, *Canadian Agriculture Policy and Prairie Agriculture*, p. 76.

11   John Spriggs and G.C. Van Kooten, "Rationale for Government Intervention in Canadian Agriculture: A Review of Stabilization Programs," *Canadian Journal of Agricultural Economics*, 36:1 (March 1988), adapted from pp. 9-10.

12   Mazankowski, "Notes for an Address."

13   Mazankowski, p. 4

14   Mazankowski, p. 5.

15   The three federal Agriculture ministers are Don Mazankowski, Minister of Agriculture, Charles Mayer, Minister of State (Grains and Oilseeds), and Pierre Blais, Minister of State (Agriculture).

16   A Green Paper sets out a range of alternative proposals for discussion before a policy position is adopted. In contrast, a White Paper is a statement of government policy. Agriculture Canada issued a previous Green Paper, *A Food Strategy for Canada* in 1977. For more details, see Audrey D. Doerr, "The Role of Coloured Papers," *Canadian Public Administration,* 25:3 (Fall 1982), pp. 366-79.

17   *The Budget Papers*, p. 65.

18   Agriculture Canada, *Growing Together: A Vision For Canada's Agri-Food Industry* (Ottawa: Supply and Services, 1989), p. 35.

19   *Growing Together*, p. 35.

20   *Growing Together*, p. 36

21   *Growing Together*, p. 50.

22   *Growing Together*, p. 52. "Decoupling" farm income and price support programs is under discussion also in other OECD agricultural producing nations.

23   *Growing Together*, pp. 52-54. The Green Paper also proposes five principles for reviewing Canada's agricultural transport programs like the *Western Grain Transportation Act*, pp. 61-62. On the controversial issue of whether to pay the WGTA subsidy (the Crow Benefit) to the railways, as is currently done, or to farmers, the Green Paper does not take a position but cautions that any changes be carefully analyzed to avoid unintended adverse consequences for the agri-food industry. This point was echoed by a recent report prepared for the Manitoba government. See Glenn Cheater, "Danger seen in blind changes to Crow," *The Globe and Mail* [Toronto], January 11, 1990, p. B4.

24   *Growing Together*, p. 74. A senior level Corporate Priorities Committee has been established in Agriculture Canada to oversee the strategic management of the policy review process. Policy review teams for each of the seven policy areas support the Corporate Priorities Committee. The agriculture policy review is expected to continue through to 1992.

25   Don Mazankowski, Deputy Prime Minister of Canada and Minister of Agriculture, "Keynote Address at the opening of a National Agri-Food conference," (Ottawa: December 11, 1989), pp. 6-7.

26   On "decoupling" federal farm income support programs, see Auer, *Canadian Prairie Farming*, chapter 6; Economic Council of Canada, *Handling the Risks*, chapter 8 and J.C. Gilson, "Early experiences with the coupling and decoupling of agricultural price supports and farm commodities," *Canadian Farm*

Economics, 22:1 (1988), pp. 40-46. These studies suggest that Canadian farm income support programs now provided to Prairie farmers and other producers could be decoupled in several different ways. Each approach, however, results in losers as well as winners. On the production and political limitations of decoupling, see R.D. Bollman and M. Tomiak, "Decoupled Agricultural Policy and the Lack of Production Alternatives," *Canadian Journal of Farm Economics,*36:2 (July 1988), pp. 349-52, and Jeffrey Simpson, "A harvest of grain subsidies," *The Globe and Mail* [Toronto], January 26, 1990, p. 6.

27   Agriculture Canada, *1990-91 Estimates*, Part III, pp. 2-8 and 5-10. The CCDA Program is projected to drop 97 per cent, from $788 million to $21 million.

28   Quoted in Geoffrey York, "Poor regions will suffer, Westerners say," *The Globe and Mail [Toronto], February 21, 1990, p. A11.*

29   *Estimates*, Part III, p. 1-7.

30   *Estimates*, Part III, pp. 5-14 and 5-15.

31   *Estimates*, Part III, p. 4-23.

32   Agriculture Canada, "Farm Income, Canada and Provinces, 1990," (Ottawa: December 7, 1989).

33   See Geoffrey York, "Devine kills gas rebate, says province under siege," *The Globe and Mail* [Toronto], March 7, 1990, p. A7, and Bob Cox, "Bleak years reduce feisty farmers to poverty, tears, revolt," *The Times-Colonist* [Victoria], February 25, 1990, p. A5.

CHAPTER 7

"SLOWING THE STEAMROLLER:"

THE FEDERAL CONSERVATIVES,

THE SOCIAL SECTOR

AND CHILD BENEFITS REFORM

Allan Moscovitch

Résumé

Un des objectifs de ce chapitre est d'éclaircir le chemin plein de tours et de détours qu'ont suivi les discussions et la réforme en matière de programmes de prestations pour enfants au cours des six années de gouvernement conservateur dans les années 80. La réforme a peut-être visé la simplification de l'enveloppe des prestations selon la définition du gouvernement (allocation familiale, crédit d'impôt pour enfants, exemption d'impôt pour enfants), mais cela n'a pas réussi. Les mécanismes de la livraison des prestations pour enfants sont en effet beaucoup plus complexes dans les années 90 qu'ils ne l'étaient avant le lancement du projet de réforme des conservateurs.

Les changements apportés à l'allocation familiale, au crédit d'impôt pour enfants et à l'exemption d'impôt pour enfants ont eu comme effet la baisse des dépenses pour l'enveloppe des prestations, ce qui a en même temps réduit encore plus le lien entre les salaires du marché et le niveau de besoin familial, lien toujours faible au Canada.

L'impact des groupes de pression de divers secteurs sociaux a été marginal. On explique comment et pourquoi ces coalitions se sont formées, ainsi que les raisons pour lesquelles leur impact a été limité.

Y aurait-il d'autres possibilités pour la réforme des prestations pour enfants? En conclusion, on examine brièvement plusieurs propositions récentes visant la réorganisation ou l'expansion des prestations pour enfants.

INTRODUCTION

Two months after election in September 1984 the new Conservative government released a statement entitled *A New Direction For Canada: An Agenda For Economic Renewal* in which it outlined principles and directions for the next several years.[1] The fundamental principles of *Agenda for Economic Renewal* were containment of the deficit and the national debt, reliance on private sector initiatives and private markets for economic growth, reduction in the size and scope of government, promotion of government efficiency and maintenance of the basic income security system with increased targeting of assistance to "those who really need it."[2]

A secondary and related objective was to review and redesign social programs "based on the twin tests of social and fiscal responsibility."[3] The former related to greater targeting of social expenditures while the latter related to the greater use of government expenditures to promote private economic growth to increase employment. *Agenda for Economic Renewal* raised four aspects of social programs for discussion: elderly benefits, child benefits, unemployment insurance and housing. Child benefits were defined to include the family allowance, the child tax credit and the child tax exemption. The document posed a series of questions for public consultation including the advantages to phasing out the child tax exemption, de-indexation of the family allowance in full or in part, surtaxing the family allowance to higher-income recipients, and substantially increasing the child tax credit.[4] In this way the document signalled not only the direction of government thinking but also a major part of the agenda for social policy reform in the following years.[5]

One purpose of this chapter is simply to unravel the many twists and turns of debate and reform that have taken place in the government-defined envelope of child benefit programs in the six years of Conservative federal government in the 1980s. While one objective of reform may have been to simplify the envelope of child benefits it was certainly not the result. The mechanisms of delivery of child benefits are, in the 1990s, much more complex than they were when the Conservative government launched themselves into their reform project.

An important aspect of this unravelling has to do with the two solitudes of social politics during this period of Conservative government. When, during the election debate of 1984, the future prime minister declared social policy to be a sacred trust, this phrase was taken by many to mean that the Conservative winds of reform would blow over social programs without touching them. Consequently *Agenda for Economic Renewal* raised many fears about the federal government's commitment to social policy. Among social reformers involved in advocacy organizations for women, and for social, family, and child welfare, (which together I refer to here as the social sector), fears aroused in the election campaign were confirmed by the release of *Agenda for Economic Renewal*. Fears turned to a sense of betrayal when the Conservatives' first budget was released in May 1985 with its array of changes in child benefits.

What becomes apparent in this review is that the government does not accept that it has betrayed a commitment to universality, or to children. At the same time social sector organizations have, with virtual unanimity, repeatedly expressed views contrary to those of the government. The meaning of the "sacred trust" and the nature of the differences between the two sides are also themes here.

For the first time two groups of social sector organizations reached agreement to form coalition lobby groups which participated in some of the many consultations on child benefits during this period. As the title of this chapter suggests, the impact of the social sector groups on child benefits reform was marginal. How and why the social sector coalitions formed, and the reasons for their limited impact, is a further theme explored here.

The reform of social policy has been shaped by both deficit reduction and, more selectivity in social expenditures. These measures are consistent with Conservative philosophy. However, while the importance of selectivity in particular has increased in the last six years, it was the Liberal government which first suggested the move to greater selectivity in its 1970 plan to change the family allowance into a family-based and income-tested program. In 1978, it was a Liberal government which reduced the value of the family allowance to contribute the savings towards the funding of the selective child tax credit.

The result of the changes to the family allowance, the child tax credit and the child tax exemption (now a non-refundable tax credit for dependent children) has been a decline in expenditures on the envelope of child benefits. As a consequence the bridge between market wages and salaries and the level of family need, always weak in Canada, has been weakened even further.

Are there other alternatives for child benefits reform? This chapter concludes with a brief examination of several recent proposals to rearrange or expand child benefits. One proposal which has recently been put forward appears in the report of the Social Assistance Review Committee (SARC) in Ontario, presented in September 1988. It is to create a substantial income-tested children's allowance based on funds currently expended as child benefits and as social assistance. A second proposal for the establishment of a universal children's allowance equivalent to the cost of maintenance of a child appears in the work of the Child Poverty Action Group; a variation appears in the statement from the child poverty coalition of national child welfare organizations. A further proposal for an income-tested Guaranteed Family Supplement appears in the Senate Committee on Social Affairs report on Child Benefits. A fourth proposal is contained in The Report of the Royal Commission on the Economic Union, for reforms similar to those proposed in the government's *Child and Elderly Benefits Consultation* paper.

THE ORIGINS OF FAMILY INCOME SUPPORT

The federal government first recognized the extra costs to familes with children when it introduced the wartime income tax in 1917. An income exemption of $200 a child was provided to taxpayers with children under the age of 21. Exemptions were introduced soon after, in recognition of the additional income necessary to support a spouse and other dependents.[6]

The early income tax was intended to be a tax on high incomes, the conscription of capital which would parallel the conscription of labour.[7] During the Second World War this tax was transformed into the modern mass-based income tax system through the reduction of the personal exemption and the growth of personal incomes. The spousal, child and dependents exemptions which had been incorporated into the original income tax were retained. In addition, tax credits for dependent children were introduced in 1940 at the rate of $4 per child with the introduction of the National Defence Tax. These credits rose to $108 in 1942 with the introduction of the graduated tax and were discontinued for the 1947 tax year.[8]

In his 1943 examination of *Social Security for Canada,* Leonard Marsh notes that the wage or salary received by the worker is the same, regardless of the number of dependents that are supported by it. The labour market does not provide supplements to ensure that the worker with dependents will have sufficient income to support them. The bridge between the labour market and family need in Marsh's visionary statement was to be the children's benefit or the family allowance as it was often called. Similarly, in planning income security programs, he believed that it would be more efficient to use family allowances as the bridge between benefits and number of child dependents.[9]

Family allowances were legislated in Canada in 1944. When they were first paid the following year, there was a direct relation between them and the wartime dependent child tax credit in the tax system. For the taxation years 1945 and 1946 family allowances were recovered on the tax form in relation to taxable income and therefore the value of the tax credits received. For 1947 this practice was discontinued; however, families not receiving the family allowance were given a higher child tax exemption. The family allowance was not considered taxable income.[10] After 1947 it was paid on a universal basis to all families on behalf of each child under the age of 16. Further, the family allowance was the first universal social expenditure program in Canada, paying between $5 and $8 per child per month depending on the age of the child.[11]

Between 1945 and 1973 the only changes in family allowances were minor alterations of the rate structure [1949, 1957] and the creation of the Youth Allowance in 1964 for children aged 16 and 17.[12] In relation to average annual male wages in 1945, the average family allowance payment of $72.48 represented some 7.2 per cent. For families with three children, the family allowance represented 24 per cent of monthly income.[13] Family allowances fell steadily as a percentage of government expenditures from 13.5 per cent in 1950 to 2.8 per cent in 1972.[14]

REFORM IN THE 1960s AND 1970s

In the 1960s the appointment of the Royal Commission on Taxation gave a focus to the reform of the income tax, and the Royal Commission on the Status of Women gave focus to the activities of government in relation to women and children.

The Royal Commission on the Status of Women recommended the payment of a "federal annual taxable cash allowance in the order of $500... for each child under 16 to be paid in monthly installments to the mother."[15] This recommendation was made at a time when yearly family allowance payments were in the order of $72 to $96. The Royal Commission on Taxation recommended the conversion of the spousal, child and other dependents exemptions to credits. Neither recommendation was acted on.

Early in the life of the Liberal government under Pierre Trudeau the family allowance became the subject of reform proposals because of its universal character. A 1970 *White Paper on Income Security For Canadians* proposed a Family Income Support Program (FISP) in which family allowances would be paid on a sliding scale from $16 to zero dollars in relation to income. The White Paper stated that:

> ...greater emphasis should be placed on anti-poverty measures. This should be accomplished in a manner which enables the greatest concentration of available resources on those with the lowest incomes. Selective payments based on income should be made where possible, in the place of universal payments..."[16]

Clearly the White Paper predated the present government's approach. However, legislation to establish the FISP failed as a result of an election being called in 1972. In 1973 during the period of minority Liberal government the value of the family allowance was increased — the first substantial increase since 1945 — and the universal character of the family allowance was retained, a condition of NDP support. At the same time the family allowance was made taxable. The family allowance and other social program benefits, as well as the child tax exemption and other parts of the income tax, were fully indexed to inflation in 1974; the lack of indexation had caused the substantial erosion of the family allowance between 1945 and 1973.

In 1978, after an inconclusive series of federal/provincial discussions over the reform of social security, the federal government instituted a child tax credit. The child tax credit was to be delivered as a part of the income tax system and in relation to the income of the family up to a maximum. An unusual feature of the child tax credit was that it was to be "refundable." It would be paid in cash, refundable, to families without taxable income. For these families it would become a tax-based selective form of family allowance paid one time per year. But, where the family allowance required only one application in the lifetime of the child, the child tax credit would require an application every year.[17]

The establishment of the child tax credit was accompanied by a reduction in the value of the family allowance from $25.68 per child in 1978 to $20.00 in 1979; the savings contributed to the cost of the child tax credit when it was first paid in 1979. The child tax credit accomplished what the early 1970s reform had not: the establishment of a selective family support program. But it did so by building the selective scheme over a universal base.[18]

THE CONSERVATIVE YEARS, 1984-1989

The Child And Elderly Benefits Consultation Paper

Agenda for Economic Renewal signalled the government's intention to review and consult on the package of programs and tax measures that it called child benefits. It was followed in January 1985 by a Health and Welfare *Consultation Paper on Child and Elderly Benefits*, which explained the government's approach as one of adjusting a fixed budget for child benefits to achieve greater fairness subject to retaining universality for family allowances. It also avowed that any savings from changes in social programs would not be applied to deficit reduction. It should be noted that the Consultation Paper only dealt with changes to this package of child benefits.[19]

The priorities for reform appeared to be a surtax on the family allowance for high-income earners and conversion of the child tax exemption in the income tax. If there were to be improvements in benefits, these would go to those in need. Finally, no funds would be available for social benefits other than those already committed for social expenditures in the 1985-86 Budget.[20]

The child and elderly benefits paper clearly defined the social policy agenda of the government as one of rearranging the distribution of benefits available from a package of child-related benefits to achieve greater targeting. The package was constituted by putting together three different types of social benefits: The first one a universal expenditure program (the family allowance), the second a tax-based refundable credit (the child tax credit) and the third a non-refundable tax exemption (the child tax exemption). Excluded were the equivalent-to-married exemption which may be claimed by single parents, the child care deduction, exemptions for children over the age of 18 who remain in school and the spousal exemption. The reason for excluding this list of child-related benefits is nowhere made clear. Some subsequently became the subject of consideration by the House of Commons Committee on Child Care.

Since the child tax exemption is considered to be the most regressive of the child benefits why not eliminate it entirely? Such a proposal is part of the first option presented in the Consultation Paper. The answer provided is that, were this to occur, a major beneficiary would be the provincial governments. It is simply assumed that the provinces would not be prepared to put the additional windfall back into social expenditures, an avowed objective of the federal government.

The second option considered in the document involved the reduction but not the elimination of the child tax exemption, the reduction of the family allowance, and an increase in the levels and availability of the child tax credit. In essence this is the pattern of reform followed by the Conservative government over the subsequent five years.

The Consultation On The Consultation Paper

The consultation which followed began with hearings by the Standing Committee on Health, Welfare and Social Affairs after the Child and Elderly Benefits Consultation Paper was tabled in the House of Commons. Between March 1 and March 25, 1985, the committee heard representations from the Minister of Health and Welfare and from 19 organizations. Of the 19, there were 12 organizations concerned with social services or social reform, four women's organizations, the Canadian Labour Congress, the NDP, and the United Church of Canada. No business organizations appeared before the committee.

Among the 92 briefs received, in addition to those from organizations also appearing, were those from the Canadian Chamber of Commerce, two local chambers, the Life Underwriters Association and the Hon. Muriel Smith representing the Manitoba government. It was not the broad scale consultation involving individuals, "organizations concerned with social policy, business, labour or provincial governments", called for in the Child and Elderly Benefits Consultation Paper.[21]

The response to the Consultation Paper on the part of social reform organizations was generally one of qualified support. In a brief to the House of Commons Committee, the Social Policy Reform

Group, (SPRG is a coalition of six organizations which is discussed below), lauded the Consultation Paper because "it seriously considers abolishing or substantially reducing the children's tax exemption," which many social reform organizations had long criticized along with other exemptions and deductions in the income tax as regressive. They were pleased to see the government linking the reform of social policy to the reform of the tax system.[22]

Concerning the two options, the SPRG was critical of the first (eliminate the child tax exemption, increase the child tax credit, reduce the child tax credit threshold level) for not protecting the benefits to moderate-income families; and the second (reduce the child tax exemption, reduce the family allowance, increase the child tax credit, and reduce the threshold level but by less than that proposed in Option 1) for reducing per child family allowance payments. In general, it supported universality and opposed a surtax on the family allowance which was suggested as an option. It also supported the progressivity of the government's proposals on tax reform but wished to ensure that benefits to low- and moderate-income families would be protected. This latter point was emphasized by the National Council of Welfare which supported the first option with a difference: The council recommended that the government **increase** the turnover point on the child tax credit and disallow the deduction of contributions to pension plans and RRSPs in the definition of family income.[23]

As the Report of the House Standing Committee on Health, Welfare and Social Affairs noted, what emerged from the briefs presented was a very remarkable level of agreement among witnesses along the lines suggested by the Social Policy Reform Group. They supported universality and therefore opposed any reduction of, or surtax on, the family allowance; they supported the elimination of the child tax exemption; and they opposed a reduction in the threshold level used in the child tax credit. They also wanted to ensure that savings from eliminating the child tax exemption be reallocated to one of the two remaining child benefits.

The committee report in April 1985 went beyond the proposals in the Consultation Paper in suggesting that the total of child benefits be above the maximum proposed in the Consultation Paper, that there be a higher turnover point for taxation of benefits in the $27,000 to $32,000 range, and that higher-income families retain after-tax family allowance benefits. It also came out against a surtax on the family allowance. Despite the committee's clear concerns in regard to deficit containment, any savings generated, the report indicated, should be directed to social affairs but not necessarily child benefits.[24]

The Child and Elderly Benefits Consultation Paper was also referred to the Senate Committee on Social Affairs, Science and Technology which held only a few hearings in May and June 1985. What concerned the senators was the relationship between the federal child benefits and the benefits available for children under the Canada Assistance Plan as administered by the provinces. They struck a sub-committee to draft two reports. The first, *An Analysis of Child and Family Benefits in Canada* was released in December 1985, and the second on child benefits in June 1987. While competent, neither report really contributed to the ensuing debate.[25]

The 1985 Budget And Child Benefits

In the spring of 1985, the Department of Finance began preparation of the Budget with a round of meetings, mainly with business organizations. On this occasion however the minister included a meeting with the Social Policy Reform Group to hear the views of representatives of the social sector.[26] Several measures related to child benefits were introduced in the May 1985 Budget.[27] These measures included a series of increases in the child tax credit for 1986, 1987 and 1988; the reduction of the turnover point for the child tax credit to $23,500 in 1986 and partial de-indexation to inflation less 3 per cent for 1987 and after; the reduction of the child tax exemption from $710 in 1986 to $560 in 1987 and $470 in 1988 and partial indexation to inflation less 3 per cent from 1989, and to the level of the family allowance for 1989; and the partial de-indexation of family allowances to inflation less 3 per cent from January 1986.[28]

In presenting these changes in the Budget Speech the Minister of Finance stated that this restricting of benefits was in response to "suggestions made by many individual Canadians, social groups and the Standing Committee on Health, Welfare and Social Affairs."[29] What he did not mention was the virtual unanimity of the opposition voiced by the organizations testifying before the House committee to de-indexation of the family allowance and the turnover point for the child tax credit, and to the reduction of the turnover rate and to retention of the child tax exemption. Neither did he mention that the House committee report had supported in large measure the position of the social groups.

The Budget's intention was the redesign of child benefits to increase the benefits available to lower-income families by increasing the child tax credit, and to reduce the benefits available to higher-income families by reducing the value of the child tax exemption and de-indexing the family allowance. It was also to generate some savings to put toward deficit reduction through partial de-indexation of the white envelope of child benefits. In opting for a reduction in the indexation of the family allowance, the government was simply following its agenda for greater targeting of benefits. As far as the government was concerned, it had responded to the social groups by retaining universality and moving to reduce the child tax exemption, measures designed to promote fairness. At the same time the government expected general agreement on the overriding priority of deficit reduction, despite the guarantees in the Consultation Paper several months earlier.

> When resources are increasingly limited, we must also adjust social programs so that benefits are targeted to those most in need and funds are freed for other social priorities. Nowhere is this more apparent than with regard to child benefits...

> These changes achieve a number of important goals. The universal family allowance is maintained. Support to lower-income families will be increased and child benefits will be made more progressive. Our child benefits system will become more effective and fair...[30]

The reception accorded the Budget by organizations concerned with the level of child benefits was not warm. The Social Policy Reform Group called the Budget "tough — but unfair." It suggested that by 1990-91 the government would save $635 million per year through de-indexing the family allowance, lowering the threshold level on the child tax credit and reducing the child tax exemption. These were savings which would not be returned to child benefits. Consequently, after full implementation the changes to child benefits would result in a real reduction of benefits in all income categories. It called for the full indexation of the family allowance and the child tax credit, and elimination in full of the child tax exemption. It also went on record as opposed to the government's tax incentives for the more affluent, the centerpiece of the 1985 Budget.[31]

Every Budget represents a set of political compromises; the 1985 Budget was no exception. Nonetheless, the Child and Elderly Benefits Consultation Paper appeared to establish firmly the government's principles for social policy reform. Consequently, the government's decision to de-index and to divert funds from social programs appeared to the social sector as a violation of these principles.

To the government, the deficit warranted reducing social expenditures. By retaining the family allowance payment to all households on behalf of all children the government argued that universality was being maintained. Targeting would simply increase the efficiency with which benefits could be directed to children in low-income families. To many of the social sector groups the issue was not simply one of redistribution but also one of "social solidarity," which one organization defined as "the realization of the common good in a given society."[32] For many, the family allowance paid by the federal government has represented a tangible means by which the community could express its concern for the welfare of all children. Their concern was one of equity among families with and without children, and among families with differing numbers of children at the same level of income, (horizontal equity). At the same time the social sector was also concerned with equity between households at different levels of income (vertical equity) but the social sector groups challenged the government's claims that the result of the changes to child benefits would be significant redistribution to low-income families.[33]

The fears of social reform groups which had been raised by *Agenda For Economic Renewal* and allayed by the Consultation Paper, were renewed by the Budget. They had been consulted by Parliament and, through the Social Policy Reform Group, by the Minister of Finance; but they had not had the impact they had wanted.

This was also the budget that proposed partial de-indexation of the old age pension, a measure subsequently withdrawn after considerable public opposition in the fall of 1985. Pensioners in particular had interpreted the change as a threat to universality as well as to the sustenance of the elderly. Similarly, it was the partial reduction of indexation for the family allowance which became a sticking point for the social sector.

After the presentation of the budget, the government tabled bills to amend the family allowance, the old age pension and the income tax. Each attracted a further round of consultation in committees of the House of Commons and the Senate. Bill C-70 to amend the *Family Allowances Act* was referred to a House Legislative Committee in September 1985. In a series of eight sessions, witnesses were heard from 18 social organizations, two-thirds of whom had testified in the Spring on the Consultation Paper, the Canadian Labour Congress and the Government of Manitoba. Again there were no business organizations testifying. What the committee heard was a strong message of opposition to de-indexing the family allowance. In November, the Bill passed third reading and was referred to the Liberal dominated Senate where yet another round of debates and hearings began in early December.

The Senate Committee on Social Affairs, Science and Technology hearings on Bill C-70 were extended to March 1986 to accommodate the many organizations wishing to testify, as well as the Minister of Health and Welfare and departmental officials, who appeared both at the opening and the closing of the hearings. The Senate committee heard from organizations that had appeared several times before committees during the year, such as: Family Service Canada, the National Anti-Poverty Organization, The National Action Committee on the Status of Women, The National Council of Welfare, the Vanier Institute, the Canadian Council on Children and Youth, the Canadian Labour Congress, and the Confederation of National Trade Unions.

However, the additional times for hearings provided by the Senate in an effort to delay passage of the Bill, allowed social organizations that had not appeared previously to testify. During 11 sessions from December 1985 to March 1986, the committee also heard from: The Native Women's Association of Canada, the Coalition du Quebec pour les allocations familiales (a coalition of 80 Quebec groups which also presented a petition with 50,000 signatures), the Fédération des femmes du Québec, the Front Commun des assistes sociaux du Québec, Solidarité populaire (a coalition of 50 Quebec-based groups), the Canadian Home and School and Parent-Teacher Federation, the Canadian Conference of Catholic Bishops, the United Church, and the Confédérations des organismes familiaux du Québec. The message which had been delivered on two previous occasions was delivered once more: Withdraw the bill, do not de-index child benefits, retain the universality of the family allowance by not eroding benefit levels, eliminate the child tax exemption, protect the incomes of the working poor and the middle class by not decreasing the threshold level of the child tax credit, and increase — not decrease — the overall level of child benefits.

Testimony also emphasized even more than had been the case previously the very fragile existence of those in poverty. Not only did poverty increase in the early 1980s, but profound poverty began to grow as well. This was evidenced by the rising numbers of homeless people and people, including children, who had become regular food bank users for survival. While the government saw the changes it proposed as very minor reductions in child benefits, the social organizations testified that what was needed was more, not less, and that even small changes could have a very serious effect, particularly on the very poor.

This was expressed eloquently by a representative of the Coalition du Quebec pour les allocations familiales:

> I have worked for more than 20 years with women: immigrant women, women on welfare, and visible minority women. These women have always had a very difficult time struggling out of poverty. Poverty remains an abstraction for politicians, but I look into the human face of poverty every day of my life and I can tell you that the family allowance benefits for these women are vital.[34]

The 1986 Budget introduced the prepayment of $300 of the child tax credit in November of the tax year to families with annual incomes below $15,000. The purpose of prepayment, it was indicated, was to "reduce the need for tax discounting."[35] This is the arrangement by which store front income tax consultants will prepare a tax return on behalf of a tax filer and then pay the tax filer the amount of any refund less a percentage. The establishment of the child tax credit as a refundable benefit under the income tax has significantly spurred the development of this business because the refund, unlike the family allowance, has been paid only once a year. The advantage of the family allowance is that it is paid monthly, largely to women across the country on behalf of their children. By moving to establish an interim payment, the government appeared to be acknowledging the administrative advantage offered by the family allowance.

Income Tax Reform In 1987 And Child Benefits

Since 1987 the Conservative government has pursued a two-stage program of tax reform, first signaled in the release of the *White Paper on Tax Reform* in June 1987. Reform of the income tax has included the lowering of marginal tax rates, the reduction of tax brackets from 10 to three, the reduction of the top income tax rate from 34 per cent to 29 per cent, the elimination of several deductions, changes in the taxation of capital gains and the conversion of several personal exemptions and deductions to non-refundable tax credits. The child tax exemption was converted to a tax credit of $65 per child for the 1988 taxation year. According to the *White Paper on Tax Reform*, this was to represent "17 per cent of the estimated value of the family allowance in 1988. This means that family allowance payments will be free of tax for individuals with taxable income up to $27,500."[36] The *White Paper on Income Tax Reform* was given an extensive review by the House Standing Committee on Finance and Economic Affairs leading up to the preparation of a report in November 1987. While the wide range of issues engaged by the White Paper drew out a similarly wide range of organizations appearing before the committee, few of them, other than the same core list of social sector groups, spoke to the child benefits proposals.

Reaction from social sector groups to income tax reform was mixed. The conversion of many deductions and exemptions to tax credits was widely welcomed. What was not welcomed was the reduction in the marginal tax rates from 10 to three, the failure to convert the child care deduction to a credit and the failure to re-establish full indexation of the family allowance and the child tax credit. Further, the conversion of the child tax exemption to a $65 tax credit was considered an inadequate substitute for the tax advantage of the child tax exemption. Analysis of the changes by the National Council of Welfare, the government's own advisory body, showed that neither vertical nor horizontal equity was improved by the proposals in the White Paper. Using the example of a double income family with two children, the National Council of Welfare showed that families in every category would lose child benefits from the proposals. The biggest losers would be middle-income families with incomes between $45,000 and $75,000 per year. As a result of the cumulative effect of the White Paper proposals and the 1985 Budget, the difference in income tax payable for families with children and without children was substantially reduced in all income classes except at $20,000 per year or lower.[37]

The effects of these changes in child benefits were recognized in the Report on the *White Paper on Tax Reform* prepared by the House of Commons Standing Committee on Finance and Economic Affairs in November 1987:

> Evidence presented to the Committee indicates that, over a span of seven years from 1984 to 1991, real child benefits will be cut by half or more for upper- and middle-income families, whereas real benefits for low-income families will end up being at the same level in 1991 as in 1984, if the government does nothing to change the effects of partial indexing and the White Paper proposals.[38]

In reviewing changes to child benefits already implemented, as well as those proposed in the White Paper, the Finance Committee expressed concern about the impact on large families of the conversion of the child tax exemption to a tax credit of $65. The committee proposed doubling the value of the child exemption credit for the third child and subsequent children. In order for families without taxable incomes to benefit, the committee also suggested that $100 per child be added to the refundable child tax credit for third and subsequent children. The additional supplement would be reduced by the amount of the supplemental child exemption credit which is claimed.

In order to slow the erosion of the child tax credit due to partial de-indexation, the committee suggested a one time increase in the turnover rate to $25,500. The White Paper proposed that either parent be permitted to claim the family allowance for the purposes of taxation, providing a tax advantage to some families. The committee proposed that the parent with the higher income be required to report the family allowance as income.[39]

In his response to the Finance Committee, the Minister of Finance accepted the recommendation to double the child exemption credit for third and subsequent children from $65 to $130. On the 1988 Income Tax return this change translated into a tax credit calculated as 17 per cent of a $776 allowance per third and subsequent child. The minister also indicated that the government would be adding $35 to the child tax credit, increasing the income threshold for dependent children to $2500 and would be making the change recommended in the reporting of the family allowance. The minister declined to raise the child tax credit turnover rate.[40]

Announced at virtually the same time, the National Child Care Strategy contained a proposal for a supplementary child tax credit limited not to third children, but to children under the age of six.

The National Strategy On Child Care

The National Strategy on Child Care, announced in December 1987 was to provide an amount of $5.4 billion on child care over the seven years from 1988 to 1994. The government confused child care with child benefits (and confounded its critics) by including $2.3 billion in the Child Care Strategy to finance changes in the child tax credit and the child care expense deduction. The bill to put the *Child Care Act* into place failed when the 1988 election was called. It has not yet been reintroduced; the 1989 Budget subsequently put it on hold.[41]

The 1988 Budget introduced the tax changes proposed in the National Strategy on Child Care, including a $200 supplement to the child tax credit for pre-school children under the age of seven at the rate of $100 in 1988 and $200 in 1989 and thereafter. In the same Budget, the child care expense deduction was increased to $4000 for children under the age of seven. The supplement was to be reduced by 25 per cent of the child care expense deduction claimed for the child and to be subject to partial indexation in 1990 and after. For the taxation year 1988, the full $100 was to be prepaid in November to recipients whose net family income for the year was not in excess of two-thirds of the threshold for the credit. In 1989 and after, two-thirds of the $200 supplement will qualify for prepayment.[42]

In 1986 the government introduced partial prepayment of the child tax credit in November of each year for recipients with net family incomes of less than $15,000. In 1988, the level of maximum net family income for the purposes of partial prepayment was changed from $15,000 to the formula of two-thirds of the family income threshold for the basic child credit.[43]

As critics of the Child Care Strategy pointed out, the increase in the child tax credit was hardly sufficient to allow families to purchase child care and would not make any new day-care spaces available. As for the increase in the child care expense deduction, it hardly seemed defensible after the government had accepted the principle of conversion of deductions and exemptions to tax credits. Similarly, critics argued that the tax expenditure could be more efficiently spent directly on day-care. Further, if the government was truly concerned about the support of young children at home, why not expand child benefits like the family allowance instead of reducing them?[44]

One of the goals of tax reform had been to simplify what had become a complex system. One important result of the changes to child benefits which were announced in December of 1987 was to add an almost bewildering complexity. As a result of the many changes, calculation of child benefits for the 1988 income tax year required the development of a supplementary Child Care Expense tax form.

The 1989 Budget And The Taxback Of The Family Allowance

The 1989 Budget introduced a clawback of payments of the family allowance from taxpayers in receipt of family allowances with annual incomes over a threshold of $50,000. They will be required to repay the family allowance at the rate of 15 per cent of their net income above the threshold. The change, which at the time of writing had not yet been approved in the House of Commons, would be phased in over the three-year period 1989 to 1991.[45]

Will this be the end of universality in child benefits? To the government the answer appears to be no:

> ...families with dependent children under the age of 18 are eligible for family allowance payments, regardless of

the need for assistance...The budget proposes to recover these payments from higher-income Canadians.[46]

The government's viewpoint is that as long as a payment is going to every family on behalf of that family's children, then universality has been retained. How the family allowance is taxed (or indexed to inflation) is irrelevant. Neither is the value of the family allowance relative to other child benefits.

But when is universality no longer universality? To the National Council of Welfare, the result of the addition of the clawback was clear:

> There is no question that the clawback puts an end to universality... A social program that delivers benefits to everyone and then collects them back from some recipients is not universal.[47]

Similarly the Canadian Council on Social Development did not accept the government's proposal. In rejecting the clawback they also rejected as well the government's view that redistribution be the primary criterion for the provision of child benefits.

> ...the clawback of...family allowances paid to households earning $50,000 or more constitutes a special surtax on...families with children — a tax which is not imposed on other individuals and households making the same income...Universal benefits to a particular group, such as families with children, are a transfer to that group from the rest of society, because society recognizes the contribution of this group, and the costs they incur.[48]

To the social sector groups the clawback was and remains a fundamental difference of principle with the Conservative philosophy of targeting benefits, and further evidence of a breech of trust. As the Canadian Council on Social Development put it:

> Universal programs are an important part of the social contract between the state and its citizens, which implies mutual trust and a commitment to continue living by the same rules.[49]

While the government estimated that 14 per cent of recipients would be affected by the clawback, this did not account for those who would be surtaxed after the phase-in period, since the clawback threshold would not be fully indexed to inflation. The National Council of Welfare estimated that 29 per cent of recipients would be subject to surtaxation within ten years.[50] Further, since the family allowance is taxable in the hands of the spouse with the higher income, the clawback will discriminate against single income families. Perhaps the most telling criticism of all is simply that the clawback breaks with the government's own philosophy: The child benefits envelope will not be fairer since there are no plans to redirect the funds saved to low-income families.

The Subcommittees On Child Poverty

The final chapter on child benefits and child poverty in the 1980s leaves the door open for more installments in the 1990s. As a result of the unsatisfactory nature of the six year debate on child benefits initiated by the government in 1984, the Senate authorized its Standing Committee on Social Affairs, Science and Technology in June 1989 to prepare a report on child poverty, social problems which manifest in adult life, and what might be done about them. A first stage report was submitted in December 1989 with hearings to follow in 1990.[51]

In the House of Commons in his final speech as a member of Parliament on November 24, 1989, Ed Broadbent spoke of the plight of the children in poverty in Canada. After he spoke, he introduced a motion calling on the House of Commons to "seek to achieve the goal of eliminating poverty among Canadian children by the year 2000."[52] A Subcommittee on Poverty of the House of Commons Standing Committee on Health and Welfare, Social Affairs, Seniors, and the Status of Women was established to develop a plan to eliminate child poverty. Its terms of reference include a review of the effectiveness of public policies in reducing child poverty. The terms of reference also suggest that special attention be given to government income-support programs.

The mandate of each of these committees appears to portend two more reviews of child benefits. Yet, unless something has changed, it is difficult to believe that these reviews will be more than a repeat of the past six years of consultation and study. In the present circumstances, it is appropriate to ask whether there are any arguments or evidence which would induce the Conservative government to act to lower the rate of unemployment, establish social assistance rates under the Canada Assistance Plan sufficient to ensure no child is in poverty, or increase family related benefits. Any of these changes could have the direct effect of reducing child poverty. If as seems clear, the answer is no, then the efforts of the House Committee might better be saved.

It is not that the information is not already available; for example the Canadian Council on Social Development has recently produced the *Canadian Fact Book on Poverty-1989*, another in a long line of studies on poverty in Canada. The National Council of Welfare has regularly made its studies on poverty available since it was established almost 20 years ago, including a report in 1975 on children in poverty. And year after year, Senator Croll continues to send out updated statistics on poverty based on the Senate Committee on Poverty *Report* of 1971.[53]

It does not appear that the answer lies in more information, it lies in the powerlessness of the people whose lives are at issue and the lack of political will to make the changes to alleviate the distress in the lives of the many children in poverty in our society. In a telling letter to *The Globe and Mail* published on New Year's Day 1990, the Minister of Health and Welfare wrote that "the facts show that we have a package of social and economic policies that are moving Canada in the correct direction." This conclusion is based on the fact that the number of children in poverty in 1988, as measured by Statistics Canada, has fallen to its lowest level since 1980.[54]

What the data also show is that in the 1988 the actual number of children in poverty was still at least 875,000. Further, the national organization of food banks which conducts a Canada-wide survey of the number of people using its facilities each year estimated that, in 1989, 151,000 children were regular monthly users of food banks and a total of 560,000 children used food banks at some time during the year. It appears that there is now a significant class of people who are in deep poverty. The redesign of child benefits of the last several years has only exaggerated their profound distress.[55]

EVALUATING CHILD BENEFITS

The intent of federal Conservative government policy was to maintain expenditures in the child benefits envelope while introducing more selectivity in the delivery of the benefits. The purpose was to tilt the distribution of the benefits towards families who are poor. While more "selectivity" could be introduced through a more steeply progressive income tax together with an expanded family allowance, the government chose to accomplish its objectives through a reduction in importance of the family allowance, an increase in the refundable child tax credit, and a shift of the child tax exemption to a dependent tax credit.

What has actually happened? Tables 7.1 through 7.8 in the Appendix to this chapter present a picture of child benefit expenditures including tax expenditures over the period 1984 to 1990. The monthly amount of the family allowance has increased by 9.3 per cent over the six year period 1984-1989. The rate increase shows the effect of the partial de-indexation introduced in the 1986 payment year; had full indexation been maintained the increase would have been 22.8 per cent. (Table 7.1) Total expenditures on the family allowance on a current dollar basis rose by 10.0 per cent over the period. Constant dollar data which capture the effect of the partial de-indexation show that family allowance expenditures over the same period fell by 12.0 per cent. (Tables 7.4, 7.5)

In 1984 the indexation of the rate of the child tax credit was suspended but restored to partial indexation for 1989. During the period 1984 to 1989 the government initiated several rate increases to a level of $565 per child seven or over, or $765 for children six or under, a 53.9 per cent increase in the basic rate over the period, and a 111.2 per cent over the same period for children six and under. The threshold for payment fell by 7.5 per cent over the same period. (Table 7.2) Total expenditures on the refundable child tax credit on a current dollar basis showed an increase of 22.7 per cent as a result of the impact of the rate increases. Constant dollar data suggest that when the effect of de-indexation is taken into consideration, expenditures on the child tax credit fell by 0.5 per cent.

In 1984 when indexation of the child tax exemption was frozen, the value of the exemption was $710. The value of the exemption was reduced in 1987 to $560 but for 1988 and subsequent tax years the exemption was converted to a credit at the rate of 17 per cent of the annual per child expenditure on the family allowance. In effect the value of the child tax exemption fell by 44.8 per cent over the period 1984 to 1990. As a result of the changes, the cost of the child tax exemption/dependent tax credit fell by 54.4 per cent in current dollars and by 63.0 per cent in constant dollars. (Tables 7.3, 7.4, 7.5)

Data on total expenditures suggest that child benefits have not been maintained over the period. Total expenditures on the three benefits fell by 3.2 per cent in current dollars over the period revealing the impact of the many changes in rates, thresholds and method of availability. Constant dollar figures which add the impact of deindexation in full and in part suggest that child benefits fell by 21.4 per cent over the same period. (Tables 7.4, 7.5)

192 / How Ottawa Spends

Assessment of the impact of the changes in child benefits over the period by income groups requires selection of representative household types because of the complexity of applying the rules of availability of the three child benefits. Constant dollar estimates supplied by the National Council of Welfare for a single income two child family (one child under seven, one over seven; neither child receives paid care) suggest that over the period 1984 to 1991 child benefits have been made more progressive and will become more progressive over time. However, only those single income families without earnings will benefit by the combination of changes introduced by the Conservative government. With de-indexation even poor families will have their constant dollar benefits eroded in the 1990s. (Table 7.6)

For the double income two child family (one child under seven, one over seven) the changes have resulted in a substantial drop in the benefits available in each income category but the first. Only families without earned income will receive an increase in benefits over the period 1984 to 1991; benefits available to other families with higher levels of income will fall. The drop in higher-income categories will be tempered by the effect of the doubling of the child care deduction for children under the age of seven. De-indexation will erode child benefits resulting in a decline in the 1990s even for families with very low incomes. (Table 7.7)

Constant dollar estimates of the impact of child benefits on single parents wih two children suggest a different result if account is also taken of the equivalent-to-married exemption/credit for the first child. While families without earnings increase their benefits by 12.8 per cent, the working poor continue to gain a higher benefit because of the impact of the dependent tax credit and the equivalent-to-married exemption. (Table 7.8)

Two effects are clear in the data: There has been a substantial decline in the value of child benefits over the period 1984 to 1989; this decline has been spread unevenly across income groups resulting in a more progressive distribution but at the cost of some weakening of horizontal equity. Only the lowest-income families have gained additional benefits over the period 1984 to 1991. One additional consequence of the many changes has been to make the family allowance substantially less important as a source of child benefits to low-income families and substantially more important to middle-income families.

THE EMERGENCE OF SOCIAL SECTOR COALITIONS

The Social Policy Reform Group[56]

In 1984, the Institute for Research on Public Policy conducted the first stage of a study funded by Health and Welfare Canada on social policy organizations in Canada. One of the issues examined was that of leadership. Consequently, the idea of forming a national social policy lobby group had already been under discussion between the leadership of the National Anti-Poverty Organization (NAPO) the Canadian Council on Social Development (CCSD), and the National Council of Welfare (NCW) when the new Conservative government released *An Agenda for Economic Renewal* in early November.[57]

The latter document raised such concern over the future of social policy that it prompted a meeting between representatives of several organizations, the purpose being to form a loose coalition which would provide a forum to trade ideas and information and to try to reach common ground on policy issues. Formed in December 1984, the membership of the Social Policy Reform Group included the core group of the CCSD, the NAPO, and the NCW, as well as the National Action Committee on the Status of Women (NAC), the Canadian Advisory Council on the Status of Women (CACSW), and the Canadian Association of Social Workers (CASW). Subsequently, they were joined by the National Pensioners and Senior Citizens Federation.

From the outset the Social Policy Reform Group (SPRG) was purposely kept to a small list of organizations. At the same time, SPRG has sponsored a once-a-month consultation with a broader network of social reform organizations. In order to facilitate the participation of the member organizations in the preparation of briefs and other materials, and in the meetings with members of the federal Cabinet, it was agreed "to provide a common response ... to social policy issues" but not to enforce decisions on each organization. It was also agreed that "each will continue to offer advice individually."[58] Nonetheless, the CACSW was uncomfortable with its status as a government advisory body participating in an organization which could be taking a critical view of federal government policy. After a sporadic record of participation, the CACSW left the coalition in 1988. (The NCW was in the same position but saw its participation as an aspect of its advisory role.)

The Social Policy Reform Group has met with the Minister of Finance regularly—roughly twice yearly—since 1985. Over the same time period there have been only a few meetings with the Minister of Health and Welfare. The group has not yet met with the new minister, Perrin Beattie. The emphasis on the Minister of Finance reflects the change in social policy formation which has taken place since 1984. The predominance of the deficit and the emphasis on tax-based social policy have led to the gradual displacement of Health and Welfare as the locus of social policy in the federal government. Health and Welfare is two departments in one, and one where health issues have increasingly occupied the attention of the minister.

The first meeting with the Minister of Finance, which took place early in 1985, was described by SPRG participants as formal; the meetings since have been described as more cordial and certainly frank. They have involved direct and wide ranging discussion with the minister on the tax system and particularly the child- and family-related benefits.

Have the meetings been useful? While SPRG members found the consultation process to be useful they came away with the view that the minister is from a different world, one which is in little contact with the world the Social Policy Reform Group was addressing. Their major disappointments were over the government's introduction of partial de-indexation of child benefits in the income tax and over government plans to increase the Registered Retirement Savings Plan limits.[59]

The government has been concerned about not appearing as though it is harming the poor. Consequently the minister was prepared to introduce a refundable sales tax credit for the poor, a move to which some SPRG members point as an example of positive influence. However, SPRG has been trying to convince the minister that he should also be concerned for the working poor. On this they believe they have been unsuccessful. As SPRG have outlined in a number of documents, they have taken the view that the income tax system has been altered such that more people at very low incomes will be paying some tax. SPRG's proposal for a tax credit for the working poor has been rejected by the minister. Instead they have been treated to a lecture on the deficit.

Has the Social Policy Reform Group been an effective way for the organizations in the coalition to press for reform of child benefits? According to one of its founding members, SPRG has made all the organizations more effective in stating their case publicly. Summing up their influence on government policy, the same SPRG member stated that "the steamroller was slowed but not stopped."

The Child Poverty Network[60]

The Conservative government's handling of child benefits and child poverty spawned the development of a second coalition lobby group. On October 27, 1988, a group of seven organizations held press conferences in Ottawa and in several other cities across Canada to release a statement and a supporting information package to candidates in the 1988 federal election. Entitled *A Choice of Futures: Canada's Commitment to Its Children,* the document called for a commitment to eliminate child poverty. The group included the Canadian Council on Social Development (also a member of SPRG) and six others including the Canadian Child Welfare Association, the Canadian Council on Children and Youth, the Canadian Institute on Child Health, the Child Poverty Action Group, Family Service Canada, and the Vanier Institute.[61]

On the basis that families with children are much more likely to be poor than childless families, the group criticized the erosion of "the value of benefits for children and families," and called for the payment by the federal government of $2300 per child in 1989.[62] Since October 1988 the network has remained active, meeting with the members of the federal caucus of the Liberal Party and of the New Democratic Party, the Chair of the Senate Subcommittee on Child Poverty, and officials of the federal Department of Finance. Its various representations suggest that members of the network lean toward the social democratic tradition of emphasis on universal payments.

Social Sector Coalitions: An Evaluation

The three most important social policy issues of the six years of Conservative government have been the de-indexation of the old age pension, the National Child Care Strategy, and child benefits. The first affected the group in society which at present is considered to be the most deserving, the elderly. Widespread protest by the elderly led to the withdrawal of this measure.

The second of these issues concerned the availability of child care. It was about removing child care from the Canada Assistance Plan where funding is limited to families that are in poverty or are likely to be so, and creating a new *Child Care Act* which would provide for capital as well as individual funding. The bottom line for the government was not spending more and appealing to its own constituency which was opposed to child care. Consequently, the resultant proposals satisfied neither the Conservatives nor the day-care lobby for whom child care is an aspect of equality rights for women. It appears from the 1989 Budget that the tax measures of the National Child Care Strategy will go ahead but not the *Child Care Act*. The National Child Care Strategy was opposed by a well organized day-care lobby with a constituency, all parents but particularly women, with some public claim to being considered deserving. The lobby has evidently had some limited effect in that the *Child Care Act* has been stalled.

Of the three, the reform of child benefits envisioned by the government has largely been accomplished. Child benefits have been reduced and made more selective. The universal base of child benefits has been substantially eroded; it continues to exist but de-indexation and surtaxation will limit its size and scope. And while there was a substantial amount of what was termed consultation, it was to little avail. In the process, universality in child benefits has effectively disappeared without a public debate.

Why was this possible? At present children, especially those living in families with low incomes, are not high on the list of those deserving of public support. On the contrary, the present government, in rejecting the claims made on behalf of children for a much larger family or children's allowance, believes that children should necessarily share the same fate as their parents. A further conclusion which may be drawn from the six years of experience with these three social policy issues is that the reductions in children's benefits appear to have been made possible by the lack of sufficient political organization on the part of those social sector groups that assumed their defence.

ALTERNATIVE REFORM PROPOSALS

The Child Poverty Action Group

Founded in 1986 and modeled on the British organization of similar name, the Child Poverty Action Group was established to lobby for all children and in particular those most at risk due to poverty. In order to correct the relative disadvantage of all children relative to adults, the Child Poverty Action Group proposed "a guaranteed income for children to match the universal old age security provision for the elderly." Using the findings of the Metro Toronto Social Planning Council that the average annual cost of raising a child from birth to 18 is roughly $3700, the Child Poverty Action Group called for the establishment of a "universal taxable child benefit to all children up to the age of 18 regardless of whether the parent or parents are in the work force or not."[63]

The proposal by the Child Poverty Action Group is very much in the social democratic tradition in Canada of approaching questions of family and child welfare through universal payments as a bridge between the labour market and family need. Leonard Marsh's 1943 study of social security in Canada advocated a similar approach to the support of children and to the establishment of horizontal equity between households with and without dependents.

The Thomson Report In Ontario

The Ontario government appointed a Social Assistance Review Committee in July 1986 under the chair of Judge George Thomson, a former Associate Deputy Minister of Community and Social Services. The purpose of the committee was to examine the administration of social assistance in the province and to make recommendations for reform. The SARC Report was released on September 6, 1988 to considerable positive response. This was a result of the philosophy of "helping clients make the transition from dependence and isolation to self-reliance and integration."[64] While there are aspects of the report worthy of criticism it is remarkable because its analysis and reform proposals are in the opposite direction from that of the federal government.

Beginning with an analysis of the number of poor children in Ontario, the report recommends that children be removed from social assistance dependency in the longer term through the development of a new benefit for children. In effect this would allow parents to apply for social assistance as individuals if need be. The committee proposed replacing "present income programs for children with a new income-tested tax credit. The credit would provide $3,300 per child in 1988 dollars. All low- and some middle-income parents would receive the credit."[65] The threshold income would be $15,000 under this plan. Above this point the beenfit would be taxed back at a rate of 25 per cent of earnings.

The proposal represents a compromise between the Child Poverty Action Group's proposal for a substantially expanded family allowance and the federal government's concern for targeting. As such, the proposal is very much in the Canadian tradition of liberal social reform. Establishment of such a scheme would require a considerable period of negotiation between the provincial and the federal governments. At the time of writing the province had not approached its federal counterparts to begin the process, largely since it appears that the Ontario Cabinet has not been able to reach agreement on pursuing such a proposal.

The Senate Standing Committee On Social Affairs, Science and Technology

The *Report of the Senate Standing Committee on Social Affairs, Science and Technology on Child Benefits,* June 1987, presented a proposal for the establishment of a Guaranteed Family Supplement (GFS). Two alternatives were suggested. In the first the value of the family allowance, the child tax credit, the child tax exemption (now a tax credit), and the equivalent-to-married exemption would be combined to finance a new GFS benefit. In the second the family allowance would be retained, the value of the other three would be combined and the new GFS would have to be boosted by additional federal funds.

The GFS would be available according to the net family income in the previous calendar year as well as the number of children in the family at that time. Families could apply if they had dependent children living at home and if their before-tax family income was below the Canadian average. Those with lowest incomes would receive the highest benefits, presumably paid on a monthly basis.[66]

To those historically inclined, the first GFS proposal is interesting for its similarity to the Family Income Supplement program proposed by the Liberal government in 1970, the purpose of which was to eliminate the family allowance as a universal payment and to replace it with an income-tested program. In its other version, the proposal would retain the family allowance as a base, but add the GFS, and income-tested program onto the top. Given the dominance of the Senate Committee by Liberal party members, it is not unrealistic to take this as an expression of current Liberal thinking.

The Royal Commission on the Economic Union and Development Prospects for Canada (The Macdonald Commission)

In its 1985 *Report*, the Royal Commission directed chapter 19 to a discussion of the Income Security System. The chapter presents two options for change in assistance to families. Under Option One, family allowances would be reduced, the child tax exemption substantially reduced to the same level as the family allowance, and the child tax credit would be substantially increased while the threshold point of the child tax credit is reduced to $20,000. The net result of this change is simply to concentrate receipt of the combination of benefits in families with incomes below $30,000.

Option Two would involve reducing the family allowance; reducing the child tax exemption substantially to the same level as the family allowance; increasing the child tax credit but by less than the amount necessary to use up the funds freed up by cutting the family allowance and the child tax exemption; and, reducing the threshold level of the child tax credit to $20,000. The net result is to remove funds from support of families.

The Commission supported Option One. No alternatives for increasing the family allowance were put forward. The options for reform of family benefits presented in the Royal Commission *Report* are very similar to those outlined in the federal government's *Child and Elderly Consultation Paper*.

The Royal Commission *Report* also presented a proposal for a Universal Income Security Program (UISP) which would involve the elimination of the Guaranteed Income Supplement, Family Allowance, Child Tax Credit, married exemptions, child exemptions, federal contributions to the Canada Assistance Plan, and federal social housing funding. In the first option, the personal income tax exemption would also be eliminated. The pool of funds would be used to create a guaranteed income of $3,825 per year for each adult (and the first child in a single parent family) and $765 per year per child. A 20 per cent tax back rate would apply at all levels of income. In Option Two, the personal income tax exemption would not be eliminated creating a benefit of $2,750 per adult and $750 per child. The Royal Commission's proposals, like those of the federal government, are best characterized as neo-conservative options based on increasing selectivity.[67]

CONCLUSION:

THE CONSEQUENCES OF THE CONSERVATIVE APPROACH TO SOCIAL POLICY

In an interview early in 1984, Brian Mulroney was quoted as saying:

I have no hesitation in reviewing the concept of universality provided its done by a tripartite committee of the House. Such a review would take a look at the concept to ensure that the delivery of public dollars is done in the most efficacious way possible.

But universality is part of our social fabric. And if it is going to be changed, there have to be good reasons to change it, and there has to be a body of opinion supporting that... However what you'll find is that any abrupt departure from universality is going to result in savings that are minimal: $100 million a year on the family allowance side. That is partially offset by the civil servants required to stagger in various programs at different income levels.[68]

Such comments undoubtedly created the impression, sustained during the election campaign of 1984, that when the future prime minister talked about social programs as a sacred trust he meant that social policies and social expenditures would be maintained whatever other changes the government might attempt.

After their election the new Conservative government made clear in the release of the document *A New Direction for Canada: Agenda for Economic Renewal* — that the business agenda of making reduction of the deficit the number one goal was also to be the agenda of the government.[69] A reduction of the deficit would require the redesign of social programs based on diverting scarce resources to those in greatest need and to generating job opportunities.[70]

Agenda For Economic Renewal revealed the government's intention to make social policy subservient to economic policy, not its equal. As a consequence, the locus of social policy making has been shifting over the period of Conservative government from the Department of Health and Welfare to the Department of Finance. The emphasis in the package of children's benefits on tax-based social programs and tax-based changes in the family allowance has served to reinforce the primary role of Finance during this period and in this debate.

The perceived Conservative threat to social program expenditures for children and the increasing extremes of child poverty have prompted the development of two permanent social policy lobby coalitions, one of which has initiated a regular consultation with the government, particularly the Minister of Finance. It has also prompted a considerable number of social policy and women's organizations to step up their lobbying efforts.

The lobby with government has been of little influence because of the strong ideological mission of the government in relation to social policy, and because of the lack of mobilization of a strong mass constituency opposed to the government's reforms.

The shift to greater selectivity does not represent simplicity, efficiency or modernization since none of these have really been at issue. What has been at issue is a vision of social responsibility in regard to the nation's children. In effectively rejecting universality, the Conservative government has rejected the concept of collective entitlement, a payment available as a right on behalf of all children, in favour of the modern version of noblesse oblige – the poor will always be with us but they are our poor and we will be seen to be taking care of them. Other arguments in favour of universality of family allowances presented by the social sector, including the value of having a bridge between wages and family need, and the importance of the payment of family allowances to mothers, have also been rejected in favour of the primacy of the deficit and the targeting of benefits.

Despite the prospect of the erosion of universality for children and the elderly as outlined in the April 1989 Budget, there has been virtually no public debate over its fate. Although other governments have attempted to limit the applicability of the family allowance as a universal program, only the Conservatives will have succeeded if the legislation authorizing the changes is passed in the present session.

The result of the debate over child benefits was unlike the fate of de-indexation of the old age pension. The elderly, because of their status in Canadian society as the most deserving of the poor and because of their political mobilization, were able to successfully press their case against de-indexation of the old age pension. The result was also unlike the debate on child care for which, as an aspect of women's equality rights, there was a large and vocal constituency. While the child care advocacy groups were not able to achieve what they wanted, they were able to press the government to a stalemate at least over the proposed *Child Care Act*. Child benefits advocates had neither the constituency nor the mobilization to press their case to the government.

When is a consultation not a consultation? By introducing several different options for the reform of child benefits and calling for consultation the government gave the impression that the reform of social policy was an open question on which they genuinely wished to take advice. Within months of the release of the consultation document, the Budget of 1985 made it clear that the government was launched into the process of reducing and targeting social expenditures. The fact that it was social sector groups who participated in this consultation publicly, while business groups declined to do so, simply reinforced the view that not only was the government not open to influence, it was in power simply to carry out an ideological agenda. This view was also reinforced by the fact that the House tripartite review called for by Mr. Mulroney in the spring was ignored by the government as well.

The debates on child benefits on Parliament Hill have taken on a strongly partisan character, particularly between the Conservative government in the House and the Liberal-dominated Senate. Extended Senate hearings have served to provide a forum for social sector groups who were on several occasions not accorded the opportunity to present their views to House committees as well as delaying passage of legislation. However, two Senate reports produced on the issue of child benefits during this period contributed little to the debate. If, in the tradition of the Senate committees on aging or on poverty, the Senate wishes to have a greater impact on the issue of child poverty then it will have to become more than a platform for the expression of partisan Liberal sentiment.

Over the course of the last six years, the number of children in poverty as measured by Statistics Canada has fallen as the effects of the recession of the early 1980s have abated. Federal child benefits have not contributed to this decline, as the level of benefits in cash has fallen over the same period. And while the number of children in poverty has fallen, the number in extreme poverty has been increasing. The Conservatives have presided over the fastest growing segment of the banking industry—food banks. There are still substantial numbers of children in poverty; the changes to the child benefits envelope have not helped to alleviate these extremes of poverty.

Changes to the child benefits envelope have resulted in the erosion of benefit levels. The government's avowed aim in its child and elderly benefits consultation document was to redesign programs to increase benefits to those who need them without reducing social expenditures. The evidence suggests that this did not happen, but rather expenditures on child benefits have suffered a decline. While child benefits have been made more progressive, only benefits to the very poorest families have increased; benefits to families at all other levels have been reduced. Over the next several years, partial de-indexation of the family allowance will erode the real value of even the increases to the very poorest families.

The government also avowed that it wished to simplify the tax system. The consequence of the list of changes to tax-based social programs has made the delivery of these benefits far more complex than they were before tax and child benefits reform. The family allowance which the prime minister noted is both simple and relatively low cost to administer has been reduced in range and value in favour of tax-based delivery devices which are more complex and cannot be cheaper to administer. If the issue was simply the complaint that bankers should not be receiving the family allowance, then the simple solution was to tell them not to apply for it. The family allowance is not compulsory; it is paid only upon application. Those who feel they should not be receiving it could be encouraged not to apply and therefore not violate the demands of their consciences.

The changes to child benefits have included the transformation of the regressive former child tax exemption, which could best have been changed into a child exemption tax credit but at a level which now produces a much lower level of tax benefit even at low levels of income. The value of the refundable child tax credit has also been increased, and has been made payable twice yearly to families with relatively low net incomes; but turnover or taxback level has been lowered, taxing back more of the benefit at middle levels of income. To compensate families unable to claim benefit from the increase in the regressive child care deduction (which was doubled to $4000 for children under six), the government introduced a special $200 addition to the refundable child tax credit. At the same time the government has de-indexed the family allowance, substantially eroding the value of the monthly payments and announced its intention to surtax family allowances to recipients with $50,000 of annual net income or more.

Finally, what are the prospects for the future? After six years of cost cutting measures and substantial increases in tax revenues, the deficit is virtually as large as it was when the government came to power in 1984. The national debt is now many times larger and it is the rising cost of financing the national debt which is the fastest growing item in the federal budget. As a consequence, the federal government is likely to redouble its efforts to reduce social spending since it continues to share the business agenda of deficit reduction. In late January in preparation for this year's budget, the Canadian Chamber of Commerce urged the federal government to cut $20 billion from government spending within three years, the Business Council on National Issues supported spending cuts, and the C.D. Howe Institute called for cuts of $5 billion a year for the next four years.[71]

Where are these cuts to come from? The answer provided by the February 1990 Budget is that social expenditures continue to be a prime target. The Budget proposed to reduce expenditures in Established Programs Financing and on the Canada Assistance Plan in Ontario, British Columbia and Alberta. While social sector organizations have not been particuarly effective in organizing resistance to the government's proposals, they have been vocal. The Budget proposes to reduce the deficit by reducing the funding available to national women's and Native organizations, a measure which will have the effect of substantially limiting the capacity of these organizations to act as critics of the government. The Budget further proposes to reduce the funds available to Welfare Grants, a program used to provide core funding to national social reform groups, although details of the reductions are not yet available.[72]

There is also a chance that the government may move to set up the much vaunted Guaranteed Annual Income to combine several family- and child-related benefit programs as a cost cutting measure, a proposal which was central to the Macdonald Commission.[73] As to the social sector proposals for an increased universal child allowance, they are simply not on the agenda.

Appendix 7.1

Table 7.1
Family Allowance, 1984 - 1990

Date	Rate	Indexation	Fully Indexed Rate	Reforms
	$	%	$	
1984	29.95	5.0	29.95	
1985	31.27	4.4	31.21	
1986	31.58	1.0	32.52	De-indexation to Inflation less 3% in 1985 Budget
1987	31.93	1.1	33.85	
1988	32.38	1.4	35.34	
1989	32.74	1.1	36.79	1/3 repayment of 15% of family allowance for each dollar of net income over $50,000
1990	33.33	1.8	38.56	2/3 repayment/full repayment in 1991.
% Change 1984-1989	9.3%		22.8%	

Sources: Health and Welfare, *Family Allowance, Historical Statistics,* Ottawa, Table 4.

Health and Welfare, *Monthly Statistics*, December 1988, Table E.

Department of Finance, *Budget Papers*, 1985-1989.

Table 7.2

Refundable Child Tax Credit, 1984-1990

Date	Rate $	Threshold Level $	Indexation	Reforms
1984	367.00	26,330	Suspended	
1985	384.00	26,330	Suspended	
1986	454.00	23,500	Suspended	Lowered the threshold May 1985 Budget; prepayment of $300 to families with incomes below $15,000
1987	489.00	23,760	Suspended	Indexation of Inflation - on the turnover rate in 1985 Budget
1988	559 - 659	24,090	Suspended	$35 increase; $100 Supplement for children under six reduced by 25% and child care expense deduction
1989	565 - 765	24,355	CPI - 3%	Indexation of rate to inflation less 3%; 1985 Budget prepayment of 2/3 of $200
1990	575 - 775	24,793	CPI - 3%	$200 supplement income to indexed less 3%
% Change 1984-89	+ 53.9% - 111.2%	-7.5%		

Sources: Health and Welfare, *Inventory of Income Security Programs,* 1988, Appendix C.

Department of Finance, *Budget Papers*, 1985-1989.

National Council of Welfare provided estimates for 1990.

Table 7.3

Child Tax Exemption/Dependent Tax Credit, 1984 - 1990

Date	Rate	Indexation	Reforms
1984	$710	Suspended	
1985	$710	Suspended	
1986	$710	Suspended	
1987	$560	Suspended	Doubled for third children or more in family in response to House Committee Report
			1987 Budget set amount at $65 or 17% of family allowance.
1988	$388 x .17 = $66 credit	Suspended	
1989	$392 x .17 = $67 credit	Suspended	
1990	$399 x .17 = $68 credit	Suspended	

Sources: National Council of Welfare, 1990.

Department of Finance, *Budget Papers* 1985-1989.

Table 7.4

Expenditures on Child Benefits, 1984-1990

Current Dollars (Billions)

Date	Family Allowances	Child Tax Credit	Child Tax Exemption/ Dependent Tax Credit	Total
1984	$2.394	$1.447	$1.272	$5.113
1985	$2.492	$1.484	$1.175	$5.151
1986	$2.528	$1.573	$1.331	$5.432
1987	$2.554	$1.639	$1.095	$5.288
1988	$2.596	$1.671	$0.543	$4.810
1989	$2.600	$1.775	$0.580	$4.951
1990	$2.633			
% Change 1984-89	10.0%	22.7%	-54.4%	-3.2%

Sources: National Council of Welfare, *Opportunity for Reform*, 1985, p. 51.

Health and Welfare Canada, *Family Allowances, Historical Statistics,* December 1986, Table 5F.

Table 7.5

Expenditures on Child Benefits, 1984-1990

Constant 1989 Dollars (Billions)

Date	Family Allowances	Child Tax Credit	Child Tax Exemption/ Dependent Tax Credit	Total
1984	$2.950	$1.783	$1.567	$6.300
1985	$2.952	$1.758	$1.392	$6.103
1986	$2.877	$1.790	$1.515	$6.183
1987	$2.785	$1.787	$1.194	$5.766
1988	$2.721	$1.751	$0.569	$5.041
1989	$2.596	$1.775	$0.580	$4.951
1990	$2.515			$2.515
% Change 1984/89	-12.0%	-0.5%	-63.0%	-21.4%

Source: National Council of Welfare, 1990

Table 7.6

**Total Child Benefits, Single Income Couples With Two Children,
1984 and 1991
Constant 1989 Dollars**

Date $ 1989	Welfare Poor $0	Working Poor $20,000	Middle Income $40,000	Middle Income $50,000	Upper Income $100,000
1984	1731	1990	1886	1469	1340
1991	1952	1946	950	402	193
$ Change **1984/91**	222	-44	-936	-1067	-1147
% Change	12.8%	-2.2%	-49.6%	-72.6%	-85.6%

Notes   Child Benefits includes net family allowances after federal and provincial income taxes (the latter an average 55% of basic federal tax); the refundable child tax credit; the children's tax exemption, replaced in 1988 by the non-refundable dependent tax credit.

One child is under seven years old, one is over seven.

Constant dollars are for 1989.

Earnings are from employment; earners are employees.

The welfare family has no earnings.

The working poor family's earnings are $20,000 in 1989.

The middle-income A family earns $40,000 in 1989.

The middle-income B family earns $50,000 in 1989.

The upper-income family earns $100,000 in 1989.

Source: National Council of Welfare, 1990.

Table 7.7

Total Child Benefits, Double Income Families With Two Children
1984 and 1991
Constant 1989 Dollars

Date 1989	Welfare Poor $0	Working Poor $20,000	Middle Income $50,000		Upper Income $100,000	
			Without Child Care Deduction	With Child Care Deduction	Without Child Care Deduction	With Child Care Deduction
1984	1731	1980	1501	1948	1287	2166
1991	1952	1946	621	1451	193	1451
$ Change 1984/91	222	-34	-880	-497	-1094	-663
% Change 1984-91	12.8%	-1.7%	-58.6%	-25.5%	-85%	-30.6%

Notes   Child Benefits include net family allowances after federal and provincial income taxes (the latter an average 55% of basic federal tax); the refundable child tax credit; the children's tax exemption, replaced in 1988 by the non-refundable dependent tax credit; child care deduction claimed by the middle income and the upper income family.

One child is under seven years old, one is over seven.
Constant dollars are for 1989.
Earnings are from employment; earners are employees.
The welfare family has no earnings.
The working poor family's earnings are $20,000 in 1989.
The middle-income family earns 50,000 in 1989.
The upper-income family earns $100,000 in 1989.

Source: National Council of Welfare, 1990.

Table 7.8
Total Child Benefits, Single Parents With Two Children
1984 and1991
Constant 1989 Dollars

Date $1989	Welfare Poor $0	Working Poor $15,000	Middle Income $20,000	Upper Income $50,000
1984	1731	2956	2996	2927
1991	1952	3092	3092	1786
$ Change 1984/91	222	136	96	-1141
% Change 1984-91	12.8%	4.6%	3.2%	39.0%

Notes Child Benefits include net family allowances after federal and provincial income taxes (the latter an average 55% of basic federal tax; the refundable child tax credit; the children's tax exemption, replaced in 1988 by the non-refundable dependent tax credit; the equivalent-to-married exemption/credit for one child.

One child is under seven years old, one is over seven.

Constant dollars are for 1989.

Earnings are from employment; earners are employees.

The welfare family has no earnings.

The working poor family's earnings are $15,000 in 1989.

The middle-income family earns $20,000 in 1989.

The upper-income family earns $50,000 in 1989.

Source: National Council of Welfare, 1990.

Notes

1   Department of Finance, *A New Direction for Canada: An Agenda for Economic Renewal,* p. 3.

2   *Ibid.,* p. 3.

3   *Ibid.,* p. 71.

4   Readers may not be familiar with the difference between the child tax credit and the child tax exemption. In general, a tax credit can be used to reduce tax payable under the income tax. An exemption can be used to reduce total income in calculating taxable income.

5   *Agenda for Economic Renewal,* pp. 72-73.

6   Canada, House of Commons, *Debates,* 1917, 3705.

7   Bob Russell, "The politics of labour force reproduction: funding Canada's social wage, 1917-1946," in *Studies in Political Economy,* pp. 14, 50-53; J. Harvey Perry, *Taxation in Canada* (Toronto, 1951), p. 19.

8   See Russell: Income Tax Forms for the years 1940 to 1948.

9   B. Kitchen, "The Introduction of Family Allowances in Canada," *The Benevolent State,* pp. 236-239; B. Kitchen, "Wartime Social Reform: The Introduction of Family Allowances," *Canadian Journal of Social Work Education*, 7:1, 1981, pp. 32-33.

10   Kitchen, *Canadian Journal of Social Work Education 1981,* pp. 36-38; Income Tax Forms, 1947; J. Harvey Perry, *Taxation in Canada,* p. 48.

11   Health and Welfare Canada, *Family Allowances: Historical Statistics,* December 1986, xiii.

12   Health and Welfare Canada, *Family Allowances: Historical Statistics,* December 1986.

13   Kitchen, *The Benevolent State,* p. 238.

14   National Council of Welfare, *Opportunity for Reform* (Ottawa: March 1985), p. 60.

15   Royal Commission on the Status of Women, *Report* (Ottawa, 1970), p. 303.

16   Health and Welfare Canada, *Income Security for Canadians* (Ottawa, 1970), pp. 2-3.

17   B. Kitchen, "The Federal Refundable Child Tax Credit," *Canadian Social Work Review*, 1983, pp. 55-76.

18   Health and Welfare Canada, *Family Allowances: Historical Statistics,* 1986, Table 4.

19   Health and Welfare Canada, *Child and Elderly Benefits,* pp. 5-6.

20   *Child and Elderly Benefits,* pp. 9-10.

21   *Child and Elderly Benefits,* 1: House of Commons, Standing Committee on Health, Welfare and Social Affairs, Report (Ottawa, 1985), p. 3.

22   Social Policy Reform Group, *Child Benefit Reform, A Response to the Consultation Paper on Child and Elderly Benefits* (Ottawa, March 1985), p. 3.

23   Social Policy Reform Group, *Child Benefit Reform,* 1985; National Council of Welfare, *Opportunity for Reform* (Ottawa, 1985), p. 20.

24   House of Commons, Standing Committee on Health, Welfare and Social Affairs, *Report,* pp. 21-23, 27.

25   Standing Senate Committee on Social Affairs, Science and Technology, *Analysis of Child and Family Benefits in Canada* (Ottawa, December 16, 1985); Standing Senate Committee on Social Affairs, Science and Technology, *Child Benefits: Proposal for a Guaranteed Family Supplement Scheme,* June 1987.

26   Interviews with Ken Battle, Executive Director, National Council of Welfare, December 1989; and Terry Hunsley, Executive Director, Canadian Council on Social Development, January 1990.

27   Canada, House of Commons, Standing Committee on Health, Welfare and Social Affairs, *Report,* April 1985.

28   Department of Finance, *Securing Economic Renewal,* Budget Papers, Ottawa, 1985, pp. 42-44.

29   Department of Finance, *Securing Economic Renewal,* Budget Papers, Ottawa, 1985, p. 42.

30   Department of Finance, *The Budget Speech*, (Ottawa, May 23, 1985), pp. 12-13.

31   Social Policy Reform Group, *The Next Budget: What Will It Do For the Poor?* December 1985; The National Council of Welfare provided detailed calculations in their publications, *Giving and Taking: the May 1985 Budget and the Poor,* and *The Impact of the 1985 and 1986 Budgets on Disposable Income,* April 1986.

32   Working Committee for Social Solidarity, *A Time to Stand Together...A Time for Social Solidarity* (Ottawa, 1987).

33   See the National Council of Welfare, *The Impact of the 1985 and 1986 Budgets on Disposable Income* (Ottawa, 1987).

34   Senate Standing Committee on Social Affairs, Science and Technology, *Proceedings,* 6, February 24, 1986.

35   Canada, *Budget Papers,* Ottawa, February 1986, p. 19.

36   Government of Canada, *White Paper on Tax Reform,* 1987, pp. 29-31.

37   National Council of Welfare, *Testing Tax Reform,* Ottawa 1987.

38   House of Commons, Standing Committee on Finance and Economic Affairs, *Report on the White Paper on Tax Reform,* November 1987, p. 32.

39   House of Commons, Standing Committee on Finance and Economic Affairs, *Report on the White Paper on Tax Reform,* November 1987, pp. 37-38.

40   Minister of Finance, *Response to the Eleventh Report of the Standing Committee on Finance and Economic Affairs,* December 1987, pp. 3-6.

41   Government of Canada, *Budget Papers,* 1989, p. 14; Health and Welfare Canada, *National Strategy on Child Care,* December 3, 1987.

42   Government of Canada, *Budget Papers,* 1988, p. 9.

43   Government of Canada, *Securing Economic Renewal,* Budget Papers, 1988, p. 9.

44   See Susan Phillips, "Rock-a-Bye Brian: The National Day Care Strategy," in Katherine A. Graham (ed.), *How Ottawa Spends, 1989-90* (Ottawa: Carleton University Press, 1989).

45   Government of Canada, *Budget Papers,* April 27, 1989, pp. 9-10.

46   Department of Finance, *Budget Papers,* Ottawa, April 27, 1989.

47   National Council of Welfare, *The 1989 Budget and Social Policy,* Ottawa, September 1989, p. 7.

48   Canadian Council on Social Development, *Social Development Overview*, 7:2, Winter 1990, p. 1.

49   *Social Development Overview,* 7:2, Winter 1990, p. 2.

50   National Council of Welfare, *The 1989 Budget and Social Policy,* pp. 9-11.

51   Senate, Standing Committee on Social Affairs, Science and Technology, *Child Poverty and Adult Social Problems,* December 1989.

52   Library of Parliament, Terms of Reference for the Study of Child Poverty, December 18, 1989.

53   National Council of Welfare, *Poor Kids,* Ottawa 1975.

54   Michael Valpy, "Tory Social Policies Legitimize Begging," *The Globe and Mail* [Toronto], January 4, 1990, p. A8.

55   Michael Valpy, "Toronto's Christmas: Nothing for the Poor," *The Globe and Mail* [Toronto], November 27, 1989.

56   I have benefited from interviews with Ken Battle, Executive Director, National Council of Welfare, and Terry Hunsley, Executive Director, The Canadian Council on Social Development in the preparation of this section. The views expressed here, however, are those of the author.

57   A.R. Dobell and S.H. Mansbridge, *The Social Policy Process in Canada* (Montreal, 1986).

58   Social Policy Reform Group, *Child Benefit Reform,* pp. 1-2.

59   Social Policy Reform Group, *Federal Report Card,* 1984-1988, n.d., pp. 7-8.

60   I have benefited from discussion with Christa Freiler of the Child Poverty Reform Group on the origins of the Child Poverty Network. While I have used the term Child Poverty Network, the group does not have an official title. The views expressed here are those of the author.

61   Canadian Council on Social Development, *Social Development Overview,* 6:2 Winter 1989, 6:2, p. 1.

62   *Social Development Overview,* Winter 1989, p. 1.

63   Brigitte Kitchen, *A Fair Chance for Children,* Child Poverty Action Group, Toronto, 1986, p. 13.

64   Social Assistance Review, "News Release: SARC Advocates New Programs for Children and People with Disabilities," Toronto, September 6, 1988, p. 1.

65   "SARC advocates...," *Ibid.*

66   Standing Senate Committee on Social Affairs, Science and Technology, *Child Benefits,* June 1987, pp. 43-44.

67   Royal Commission on the Economic Union and Development Prospects for Canada, *Report* (Ottawa, 1985), Volume 2, Chapter 19, pp. 772-793.

68   The original was from an interview in *The Financial Post,* March 15, 1984. It was quoted in an editorial in *The Financial Post,* September 15, 1984, p. 9.

69   Department of Finance, *A New Direction for Canada: An Agenda for Economic Renewal*, November 8, 1984, pp. 1-3.

70   *Ibid.,* p. 71.

71   Don McGillivray, "Bank is driving us deeper in debt," *The Ottawa Citizen,* January 2, 1990, p. A6; Eric Beauchesne, "Cutbacks campaign a holy war," *The Ottawa Citizen,* January 27, 1990, p. B8.

72   Government of Canada, *The Budget,* February 20, 1990. See esp. pp. 75-81.

73   Such a proposal was recently supported by the Ontario wing of the Liberal Party, contradicting John Turner's defence of universal social programs. See Rosemary Speirs, "'Clawback' endorsed by group at meeting," *The Toronto Star,* January 28, 1990, p. A4.

CHAPTER 8

"IF YOU'RE SO DAMNED SMART WHY DON'T YOU RUN GOVERNMENT LIKE A BUSINESS?"

C. Lloyd Brown-John

Résumé

Les conservateurs sont arrivés au pouvoir prédisposés à faire fonctionner le gouvernement de façon plus efficace et moins coûteuse. Après cinq années il faudrait en faire le bilan.

En 1983 le vérificateur général a identifié trois contraintes significatives à une gestion productive: 1) l'impact des priorités politiques; 2) des contraintes au niveau de l'administration et de la procédure; et, 3) le peu d'incitations et le grand nombre de mesures de démotivation qui influencent une gestion productive.

On examine chacune de ces contraintes à la lumière des efforts pour améliorer la productivité du secteur public. Ces efforts ont compris le concept de l'accroissement des pouvoirs et des responsabilités ministériels (APRM), l'évaluation des programmes, le recouvrement des coûts et les frais pour services, la réduction du nombre d'années-personnes ainsi que des réformes en matière de gestion foncière. On évalue les efforts d'améliorer la productivité et l'environnement des gestionnaires du secteur public à la lumière des observations du vérificateur général en 1983.

On conclut qu'une bonne partie des efforts viennent de l'intérieur du secteur public même et que, si les conservateurs ont appuyé de façon enthousiaste les efforts d'améliorer la gestion au sein du secteur public, ces efforts sont antérieurs à l'avènement au pouvoir des conservateurs et ne donneront sans doute pas de résultats à court terme.

I hope we can move on to important things like accountability in government, more responsive government,
more efficient government.

former Ontario Treasurer Darcy McKeough. Interview,
The Financial Post, May 15, 1982, p.25.

All told, the structure of control built up between 1918
and 1951 was impressive — and unique. Measured against
the most narrow objectives, it was also unquestionably
effective: the standards of probity reached by the Government of Canada in its use of people and money are high.
But good management consists in more than the
avoidance of sin, and this Calvinistic approach to public
administration, while well designed to discomfit bad
managers, was bound to prove most frustrating to good
ones.

Report of the Royal Commission on Government Organization (Glassco Report), July 18, 1962, Volume 1
"Management of the Public Service," p.44.

Almost anything you read or anybody you talk with in Ottawa about
internal management of the Government of Canada will reference the
1962 Glassco Report. Like a Holy Grail, the Glassco Report serves to
bolster almost any argument for reform or change. True, there was the
1979 Royal Commission on Financial Management and Accountability
(the Lambert Report), but the Glassco Report (or, at least, portions of
it) has acquired a certain gospel quality as the myth and reality of
"letting managers manage" seep into the public sector.

Two points must be stressed at the very beginning of this brief
discussion: First, the concept of "management" has relatively recent
origins in the public sector in Canada and certainly cannot be traced
back much further than the 1962 Glassco Report. Second, movement
towards improved public sector management is not something which
can be attributed exclusively to the Conservatives since 1984 nor will it
necessarily be their legacy. On this latter point, I must stress that since
the election of the Conservatives in the autumn of 1984 there has been
far more stress upon management improvement. Thus, practices which
could improve internal managerial capabilities have been in the

forefront of the government's plans. Furthermore, as improved internal management practices mesh rather symbiotically with the government's pursuit of debt and deficit reduction, then all things contributing to improved "efficiency, effectiveness and even economy" are worthy in principle.

While persons of the business persuasion are wont to accord the emphasis upon improved productivity and managerial capabilities (that is, the ultimate blessing of "running government like a business") to the particular disposition of the Tories, I am inclined to suggest that, no matter which political party had occupied the PMO's office after 1983 the direction generally would have been much the same. Initiatives at the federal level are part of a general movement to enhance productivity and the management capabilities of government in the western world, although, as I shall suggest later, the emphasis may not have been quite so strident if the Conservatives had not been in power.

In this discussion I shall not begin at the beginning, instead I shall return only to 1983 and the Report of the Auditor General of Canada. In his 1983 Report, the Auditor General presented results of a study titled: "Constraints to Productive Management in the Public Sector."[1]

The study identified three "significant constraints to productive management" as follows:

° The impact of political priorities on the achievement of productive management;

° The many administrative and procedural constraints with which management is burdened; and

° The few incentives, but many disincentives, which influence productive management.

These "significant constraints" serve as a useful framework within which to conduct a modest — and perhaps selective — appraisal of "the Tories as business managers."

The discussion is structured as follows. First, I examine the Auditor General's study and explain briefly the context and interpretation of each of the constraints identified; second, I take each "constraint" independently and look at a few examples of what has and has not transpired at least since 1984; and, third, I return to the collectivity of constraints and do a little evaluation of the headway (or lack thereof) achieved to date.

CONSTRAINTS ON PRODUCTIVE MANAGEMENT: THE PROBLEM IDENTIFIED

In the Annual Report for 1976, the Auditor General of Canada observed: "The present state of the financial management and control systems of departments and agencies of the Government of Canada is significantly below acceptable standards of quality and effectiveness (p.9) ...it appears that effective control over the public purse has been deteriorating steadily for up to 15 years (p.19)."[2] The estimated 15 years places commencement of deterioration right back to the middle of the Glassco Royal Commission undertaking and suggests that governments since Glassco's Report (all Liberal governments) cared not much about controlling spending but, rather enjoyed the luxury and benefits of virtually unrestrained spending.

In an appearance before the Parliamentary Public Accounts Committee on April 1, 1976, Canada's then Auditor General, J.J. Macdonell observed:

> I have not been persuaded that the requirements for good financial management and control differ or need to differ at all in government from any other corporation in the country, with this additional point — that I think they have to be more stringent because in government we are dealing with what I regard, in a sense, as trust funds which are provided by the taxpayers...[3]

The theme that "government could/should be operated more like a business" was well entrenched in the psyche of some senior public managers by 1976.

The dual themes of improved financial management practices and the business model appear relatively frequently in the 1979 Lambert Report on Financial Management and Accountability. For example, the Royal Commission noted: "It is not an exaggeration to say that, in most departments, financial management considerations do not enter into the senior management decision-making process."[4] Also illustrative of this ethos is the series of recommendations pertaining to "Funding the Common Service Organizations" (8.1 to 8.6).[5]

The point I stress here is that by the time the Auditor General chastised the federal government for its shoddy management practices in the 1983 Report, the ground had been thoroughly worked. Thus when the Conservatives came into office in the autumn of 1984, the stage was well set for a government inclined towards, and prepared to undertake significant internal management reforms. What the Conservatives brought to the problem were three things. First, an ideological predisposition toward running government "like a business;" second, an almost obsessive preoccupation with the party's traditional assumption that public bureaucrats were too intimately involved in policy decision-making (this bias surely was a dominant motivation behind Prime Minister John Diefenbaker's creation of the Glassco Royal Commission in 1960); and, third, the slow realization that not only was the ballooning debt and current account deficit a serious problem but that its management had potential as a potent political weapon. The comments of the Auditor General in the 1983 study on constraints on productive management serve as a convenient framework upon which to construct some contemporary observations about how the Conservatives have acted, given their initial predilections concerning management productivity.

Political Priorities Have A Major Impact On Productive Management

The essential point is that politicians rarely receive electoral credit for being responsible for productive management. (The same thing has been noted of senior public managers. They are rewarded for good policy advice and for keeping their ministers out of trouble. They are not often rewarded for being good managers). The point should be obvious, politicians gain support through "announcement of policy initiatives and new programs."[6] Consequently there can exist a fundamental incompatibility between the goals of effective management and "good government." Compounding the problem for public sector managers is the simple fact, as the Auditor General noted, that "government operates in a fishbowl."[7] Even small instances of mismanagement or abuse — often, ironically, identified in the annual Auditor General's report — can become a political quagmire and a media event. What the Auditor General did not add was the observation that there appears to be an almost inherent predisposition among members of the public to find public sector officials abysmally lazy, incompetent and even slow of mind. Despite the absence of any systematic empirical evidence in Canada to support such assumptions, the impression seems almost characteristic of North American social culture.[8] Politicians seeking to enhance their own profile are more inclined to contribute to the problem of improving public sector management than they are disposed towards contributing to a solution to the problem. The temptation for politicians to use the bureaucracy as a scapegoat is sometimes overwhelming.

Public sector managers, concerned about their own careers, come to understand that there may be benefits from process management rather than from resource management. Simply stated, "process management" addresses adherence to prescribed and appropriate procedures such as form and format. Thus, sticking to the rules as laid down in relevant central agency manuals and guidelines, and the absence of performance-based measures of productivity suggest an organization geared to process management. "Resource management", by contrast, stresses effective utilization of an appropriate mix of human, material and financial resources adapted to suit the needs of a specific situation. Process managers are more easily identified and, hence, rewarded because they do things "by the book." Resource managers, on the other hand, are much more flexible (perhaps even somewhat eclectic) and thus are more difficult to evaluate.[9] However, as I suggest later, the entire Increased Ministerial Authority and Accountability (IMAA) impetus is directed toward improving the environment for resource managers.[10] Yet, one is reminded of what the Auditor General noted in the 1983 Report "...departmental proposals to reduce operating costs are sometimes not compatible with political priorities."[11]

To their credit, the Conservatives appear to have delivered some encouragement to the improvement of productive public sector management. For, while the Centre for Executive Development at Touraine, Quebec, flourished after its creation in 1981 there can be no question that the expanded version known as the Canadian Centre for Management Development (CCMD) has a broader and more aggressive mandate since its inception in 1988. Furthermore, as suggested later, announcements of December 1989 pertaining to the Public Service 2000 Task Force headed by John Edwards and the Special Operating Agreements (SOAs) outlined by Treasury Board President Robert de Cotret in December 1989 all support the view that at minimum, the Tories are trying.

Management Feels Unduly Constrained by Administrative Procedures and Conflicting Accountability Requirements

Essentially the issue here harks back, again, to the Glassco Commission. Simply stated, if managers are to manage then they need the flexibility to be able to employ their available resources in a manner which most effectively achieves the purposes and goals of the organization. Excessively detailed — often picayune — rules and regulations restricting the selection and hiring of staff, the development of unique local condition practices and "the discretion to choose an optimum mix of resources for maximum productivity"[12] were viewed as major impediments to more productive public sector management. Inflexible central agency rules impose two major constraints upon the productivity of public managers. First, there is what Stuart Nagel referred to as "non-randomness in adaptability,"[13] that is, because public managers are enjoined to function in a context where equity is the norm, policy delivery programs cannot readily be adapted to the particular environmental or contextual circumstances which may prevail for some groups or in some locations. For example, standardized living allowances may prove to be a major impediment to the transfer of a person from a regional office in Regina to the highly-charged economy of Toronto.

Second, again because of the requirement to standardize program delivery processes in order to ensure equity, public managers are often faced with "either/or" situations — we either provide the service or we do not provide the service, we cannot accommodate localized or individualized variations. Again, Nagel referred to these as "non-divisible alternatives" which he suggests are the inability to make marginal adjustments to the resource-mix in order to accommodate revised objectives or altered circumstances.[14]

Compounding the problem was the over-arching issue of accountability. For, as central agencies had emerged as key participants in the overall management of government, they also had come to represent overlapping and often contradictory sources of formal direction to which, in return, accountability was claimed. Including the then Ministries of State for Social, Economic and Regional Development, the Auditor General identified a total of eight central agency accountability relationships: Privy Council Office; Treasury Board Secretariat and Comptroller General; Department of Supply and Services; Department of Public Works; Public Service Commission; Department of Finance; and Department of Justice.[15] Each of the central agencies had its priorities and none seemed willing or able to see the encompassing responsibility of each department as a whole. Almost echoing Glassco, the Auditor General concluded:

> Productive management is not likely to be brought about by control systems, regulations and standards. These can, at best, help to prevent outright "bad" management. Productive management results to a large degree from the initiative of competent managers.

There Are Few Incentives For Productive Management, But Many Disincentives

Not surprisingly this constraint on productive management reflects the obvious: public servants are human! Good private sector managers long ago realized that increased productivity could be related directly to increased motivation and motivation begins with incentives. This becomes especially crucial in the public sector where the habitual private sector incentives of increased salary, bonuses and stock options are largely unavailable.[16]

If there was a paucity of incentives for productive management, according to the Auditor General there was no shortage of "disincentives" ranging from manipulation of person-years, "across-the-board" budget cuts and government-wide administrative regulations which cannot accommodate the uniqueness of the environments within which many departments and agencies operate. There was also the traditional problem of "lapsing balances," the requirement that managers return money left over at the end of each fiscal year, which acts as a disincentive to economize or even return non-essential funds. Not only was the list of disincentives long but, more to the point, when the system did reveal its internal glitches, public criticism spawned cynicism within public employee ranks.

While enormous improvements ensued in the 20 years after Glassco (the innovative years of Trudeau's first government), there is no doubt that by 1983 the internal management of the Government of Canada had a long way to go to demonstrate that productive management systems were in place. The door was wide open for a government — any government — to respond affirmatively. The Conservatives got their opportunity with their election in the autumn of 1984. The question we can now ask is: given the need, the opportunity and the inclination, has the Conservative government done the job?

UNCONSTRAINING ADMINISTRATION

Essentially the problem is fairly simple: how does one balance the freedom to manage with public sector accountability? As I have suggested, constraints on management as perceived by public sector managers, in large measure, stem from the myriad of rules, regulations, directives and assorted minutiae-based objectives of central agencies. The objective — not only that accountability should prevail but that it be seen to prevail — is defined in service-wide regulations which defy in principle the very logic of adaptable and flexible management.

Program-based concepts which emerged in the mid-60s along with systems analysis opened the door to alternatives, but while program budgeting and the now-defunct Policy Expenditure Management System (PEMS) precursed the direction of change, central agencies appear to have been reluctant to pick up the challenge and pursue the logic. But change, perhaps out of necessity, is occurring. In this section I shall note a few of those changes and, later, attempt to evaluate their results.

I shall note five selected areas: the Increased Ministerial Authority and Accountability (IMAA) agreements; program evaluation after 10 years; cost recovery, fees for service, and contracts; initiatives to cut the size of the federal public service; and, property management.

Increased Ministerial Authority And Accountability (IMAA)[17]

Ostensibly IMAA is the darling of Treasury Board — or, at least, of the Program Branch, which is essentially the driving force behind the concept. In an address to the Financial Management Institute in November 1986, Treasury Board President Robert de Cotret described IMAA as concerned "with what departments do both in program results and in meeting service-wide policy objectives" and less concerned "with how well procedural rules are followed." IMAA agreements are concluded between departments and Treasury Board through negotiation of a Memorandum of Understanding (MOU). As of the end of 1989 there were seven agreements with two more close to conclusion.

Under the IMAA agreements, "Ministers gain increased authority to reallocate resources internally, along with greater administrative flexibility, subject to understood conditions."[18] Negotiation of agreements begins with a "full and frank" discussion between Treasury Board and the department in which the basic question, "how do you want to manage your department?" is posed. Departments are asked to identify Treasury Board procedures which are counterproductive from the departmental perspective and eventually an agreement (MOU) is worked out. The MOUs specify clear objectives and clear measures of performance along with explicit delegations of authority. Annual Management Reports (AMRs) are submitted to and reviewed by the Treasury Board Committee of Cabinet.

The IMAA concept has several identifiable benefits:

° It forces departmental managers to carefully think through both "common sense" objectives and performance standards. These are based upon "management representations" of effectiveness and originate in the concept of value-for-money auditing. "Management representations" are a sort of personal attestation by a responsible deputy minister about the effectiveness of programs, personnel and administrative policies – that is, resource-based management as opposed to strict "process" management;[19]

° Treasury Board, while still retaining its responsibilities under the *Financial Administration Act* has undertaken a policy review designed to permit greater flexibility for departments, including a reduction in reporting requirements;

° Deputy ministers may now be held directly accountable for – and are evaluated upon – their Annual Management Reports.

As Veilleux and Savoie have suggested, "IMAA represents a shift in emphasis toward management and policy planning and away from detailed controls."[20]

But what is the downside of IMAA? Treasury Board President de Cotret apparently is a great supporter of IMAA because the concept accords well with the government's emphasis upon both downsizing the public sector and improving productivity through the implicit model of business management. Yet criticism abounds, in part because IMAA is much too closely associated with the Program Branch of Treasury Board while many of the aggravations relate to human resources management and routine administrative procedures.

Furthermore, while Treasury Board says it is prepared to loosen the strings, in practice the results are still open to query. Indeed, some deputy ministers apparently rather like Treasury Board performing its traditional "scapegoat" role for why things cannot get done. There are two additional criticisms. First, the paperwork burden. For example, while there has been a significant reduction in the number of submissions to the Administrative Policy Branch of Treasury Board and a rationalization of authorities into four subject areas, there is still perceived to be an inordinate amount of paperwork required to accommodate Treasury Board requirements. Second, there is a sense among departmental officials – and this may explain some of reluctance to enter into MOUs—of what my colleague Brian Marson referred to as "BOHICA."[21] Another grand scheme, some more fancy manuals and some more Treasury Board officials seeking to propel themselves into higher office — is that really true?

Finally, there is a sense that if the IMAA concept is such a great idea, why are departments not beating down the doors at Treasury Board trying to get their MOUs signed, sealed and delivered? One encounters various explanations for this but the most frequent is that "they're not worth the trouble." If that is perceived to be the case then either somebody has to re-think the concept or re-communicate the purpose. If the idea is allowed to prevail that IMAA is nothing more than a window-dressing designed to permit Mr. de Cotret to claim productivity gains, then we are all losers because intuitively the IMAA initiative seems to be a most appropriate direction.

Program Evaluation After 10 Years[22]

In principle there can be nothing wrong with program evaluation. After all, if improved productivity is the objective of improved management processes then evaluating what you said you would achieve makes common sense. But, under a "business-biased" government, what has been achieved?

Every federal department has an evaluation function but — and this is the major problem — not every department has taken over "ownership" of the function. In other words, some departments are "doing" program evaluation "for the Office of the Comptroller General" and they have not yet fully integrated the value of program evaluation into program delivery and management. IMAA has helped focus attention on the value of program evaluation but, as noted above, only a minority of departments have concluded Memorandums of Understanding under IMAA. Were more departments firmly fixed on demonstrating results and reaping some of the modest advantages to be garnered from the IMAA program (e.g. the ability to use saved resources), then program evaluation would more clearly achieve many of its mooted advantages.

Cost Recovery Fees-For-Service And Contracts[23]

The matter of collecting fees for government goods and services provided is not new. To some extent the Glassco Royal Commission raised the subject in Volume Two of its Report when it discussed the "make or buy" problem. More recently, former Liberal Agriculture Minister Eugene Whelan set off a small tempest in a teapot when he announced that his department would impose fees for in-plant inspection services in some sectors of the processed food industry. But under the Conservatives, fees have been extended much further and now include contracting out of functions in lieu of government-initiated user fees. The rationale for contracting out is that the private sector can offer the service at a lower cost — or, at least, more competitively — than the public sector.

There is evidence that fees-for-service effectively restrict access to government, for example, in the provision of public information. It could also be suggested that fees-for-service have been employed as a pretext upon which to base an argument that what had been hitherto provided to the public as a service can now be provided "competitively" by the private sector. On this latter point, an anonymous observer commented, "there's a lot of self-fulfilling of prophecy" in the fee-for-service-private sector relationship. Furthermore, there is the question of whether the public is paying for services which may very well be deemed essential.

There is no question that by converting to a fee-for-service basis for public documents the Tories effectively have limited the public's capacity to hold them accountable. Basic documents such as the Public Accounts, the annual Estimates,[24] revenue budget documents and many more now cost significant sums. For Canadians who might have an interest in reviewing such documents the cost of obtaining them is so prohibitive that they are effectively only in the public domain to the minimal extent required by law. Moreover, to argue as Finance Minister Wilson did, that "in any case, such documents are available in libraries" ignores the simple fact that many Canadians do not live near depository libraries.[25] Consequently, other than the controlled ministerial press releases, there has been a very noticeable downturn in the availability of information from the government.[26]

With respect to contracting out for services, there is some evidence that contracting out has been employed as a concealed form of patronage. For example, historically the Department of Justice retained the services of its own in-house legal counsel in cases involving the Crown. These were internally costed-out and carried as a fee-for-service either within the department or charged to other departments. However, there have been suggestions that legal services are now routinely contracted out to known Conservative lawyers and law firms and that these firms and individuals are charging high fees. Apparently there is no evidence to suggest that these higher costs are resulting in the Crown being more successful in litigation.[27]

Of course, the government is continuing with its "fees-for-service or cost-recovery" initiative. In December 1989, Robert de Cotret announced that the government anticipated increasing revenues by $390 over three years through higher fees to recover unspecified but presumed costs associated with providing certain services.[28] Higher fees will apply to entry to national parks, temporary work permit applications, processing of student loans and passport fees. Departments will be able to retain a portion of the proceeds for reinvestment to improve services. A quick glance over the areas targeted for higher fees-for-service suggests that many of them could easily fall into the "essential" category. For example, where else can you go but to government to obtain a passport? Thus, what opportunity does the individual have to decide to "shop around;" where are the "market forces?"

There are other serious concerns relating to the general topic of contracting which cost the government money and undermined attempts to improve productivity. These relate to contracting procedures for services rendered to government. For example, the Auditor General's 1989 Report[29] identified the Department of Supply and Services (DSS) contracting process as seriously wanting. Two things stand out about the Auditor General's observations. First, many of the corrective actions suggested are both obvious and make enormous common sense; in some instances, the suggestions have been on the books at least since the Auditor General's 1987 Report. In addition, several of the problems relate very clearly to issues identified in the Auditor General's 1983 Report and to matters which the IMAA program was designed to reduce — for example, more than 40 per cent of the contracts handled by DSS are worth less than $2,500 yet they account for less than two per cent of the value of all contracts awarded. Line departments are required to use DSS for every purchase of $500 or more. From a cost-effectiveness perspective this is an abysmally low level and clearly represents the type of constraint on good management which was identified in the Auditor General's 1983 Report.[30] In a survey of DSS clients conducted by the Auditor General's Office, respondents indicated that "increasing the dollar value limit of their direct buying authority would reduce the extent to which the DSS system is clogged by contracts of small dollar value."[31]

There is some reason to suppose that things are changing at DSS. Something called an Acquisition Service Line (ASL) has been developed, part of the purpose of which is to direct more of the expertise of DSS contracting personnel to higher value-added acquisition functions while standardizing routine commercial transactions. Furthermore, the Treasury Board Secretariat indicated in its 1990-91 Estimates that "in keeping with the IMAA philosophy, a reformated and less prescriptive contracting policy was issued."[32] Details were not provided.

Reducing The Size Of The Public Service

At the First Ministers' Conference in November 1989, Prime Minister Mulroney claimed that "since we came to office, we have reduced the federal public service by 12,000 person-years."[33] There is neither reason nor basis to doubt the generality of Mulroney's claim, but one can query the statistic. First, person-years (PYs) tell us nothing qualitatively about the reduction. Thus, if it were a reduction of 12,000 PYs with an average salary of $15,000 that would be a reduction of $180 million in salaries. But, if it were a reduction of 12,000 PYs with an average salary of $40,000, that would be a reduction of $480 million. Like any other public statistic (e.g. unemployment levels), it can be manipulated and used and abused to accommodate whatever serves the promoter's best interest.

Second, one should suspect a little "smoke and mirroring" in this statistic. For example, if the federal government transfers management of a program to the government of the Northwest Territories (as it has done) that surely can be shown to result in a net loss of PYs at the federal level. However, if the federal government continues to fund that program (as it does) then the resulting net cost can be virtually the same to the Canadian taxpayer. Thus the reduction of 12,000 PYs very well may obscure program transfers, the funding for which remains still as an obligation of the federal government.[34]

Property Management

Once again, one can return to the Glassco Royal Commission for comment on the subject of property management by the federal government.[35] Despite implementation of several recommendations in the 1960s, the problem of effectively managing properties owned and leased by the federal government was not fully solved. Thus, in 1986, a new branch of Treasury Board Secretariat was created—the Bureau of Real Property Management—to act, "as a central coordinating mechanism to reduce fragmentation and duplication in approving, designing, building and contracting for the government's real property."[36] The Bureau's role is to monitor and set guidelines for departments and agencies to manage the property entrusted to their care. Broadly defined, the objective is in accord with the overall direction of management in the public sector—greater delegation of responsibility with commensurate accountability systems in place—the same fundamental principle which drives IMAA.

Yet, despite the best intentions, difficulties do occur. While they may be exceptional they are of such a nature (and, often, magnitude) as to place into serious question the government's intentions. Take the case of developer Robert Campeau.

An office building owned by Campeau Corporation in downtown Ottawa was found to be contaminated with asbestos. The building is occupied by Transport Canada. Apparently, the federal government was on the verge of consolidating all of Transport Canada's 5,000 employees under one roof by moving them to a new building somewhere in the Ottawa region. The figure of $200 million was mooted, but not confirmed, as the prospective cost for the consolidation and move to a less dangerous working environment (apparently there was to be a lease with an option to buy on another building). In January 1989 a spokesperson for Public Works Canada (PWC) said that the Campeau building lease could not be renewed because of the asbestos.[37] But among the budget cuts announced by Finance Minister Wilson in his 1989 Budget was cancellation of Transport Canada's move accompanied by a claim that this was saving the government $200 million.

What makes the story noteworthy is that the following day Public Works Minister Elmer MacKay announced that the federal government would split the cost of cleaning up Campeau's building with Campeau Corporation. He cited the figure of $35 million for the clean-up of the asbestos, which will be done **while** 3,000 Transport Canada employees continue to occupy the building.

The case illustrates a continuing problem that was identified in the 1962 Glassco Report. Real property management requires a constant awareness of what both hands are doing. The Campeau case seems to hinge upon a breakdown in communications in PWC between those conducting negotiations for new accommodation and those pressed by short-term notice into finding "quick-fix" budgetary cuts to accommodate the government's sudden discovery of the debt and deficit crisis. Like responsive managers should, PWC has apparently learned something from embarrassing moments like the Campeau affair and efforts are being made to rectify procedures. All too frequently what is assumed as mismanagement can be attributed to overriding, and often short-term, political considerations — the very first point identified by the Auditor General in the 1983 Report. With that preliminary observation I shall turn to a cursory evaluation.

RESULTS EVALUATION

I begin by reiterating observations by the Auditor General in the 1983 Report. This Report is frequently cited by federal public sector managers as the driving impetus behind the contemporary move toward much improved public sector management. The Auditor General's observations in 1983 could not have been better timed, for the door was clearly open for major change and innovation in public sector management. Thus when the Conservatives came into office in the autumn of 1984 the public sector was ready for a new approach to internal management. Moreover, as suggested earlier, for various reasons the new government was very predisposed to introduce improved managerial concepts and to foster a more cost-oriented mindset for public officials.

What the Conservatives apparently have not fully appreciated is that within the federal public service there are many senior public officials seeking the opportunity to become full-fledged public managers (a "cadre of managerial evangelists"). Consequently, among some senior- and middle-ranking public officals there has been an expectation that the new government finally would begin to "let managers manage." (I do concede that there are some senior officials who have not been excited at the prospect but I submit that, on balance, they are a minority.) The conditions are ripe on both sides of the fence for major changes in public sector management. But what has happened?

I propose to evaluate by referring back to the three "constraints on productive management" identified by the Auditor General in 1983. However, I shall do this in reverse order for a reason which should become apparent at the bottom line.

Incentives And Disincentives

The concept of "ministerial representations" in the IMAA program closely links a deputy minister's statement of productivity goals to final results. In other words, the very nexus of accountability — "enforced responsibility" — is made explicit. Senior managers' successes and failures can be clearly pinpointed and executive careers can be accelerated or diminished accordingly. The Annual Management Reports do go to Treasury Board where Cabinet ministers apparently do review them and ask probing questions. Clearly, that is how it should be if responsibility is, first, to be accorded and second, enforced. Deputy ministers who can demonstrate a record of effective and productive management deserve to be rewarded. In the absence of stock options and very high salaries, those rewards will have to be confined to assurances that their achievements are being recognized, that they will have security in their positions and to a demonstrated commitment to effective management.

Some of the incentives of the latter type were outlined in Treasury Board President de Cotret's federal spending cuts announced on December 15, 1989. Pilot projects to launch Special Operating Agencies (SOAs) for sub-units within departments or to consolidate units from two or more departments were explained as "management improvement initiatives, to support managers as they economize, and to restructure government services more efficiently."[38]

De Cotret's December 15 announcement of measures to improve efficiency was couched in business terms. Thus, the measures include:

○ "developing special businesslike agencies within the Public Service for business-type operations that supply goods and services, such as passports, internal telephone systems and the printing of Hansard;[39]

○ better management of year-end spending, better management of government assets, more authority for managers to make purchases directly."

De Cotret added that the SOAs will have a multi-year business plan and that Treasury Board would approve flexible guidelines to achieve agreed-upon business targets. Accountability will be ensured by retaining SOAs within the structure of departments under the responsibility of ministers. On paper, the SOAs appear to be another good idea, providing we do not lose sight of an important principle — that governments exist to serve the public in a manner which is **not** identical to that of a business in the competitive marketplace.

Other incentives de Cotret outlined will include authority to increase fees-for-services and permission for managers to carry over up to three per cent of non-salary operating funds at the end of the fiscal year. This latter inducement is designed to rectify some of the abuses traditionally associated with lapsing balances at the end of fiscal years.

Administrative And Procedural Constraints

There is little doubt that the Conservatives are emotionally and ideologically committed to running government like a business. The concepts of SOAs and the "wage envelope" (for example, as negotiated between Treasury Board and the Canadian Centre for Management Development (CCMD) whereby the latter, within the broad framework of the merit system, will have much greater flexibility to manage its PYs within a total salary package) are major innovations. Indeed, I would suggest that more than ever before in the history of our public service there are opportunities for good managers to excel and for solid innovation in managerial techniques to be introduced. One should understand, of course, that the pay-offs, aside from generating enthusiasm among managers, should be improved productivity and cost-effectiveness and, it is hoped, no significant loss in the fundamental raison d'etre, serving the public.

The downside is that there are bound to be errors made and accountability structures thwarted and even broken. But the errors should be exceptions as long as we all understand that accountability of public managers at all levels is first and foremost to the public and its elected representatives.

Another downside, and one I consider more serious, is that in the enthusiasm to manage government more like a business both our politicians and public managers may lose sight of the very fundamental fact that government exists to serve the public. If "leaner" really is "meaner" (as Mulroney said) then I submit that mean government is not what Canadians want. I would submit that Canadians expect their governments to be tolerant at worst, if not somewhat benevolent. Business does not have a reputation for benevolence and thus, if one too forcefully translates that ethic to government, it seems to follow that public managers—in their passion to achieve improved productivity—will become less sympathetic to the public they serve.

If the IMAA initiative is permitted to continue and given greater impetus, if the Public Service 2000 renewal of the public service initiative bears the fruit its proponents anticipate, if departments and agencies are given more opportunities to be innovative and if the SOAs succeed within the limited terms set forth by de Cotret, we should see some improved productivity down the road. It will not, as noted earlier, manifest rapidly, for government is an enormous and complex administrative structure. Thus, any short-term statistical claims such as Mulroney's 12,000 PYs reduction must be viewed with caution, not because we doubt the intent but because we must constantly be wary of complexity reduced to catchy statistics.

As the federal public sector moves towards an era of reduced procedural and administrative constraints to effective and productive management, the public must ask three questions:

°   Is this the type of government we want — leaner and meaner?

°   Is the merit system as a basis for public service entry and promotion being eroded? and,

°   Can responsibility continue to be enforced so that meaningful and effective accountability is ensured?

There are grounds for considerable optimism and I suspect that while the Conservatives can rightfully take credit for the most recent impetus towards improved productivity and innovative public management, the roots of desire for change are well embedded in the fertile soil of Canada's federal public service.

Political Priorities

Mr. de Cotret personally seems fully committed to improved managerial practices and productivity. But the environment under which all those improvements are to take place constantly changes — you cannot build solid structures on quicksand. To allege managerial inertia when short-term political considerations must constantly override long-term management development is to miss the essence of the critical difference between management in the private and public sectors. That observation further suggests that de Cotret's "business model" may be a misguided intention and even somewhat inappropriate for government. Lest we overlook the obvious, governments are **not** businesses. They serve, and are servants of, the public. As Hyman Solomon said in commenting on de Cotret's December 15 announcements:

> Whether it results in real change or not remains to be seen. No one seriously questions that public service productivity today is abysmal. But it takes political will to push against institutional inertia and rigidities. The Tories can always make political hay out of bashing the public service and Fat City. But whether they want to undergo the thankless task of reforming the institution is another matter. De Cotret can't do it alone.[40]

I do not fully agree with Solomon's popular view that "productivity is abysmal" and that there exists "institutional inertia." If he is correct, then many of the innovations I have discussed herein, such as IMAA, would not have come to pass. Many innovations have been internally generated within the public sector even including, in part, the very re-structuring of Cabinet. There is a cadre of "managerial evangelists" within the federal public service and many of them are the driving forces behind the initiatives taken over the past four to five years. It is true that the Tories have created the "business climate" but the impetus for, and mechanics of, change are largely emanating from within the public service and, to the Tories' credit, they have responded favourably to new ideas. Thus, with these exceptions noted, I could not have said it more succinctly than Hyman Solomon.[41]

The bottom line is that if the Conservatives want to receive credit for improved management and productivity in the public sector then they are going to have to examine the longer-term, less rewarding, haul. Running government more like a business will not have a short-term high rate of return on current investment in innovation. To increase productivity requires constant reminders and pressure; results can be achieved only over a long period of time. The Tories may not want to afford that luxury.

Notes

1   Canada, *Report of the Auditor General of Canada to the House of Commons*, fiscal year ended March 31, 1983 (Ottawa: Auditor General of Canada, 1983), pp. 53-87.

2   These statements reinforced a theme identified in the Auditor General's Report of 1975.

3   Quoted in: Canada, *Report of the Auditor General of Canada to the House of Commons*, for the fiscal year ended March 31, 1976 (Ottawa: Supply and Services Canada, 1976), p. 10.

4   Canada, *Royal Commission on Financial Management & Accountability*, Final Report, March 1979 (Ottawa: Supply and Services Canada), p. 45.

5   Specifically, these paragraphs refer to: Funding common service organizations on a full-cost recovery basis (8.1); Unit-pricing of goods and services provided by common service organizations (8.2); Funds for common services, including accommodation/rental, to be provided in Estimates of user departments and transactions between common service and user departments to be actual transactions (8.3); The Comptroller General (acting as a "rate review board") to conduct public hearings on fees charged (8.4); Transfer of Bureau of Translation and Government Telecommunications Agency to Supply and Services (8.5); and, Functions of S&S be under one deputy minister (8.6).

6   *Report of the Auditor General of Canada 1976, op. cit.,* p. 56.

7   *Ibid.,* p. 57.

8   Charles T. Goodsell in his refreshing book, *The Case for Bureaucracy: A Public Administration Polemic,* (2nd ed.), (Chatham, N.J.: Chatham House, 1985), p. 37, observes:

   ...A fundamental feature of bureaucracy is that it continually performs millions of tiny acts of individual services,...[but]...Because this ongoing mass of routine achievement is not in itself noteworthy or even capable of intellectual grasp, it operates silently, almost out of sight. The occasional breakdowns, the unusual scandals, the individual instances where a true injustice is done, are

what come to our attention and color our overall judge-
ment. The water glass of bureaucracy is quite full, and
we have difficulty realizing it.

9   As Zussman and Jabes have suggested, there is also a problem
        of "job ambiguity" arising from alterations in government
        priorities. Performance goals become ambiguous and not
        readily susceptible to quantitative evaluation. Process manage-
        ment at minimum permits a manager to fall back upon routine
        and relatively known and consistent performance evaluation
        criteria. *The Vertical Solitude: Managing in the Public Sector*
        (Montreal: Institute for Research in Public Policy, 1989), p. 130.

10   Ironically, several of the Audit Guides produced by the Office
        of the Auditor General stress the importance of auditing as a
        process. For example, the Audit Guides: "Auditing of Proce-
        dures for Effectiveness" (August 1981); "Auditing the Planning
        Function and Processes" (August 1984); and, "Payroll Costs
        Management: Human Resource Planning" (June 1981) all
        characterize the manager's role as process-based.

11   *Report of the Auditor General, 1983, op. cit.,* p. 58.

12   *Report of the Auditor General, 1983, op. cit.,* p. 61.

13   Stuart Nagel, "Public and Private Management Science:
        Similarities and Differences," Section in *Management Science
        News,* Winter 1983, pp. 3-7.

14   Stuart Nagel, *Ibid.;* and, Robert P. McGowan, "Improving Ef-
        ficiency in Public Management: The Torment of Sisyphus,"
        Public Productivity Review, Vol. VIII (2), Summer 1984, pp.
        162-78 at p. 165.

15   Gordon Osbaldeston in his fine study, *Keeping Deputy Ministers
        Accountable* (London, Ontario: National Centre for Manage-
        ment and Development, 1988), p. 18, depicts the matter some-
        what differently. Describing the "Deputy Minister's
        Management Environment" he portrays the relationship some-
        what like a wheel-within-a-wheel. Thus, he defines four central
        relationships: Prime Minister and Clerk of the Privy Council;
        Minister; Treasury Board; and, Public Service Commission.
        These, in turn, are surrounded by 20 other relationships ranging
        from Treasury Board Secretariat to the general public.
        Osbaldeston's environmental model, while probably an ac-

curate picture, is not especially helpful for an appreciation of the day-to-day management context and its conflicting channels of direction and accountability.

16   I am reminded here of an observation contained in the 1908 *Report of the Royal Commission on the Civil Service* (the Courtney Commission) pertaining to salaries and motivation:

> Your Commissioners have found in their examinations that as a rule the salaries laid down in the Civil Service Act have been pretty constant for the last 30 years...the civil servant, rejoicing still in the same salary which was paid 30 years ago, finds his purchasing power sadly diminished. ...[we] have heard from officials and groups of officials...the most harrowing details of privations endured by them in providing for those dependent upon them. And as nothing so unfits a man for the faithful performance of his daily word as the constant worry over money matters...greater consideration should be shown to the very different circumstances existing at the present time than existed 30 years ago.

Clearly money has not always been motivating factor in public service! 7-8 Edward VII, Sessional paper No. 29a, A1908, p. 17.

On the modern problem of public sector management productivity incentives, see: Zussman and Jabes, *The Vertical Solitude, op. cit.,* pp. 152-53.

17   There is a fair literature on IMAA and I supplemented that with interviews in Ottawa in December 1989. The literature includes: Gaetan Lussier, "IMAA: The Employment and Immigration Canada Perspective," and, Georgina Wyman, "IMAA, The Supply and Services Canada Perspective," both in *Optimum*, 18(4), 1987/88, pp. 16-21 and 22-29 respectively; Barry Lacombe, "IMAA and the Operational Plan Framework," and, Guy Leclerc, "IMAA and Management Representations - meeting accountability requirements," both in *Optimum*, 19(2), 1988/89, pp. 70-80 and 90-96 respectively; Donald Roy, "Making IMAA Work - A look at five key issues," *Optimum*, 20(1), 1989/90, pp. 56-64; Gordon F. Osbaldeston, *op. cit.*, pp. 75-78 snf 167; Gerard Veilleux and Donald Savoie, "Kafka's Castle: The Treasury Board of Canada revisited," *Canadian Public Administration* 31(4), 1988, pp. 5176-38 at 535-38; and, Donald

Savoie, *The Politics of Public Spending in Canada* (Toronto: University of Toronto Press, 1990), pp. 117-20 and 122-25.

18   Lacombe, *op. cit.,* p. 72.

19   To reiterate, resource-based management suggests greater flexibility in developing a mix of resources whereas process-based management is driven by those proverbial abstract and detached rules. For a modest insight into resource-based management, see: Canadian Comprehensive Auditing Foundation, *Effectiveness: Reporting and Auditing in the Public Sector* (Ottawa: CCAF, 1987). Also see: Brian Usilaner, "Can we expect productivity improvement in the [U.S.] Federal Government?" *Public Productivity Review,* (September 1981), pp. 237-46.

20   Veilleux and Savoie, *op. cit.*, p. 537. Also see Savoie's comments in: *The Politics of Public Spending..., op. cit.,* p. 123 where he discusses the cynicism of departmental managers towards IMAA.

21   There is always somebody with a new scheme to do something. Brian Marson, Comptroller General of British Columbia, dubbed this "BOHICA" at the Institute of Public Administration's National Seminar at Harrison Hot Springs, B.C. in December 1989. BOHICA, Marson explained, is a mnemonic for "Bend Over Here It Comes Again" in the sense that we've been down this road before with somebody else's high-flying scheme and fancy manuals and presentations. He was not referring to IMAA but I am tempted to ask, "has anybody very clearly—and in plain language—communicated the objectives of IMAA to prospective users?"

22   There has emerged in Canada a healthy community of people interested in program evaluation and some of the product appears in the *Canadian Journal of Program Evaluation.* The Program Evaluation Branch of the Office of the Comptroller General also has some very useful material including an extremely helpful document, "Program Evaluation Methods: Measurement and Attribution of Program Results," dated September 1989. To this might be added: John Mayne, "Evaluation in the Government of Canada," Paper, American Evaluation Association, San Francisco, October 1989; Program Evaluation Branch, "Organizing for Program Evaluation," December 5, 1989; and John Mayne, "Establishing and Renewing Internal

Evaluation: The Federal Experience," August 23, 1988. The latter two articles are both mimeographed.

23 The subject is discussed by Hari Johri, Phil Charko and David Wright, "Assessment of fee charging for internal government services," *Optimum*, Vol. 19(4), 1988/89, pp. 29-48. As they point out, the effectiveness of "fees-for-service" depends upon a diminution of "external budgetary controls over how revenues may be spent", p. 34. Treasury Board Secretariat estimates that external (i.e. the public) user fees will generate $3 billion in revenues in the 1990-91 fiscal year. Canada, Treasury Board Secretariat, *1990-91 Estimates*, Part II, p. 2-7.

24 Ironically, when the Part IIIs of the Estimates were introduced in 1980, they were intended to provide a clear and concise picture of how public money was to be spent for each department and agency. But two things have happened: first, departments have learned how to prepare the Part IIIs much more skilfully and, second, they have become expensive to obtain. The end result is that even if one can afford them, they are not nearly as useful as was intended.

25 Correspondence, Hon. Michael Wilson, 1989. On the closed-door nature of the Tory government, one could add the ongoing sage of the Auditor General's efforts to obtain information on ministerial travel, the purchase of Petrofina, etc. "The Conservatives,...have made secrecy a cornerstone of power. And what Brian Mulroney once condemned as a 'totally unacceptable' practice during the Liberal tenure has become a trademark of his own government," Eric Beauchesne, Southam News Service, *The Windsor Star,* October 26, 1989.

26 To this one should add the apparent almost universal inability of ministers' offices to turn around correspondence. My experience suggests that a minimum of two months and more frequently, three months, exists between when one sends a letter and when one receives a reply.

27 *The Globe and Mail,* [Toronto], December 21, 1989.

28 Canada, Treasury Board News Release, December 15, 1989. The document released by Treasury Board in conjunction with Tabling of the *1990-91 Estimates* on February 22, 1990, titled: "Managing government expenditures," has a section titled *Management Measures* (pp. 52-57). Beyond a few cosmetic

tinkerings with Revenue Canada's (Taxation) Accounts Receivable, I can find absolutely nothing which even hints that the Tories have progressed beyond a most rudimentary understanding of what improved management practices means.

29   Canada, *Report of the Auditor General of Canada to the House of Commons*, fiscal year ended March 31, 1989 (Ottawa: Supply and Services, 1989), paragraphs 21.24 to 21.51, pp. 443-459.

30   Department of Supply and Services' reluctance to give up control over petty purchases may have much to do with "fees-for-service" as DSS charges an administration fee — a minimum of $50 (or 10%) — for all those small contracts.

31   Auditor General's Report, 1989, p. 457.

32   Canada, Treasury Board Secretariat, *1990-91 Estimates*, Part III, pp. 2-8.

33   Office of the Prime Minister, "Notes for an Address," November 9, 1989, p. 6.

34   Of course, such transfers also permit the Prime Minister to argue, as he did in the same November 9 speech, that even in "an election year we held the growth of spending on government programs to 3.1 per cent." To be absolutely precise, what he should have added is that program transfers can move actual expenditures from non-statutory (program) estimates to statutory estimates, thereby actually showing a reduction in "spending on government programs" but obscuring that same expenditure as an increase in federal transfer payments or conditional grants to a province or territory. The net result may very well partially explain why on the one hand the Tories claim to have reduced federal public service employment by 12,000 PYs while simultaneously the debt increased.

35   Canada, *Report of the Royal Commission on Government Organization*, Vol. 2(5), October 1962, pp. 19-68.

36   Veilleux and Savoie, *op. cit.,* p. 532.

37   *The Toronto Star*, May 31, 1989.

38   Canada, Treasury Board, "New Release," December 15, 1989. Mr. de Cotret explained the SOAs as follows: "These agencies

will have multi-year business plans, and Treasury Board will approve any special flexibility necessary to achieve agreed-upon business targets. The agencies will remain within government departments under ministers, and will continue to be answerable to senior management and ministers. Their business goals will be very clear, and in some cases, they will compete with the private sector for the opportunity to supply services to government."

39   One could extend this initiative to argue for greater adaptability in provision of public services. Thus, providing public managers with opportunities to systematically reduce services offered (while still maintaining adequate service delivery levels) might be feasible. Victor Murray and Todd Jick, for example, outlined a framework for such strategic public service delivery adaptation in "Strategic Decision Response to Hard Times in Public Sector Organizations," *Academy of Management Proceedings* (San Diego, CA: 1981), pp. 339-43.

40   "Innovative programs may be the right path," *The Financial Post,* December 21, 1989.

41   Apparently there is one rather reluctant partner in the move towards greater managerial autonomy and that is Finance Canada. I note this without prejudice because it has only been "said" to me by several officials but it remains unconfirmed.

CHAPTER 9

MANAGING THE FEDERAL PUBLIC
SERVICE AS THE KNOT TIGHTENS

David Zussman

Résumé

Le 12 décembre 1989 le premier ministre a annoncé la création d'un groupe de travail nommée Fonction publique 2000 dont l'objectif était de renouveler la fonction publique fédérale. En général, la décision d'initier ces changements avait été animée par le sentiment du besoin d'améliorer la gestion des ressources humaines, d'attirer les jeunes Canadiens vers la fonction publique, de motiver et de retenir les fonctionnaires et de favoriser un sens de l'excellence à tous les niveaux.

Dans ce chapitre on discute un nombre de défis auxquels doit faire face le groupe de travail. En particulier, la fonction publique doit faire face aux changements intervenant dans la valeur du travail au sein de la main-d'oeuvre du pays, à l'accroissement des responsabilités individuelles dû à la décentralisation du travail, à l'effet contraignant du profil démographique de la fonction publique fédérale, et à la perception que le travail bien accompli et les récompenses ne sont pas suffisamment reliés. De plus, de nouvelles analyses de l'Enquête auprès des gestionnaires de l'Etat laissent entendre que l'importance du ministère, la mobilité des sous-ministres, et le nombre des cadres supérieurs ont des effets différents sur la satisfaction au travail. On tire plusieurs conclusions pour la gouverne de ceux qui s'intéressent à améliorer l'état de la gestion au sein de la fonction publique.

INTRODUCTION

On December 12, 1989, Prime Minister Mulroney announced a new initiative to renew the public service of Canada. The objective of this exercise, named Public Service 2000, is "to enable the public service to provide the best possible service to Canadians into the 21st century." At the time of the announcement, the Prime Minister claimed that since taking office there had been "a number of significant improvements to the way in which services are delivered and to the way in which government is organized and managed." He went on to say that "significant change is necessary to the way in which the public service is managed if it is to continue to be as effective as possible in the context of continuing fiscal restraint."

By this statement he made it clear to the public service that restraint would continue to be an underlying principle of public administration at the federal level. Whatever increases in productivity the government needed in order to carry out its varied mandate would be found in new efficiency measures and better management techniques.

In appointing John Edwards, a senior public servant, to direct this task force and by announcing the creation of the task force in a fairly unobtrusive way,[1] the Prime Minister indicated to the nation, and especially to public servants, his desire for a low-key approach to change that would not attract much public discussion and scrutiny but that would be an effective way of addressing this serious problem.

Paul Tellier, as Clerk of the Privy Council, signalled his concern for the well-being of the public service in a speech he delivered in the summer of 1988 when he argued that "if I had to choose a single major challenge facing the public service, I would say it is to find ways of countering the now widespread disinterest and skepticism about the value of public life in all its manifestations, political as well as public service."[2] From this perspective, he saw six broad challenges, among them was the need for the better management of human resources. By this he meant being able to attract young Canadians to the public service, to motivate and retain members of the public service, and to foster a sense of excellence at all levels.

This sentiment was also echoed by Don Mazankowski who argued at the 1988 meeting of the Public Policy Forum that "a competent, highly motivated public service is a key element in a well organized and competitive economy. We must guard against unfair criticism of public servants. [New recruits] will devote their professional lives to public service only if the institution in which they can serve is widely respected."[3]

While the Prime Minister has chosen to emphasize the need for improved service to Canadians in the years to come, there have been many more reports during the last few years of severe morale problems in the Canadian public service. What is fundamentally important in the context of these reform initiatives is that, given the enormous role the public service plays in this country, public servants must, as a consequence, be productive and satisfied with their work. Morale is important because it has a long-term effect on productivity. As well, low morale also serves to signal potential recruits to look for employment elsewhere. In time, if the root cause of these morale problems is not addressed, the public service will be unable to attract the best and the brightest graduates of Canada's universities and it will have trouble keeping the best of its managers in the public service for the length of their working careers.

Most Canadians are not aware that an excellent public service is both a tradition in Canada and a necessity given the political, institutional and geographical structure of the country. While organizations like the Public Policy Forum have been formed over the years to raise public and private sector awareness of the need for a first-rate public service, the general public remains somewhat ignorant and certainly very skeptical of the role that the public servant plays in Canada.

While an economic downturn forced the private sector in the early 1980s to address the issue of good management in its own industries and organizations, it has taken almost a decade for the public service to respond in much the same way. The growing recognition that people are the most important resource of any given organization is now firmly part of the management culture in the private sector and it is becoming increasingly so in the public sector. This is due in part to proddings from academics and management consultants and also because of the commitment of the current Clerk of the Privy Council, the Secretary of the Treasury Board and the President of the Public Service Commission.[4] The task force on the revitalization of the public service is the most demonstrable evidence yet that the government wants to maintain and improve the state of management and the management cadre in the public service of Canada.

Over the last decade but especially since the Conservatives were elected in 1984, demands have increased for public services. At the same time, due to a shift in political orientation about the role of government in society, we have witnessed a number of exercises which have been designed to limit the size and influence of the public service. It must be recognized that although downsizing has a huge political appeal it only increases the workload of those public servants who stay on the job. Ironically, at the point in time when the downsizing exercise is almost complete, we have discovered that work demands as well as the stress on individual public servants, particularly managers, have increased dramatically. At this point, the principal way of dealing with this situation has been to increase the efficiency and effectiveness of government services in order to meet the higher level of demands.

In 1986, I wrote a report in *How Ottawa Spends* entitled "The Mulroney Government: Walking the Tightrope." The general theme of the article was that Mulroney as Prime Minister was caught between the conflicting demands of two different constituents. On the one hand, many of his supporters felt that he had been elected, *inter alia*, to do away with what was perceived to be a fat, lazy, partisan, and largely inefficient public service. On the other hand, he soon discovered that very few of his policies could ever be initiated, developed or implemented without a highly motivated professional non-partisan public service which considered itself to be an integral part of the government's apparatus. For the next three or four years, he walked the tightrope. At times he pandered to the conservative elements in his caucus which wanted to see a more limited role for the public service. This was accomplished by creating positions like chiefs of staff, centralizing the allocation of contracts for survey work, and generally speaking out against the public service at partisan events. However, he simultaneously implemented a number of progressive policies such as early retirement schemes, resisting pressures of politicization of the public service by appointing career public servants to deputy minister positions, and improving executive compensation.[5]

By the end of 1989, Mr. Mulroney once again discovered he was walking this now familiar tightrope since the anti-public service faction in his caucus had not dissipated its animosity. In fact, the perception persisted that Ottawa continued to be "Fat City" and anti-conservative, given the way in which the Ottawa electorate (which is significantly made up of federal public servants) had rejected all of the Conservative Party candidates in the 1988 general election. At the same time, Mulroney discovered that the once proud, professional and dedicated federal public service had been reduced to one that saw its role as marginalized, its direction ambiguous and the leadership which it had learned to expect from its senior public servants as having declined in strength and conviction.

These factors convinced the government that there was an urgent need for some reflection and reform because the current system could no longer live on its past accomplishments, traditions and values. Some observers thought that the system was hemorrhaging in a number of places due to the retirements and departures of certain key people. Moreover, it was seen by managers farther down the ranks as having lost its overall direction and purpose.

This chapter is about some of the problems currently facing the Canadian federal public service. These problems must be resolved immediately because they underlie the fear that they have produced a public service which has lost its traditional drive for professionalism and its commitment to excellence. This has also led to significant morale problems and to a failure on the part of management to resolve these issues. There is reason to be especially fearful of the present situation because it is more than likely that the public service will be mandated with increased responsibilities over the coming decade and not fewer, as many people speculate. Given this expectation of increased responsibilities, it is now even more important that the federal government attract the very best young men and women that this country produces. Failure to do so will create a management cadre that will likely not be able to meet the challenges of the 1990s and beyond.

We also know, from a long line of research activities that morale problems lead to low work satisfaction which in turn affects productivity.[6] Productivity, of course, is one of the key measures of an organization's effectiveness and it is more than likely that over the coming years, the public will expect more productivity from each of its public servants. My hypothesis is that low worker satisfaction is the result of a number of factors including changing work values, institutional barriers which make it difficult for people to do the jobs for which they were hired, demographic and other profiles which constrain upward mobility and changing perceptions of the value of public service.

In order to explore this problem, this chapter discusses changing work values, looks at the demographic characteristics of the management cadre in the federal public service and analyzes the impact some institutional characteristics have on work satisfaction.

WORK VALUES

Since 1986, there have been some dramatic shifts in attitudes, values and behaviours in the Canadian work force. In the next few pages, some of these changes are discussed in the context of the public service although the discussion has equal application to the general work force.

Ever since the recession of the early 1980s, Canadian workers have changed their view of their work and their own place in the work force. In general, it appears that Canadians have changed their value structure by becoming more hedonistic and more self-centred with regard to their work activities. It is becoming increasingly difficult for employers to move their employees around and to offer them the same financial and other incentives that were successful motivators in the 1950s. The 1980s has produced workers who have a strong view of what they want and will usually measure their needs against what the company can offer. When these two factors are at odds with one another, the employee most often follows his or her own self-interest.

Moreover, the dramatic increase in the number of two-income families has made the worker more mobile and less loyal since individual jobs are no longer as important as they once were to the economic survival of families. Two-income families have given many workers a sense of financial independence but have also placed greater stress on individuals since managing family obligations must be balanced against professional demands. These added pressures have contributed to the further weakening of work values. All of these changes suggest that employee attachment to compensation packages and rapid career advancement may be relatively less important than they once were. It has also meant that leisure time and quality of life have become increasingly more important in the value structure of the typical manager.

Not only have work values changed in Canada over the last few years, but so has the nature of the work. It now appears quite obvious that workers are more accountable to their employers and to their superiors due to the greater quantity and quality of information and to the general trend in large organizations towards decentralized decision-making. The introduction of the personal computer as a standard work tool has sped up the decision-making process, adding additional pressures on employees since they now have less time to contemplate a particular decision and to consult with colleagues.

When one factors in the increased levels of public scrutiny in both the public and private sectors through the enhanced role of interest groups and the increased popularity of access to information, we find that, in general, the nature of work has shifted towards a more open, complex and rapidly changing decision-making environment. This, in turn, has resulted in a more stressful and unpredictable work environment.

The public service is also subject to other pressures and constraints which are still relevant today. In surveys which were conducted of senior managers and executives in 20 federal departments in 1986 and 28 departments in 1988, a number of very consistent findings were found.[7] In particular, the survey data revealed that there was a wide gap in perceptions between public and private sector managers, regardless of their level in the management structure. But more important, it was discovered that within the public service, managers who worked lower down in the organization were less satisfied, less generous in their appraisal of their jobs and of the departments for which they worked. This "Vertical Solitude" as Jabes and I have labelled this phenomenon did not exist in the private sector among our 13 control group companies.[8]

While there have been many different findings resulting from these studies, three are most relevant for the discussion in this chapter. The first concerns the fact that senior public servants did not see a link between their level of performance and their rewards. The second is the perception that deputy ministers and other senior managers in the executive echelon of the federal public service were not providing adequate leadership. Finally, senior managers were uncertain of the goals and objectives of their organizations.

Despite these negative findings, we found that work satisfaction, and particularly job satisfaction, were quite high given the perceived constraints and problems in the existing system. Our conclusion two years ago was that although serious problems existed in the public service, there was enough goodwill and enough commitment to the job to bring about some dramatic and important changes if proper steps are taken to remedy the situation.

EXTERNAL ENVIRONMENT

Managing in the public service has not been easy recently and it is important to review some of the external environmental constraints facing public servants. Most people recognize that the Conservative government elected in September 1984 had a fundamentally different philosophy towards the role of government in society than had previous governments. On the campaign trail, the Conservative candidates made it amply clear that the marketplace as opposed to government intervention was the way in which the country should make its important decisions. As a corollary to this statement, there was a persistent view which emerged subsequent to the election that the public service and its mandarins would play a less important role in the determination of policy and its implementation than in the past. This was because government officials were seen to favour "liberal" policies of public ownership and state intervention.

The government did hold true to its philosophy of dependence on market forces by privatizing companies like Air Canada, de Havilland and Canadair, by reducing the size of the Canadian public service by almost 15,000 jobs and by exercising strong expenditure restraints in some areas through decreases in publicly-funded programs. Unfortunately, many of these actions were accompanied by personal attacks on the public service by politicians, which led to some very important and well-noted incidents between the public service and its political masters. The treatment that Gaetan Lussier as Deputy Minister of Employment and Immigration received before the Labour, Manpower and Immigration Committee at the hands of Ferdinand Jourdanais is an obvious example of the problems the public service had to deal with in order to maintain its credibility and the notion of a professional public service.[9] One important spinoff of these attacks on the public service has been the progressive decline in public confidence in government institutions, both political and bureaucratic.

Moreover, since the public has a great deal of trouble distinguishing between the public service and its political masters, it usually characterizes both institutions in the same negative way.[10] As a consequence, many of the political scandals which rocked the Mulroney government from 1985 to 1988 have inadvertently washed over the public service giving it the same negative reputation as its political masters. Given the usual incentives for self-survival, politicians have done very little to correct the situation while public servants are hardly in a position to influence public opinion.

ANALYSIS

The second half of this chapter looks at various data describing the state of the federal public service with an emphasis on the management cadre. The analysis is divided into two sections. The first looks at issues which affect the public service on a macro level where seeds of this problem were sown some years ago when the government adopted its current hiring practices.[11] The second part addresses issues which have arisen as a result of personnel and organizational decisions that have their full impact on a departmental basis.[12] In this instance, I have concentrated on a number of variables which were first noted by Gordon Osbaldeston who argued that the rapid mobility of deputy ministers has produced a system of inexperienced managers who often possess inadequate knowledge about the departments or agencies that they are supposed to run and the nitty gritty policy and program issues that they form.[13] The question which arises from his work is whether the current organizational structure may be inadvertently encouraging low levels of work satisfaction among managers.

Specifically, the data presented here look at the age distribution of the federal public service, actual mobility patterns of public servants, the number of Francophones and females in the federal public service, and the projected occupational demands for public servants by the year 2000. Once having examined the impact that macro demographic and institutional factors may have on employee performance, the paper considers the impact that some department-specific data such as deputy minister mobility and departmental size and type have had on work satisfaction. The paper concludes with a general discussion about the potential impact of these factors on public sector management.

I have hypothesized that departments in which deputy ministers spend a relatively long period of time will produce employees (i.e. managers) who have higher levels of satisfaction with their jobs and their departments.[14] I also hypothesize that managers of smaller departments will be relatively more satisfied with their jobs than those in larger ones, given that the communication lines are shorter, although all of them are largely decentralized in keeping with government policy. I have also hypothesized that policy departments and central agencies will produce the most satisfied employees because they are closer to the central decision-making processes and are therefore more likely to be better informed about government priorities and goals.[15] The analyses are based on an analysis of variance and person-product correlations which were used to interpret the data.

With regards to demographic data, it seems clear that a number of factors are having an enormous impact on public service attitudes and work satisfaction. One of the most important of these factors is the age of the average public servant. According to the Public Service Commission *Annual Report* (see Chart 9.1), the average age of the public service has increased from 40 years in 1978 to 41 and one half years in 1990. It is projected that, by 1998, the average age of public servants will be almost 43 years. While the average age itself is not an indicator of future difficulties, the data suggest that over the years little effort has been made to systematically replace those who have retired with younger, albeit less experienced, entry-level employees.

Table 9.1 supports the contention that the average age tenure is a significant indicator of a serious age imbalance within the public service. Overall, only a little more than three per cent of public servants are 24 years or younger while 11.2 per cent of them are 55 years of age or older. The vast majority of federal public servants are baby boomers between the ages of 35 and 44 years. This cohort makes up 36.5 per cent of the total population of public servants in Canada, a percentage much larger than that found in the general work force in Canada.[16]

Table 9.1

Age Distribution of Full-Time Federal Public Servants

Age (in years)	Number	Per Cent
Under 24	6,550	3.09
25-34	59,092	27.86
35-44	77,482	36.52
45-54	45,020	21.22
55-64	22,843	10.77
Greater than 64	1,151	0.54
Total	212,138	100.00

Source: Treasury Board of Canada, *Public Service Work Force 2000*, Phase 1 Report, 1989.

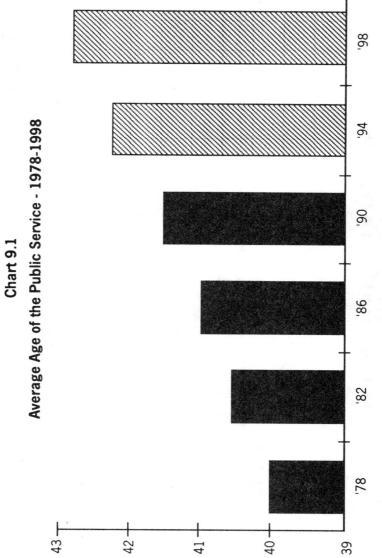

Chart 9.1

Average Age of the Public Service - 1978-1998

Source: *Annual Report*, Public Service Commission, 1988.

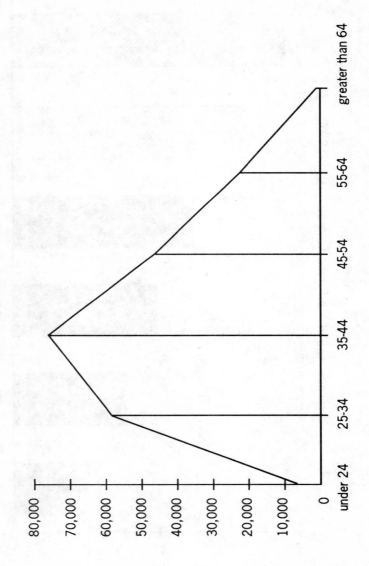

Chart 9.2

Age Distribution of Full Time Public Servants

The danger which arises from this clustering around a middle-aged cohort lies in the fact that such a large proportion of public servants are trapped in a fairly rigidly controlled bureaucracy. Few of their seniors are in a position to retire, depriving many of those in the middle-aged cohort of promotional opportunities (see Chart 9.2). At the same time, the large middle-aged group will also have a debilitating effect on relatively young and more junior public servants whose ambitions for promotions will be stymied. Consequently, the "normal" shape of the age distribution has the dual impact of offering few promotional opportunities for those who occupy the middle-aged cohort, and at the same time, this large group hinders and frustrates those who are younger and less advanced in their careers. Given the fact that promotions tend to motivate employees, especially those who work in large organizations, the relative absence of this important management tool will likely have a significant impact on morale.[17]

Coupled with the problem of age distribution is the absence of opportunities for public servants to achieve mobility through promotions, lateral transfers or other means of job advancement. Table 9.2 contains some interesting findings about the way in which the government went about finding solutions to the demographic conundrum.

Although more than 9,000 individuals were appointed to the Public Service of Canada in 1988, most of these new employees were hired into lower level, operational-administrative support groups, although there is no evidence to suggest that this group was most in need of rejuvenation. Rejuvenation through outside appointments was least prevalent for members of the policy-oriented management and administrative/foreign service officers group, where only 64 and 1,623 outsiders respectively were appointed.

Since outside appointments to the management and administrative groups did not contribute in any meaningful way to rejuvenation, relative to the other groups of public service employees, mobility was supported through internal promotion. The largest number of actual promotions in 1988 was within these two groups, when over 13 per cent of the management cadre and a similar percentage for the administrative and foreign service officers group received promotions within their respective groups.

Table 9.2

Mobility in the Federal Public Service
(number of ps and appointments)

Classification*	Number of full time employees	%	Appointments to the public service	%	Promotions	%	Lateral transfers and deployments	%	Layoffs	%
Management	4,537	2.1	64	1.41	623	13.73	523	11.53	8	0.18
Scientific and professional	22,756	10.7	1,428	6.28	2,348	10.32	1,849	8.13	245	1.08
Administrative and Foreign Service	55,912	26.4	1,623	2.90	7,582	13.56	5,478	9.80	112	0.20
Technical	25,927	12.2	1,007	3.88	2,422	9.34	1,763	6.80	69	0.27
Administrative support	65,421	30.8	2,877	4.40	5,899	9.02	10,462	15.99	208	0.32
Operational	37,174	17.5	2,439	6.56	2,039	5.49	2,880	7.75	277	0.75
Total	211,993	99.7	9,443	4.45	20,913	9.86	22,959	10.83	919	0.43

*See Public Service Commission *Annual Report* for definitions of this classification system

Source: Public Service Commission *Annual Report*, 1988

The overall rate of outside hiring and promotion reveals a need for other administrative measures to offer employees new challenges. In this regard, the Public Service Commission effected almost 23,000 lateral transfers or other types of deployment in 1988. The group receiving the greatest proportion of lateral transfers was the administrative support group which received almost 1,500, effectively giving almost one in six of their members an opportunity to work in a new environment through a lateral transfer without the benefit of higher compensation.

While it is obvious that there has been considerable movement within the public service, layoffs have not been a popular management tool. Despite the rhetoric describing the public service as over staffed and in need of massive cutbacks, in reality, fewer than 1,000 full-time federal government employees were laid off last year, representing a very small proportion of the total government work force.[18] Of those who did receive layoff notices, proportionately the largest number of people were those who worked in the operational group although, even in this instance, the numbers are relatively small.

The overall impression one develops from these data is that there is very little rejuvenation of the public service from outside and whatever attempts have been made have been largely concentrated in the lower management and operational structure of the public service. With regard to promotions, the management and the administrative/foreign service officers groups appear to have reaped the greatest benefits from promotional opportunities while the operational groupings have received the lowest level of promotional support. From a management perspective, one can only be dismayed by these findings since promotions have been disproportionately assigned to employees who already occupy the better paying, demanding and more interesting jobs. The growing popularity of lateral transfers which are used slightly more often than promotions, is an interesting way of offering people new enriched jobs[19] although the full impact of these measures on productivity and satisfaction is unknown. As a final note, layoffs, although publicly championed by the government, actually played a very minor role in reducing the size of the public service in 1988.

To further compound the problems created by demographics and policies regarding internal mobility are the increased efforts being made by the federal government to remedy a number of employment equity issues which exist in the Canadian federal public service. In particular, over the last decade, the Public Service Commission has actively supported the advancement of women and Francophones into and within the senior management category of the public service.

Table 9.3 provides some interesting information about the distribution of women and Francophones in the federal government. Overall, women comprise 42.9 per cent of the public service but, when one looks at their degree of representation in the management and executive ranks, one finds that even in the group in which the largest representation is found, women make up only 12.3 per cent of the upper management cadre.[20] Moreover, their representation is highest in the senior management (SM) group which is the most junior level within the management category. As well, the higher one moves up the executive category, the fewer numbers of women are found. As an example, within the executive group, 13.8 per cent of the 1,002 EX-1s are women while only 2.1 of the 95 EX-5s are females.

Table 9.3
Sex and Linguistic Distribution
of the Management Category
in the Public Service

	Men %	Women %	Francophones %	Anglophones %	Total N
EX-5	97.9	2.1	22.1	77.9	95
EX-4	90.6	9.4	25.6	74.4	223
EX-3	93.4	6.6	18.9	81.1	471
EX-2	90.4	9.6	22.6	77.4	815
EX-1	86.2	13.8	21.6	78.4	1002
EX Total	89.6	10.4	21.8	78.4	2606
SM	85.0	15.0	21.0	79.0	1931
Total	87.7	12.3	21.4	78.6	4537
Total Public Service	57.1	42.9	28.5	71.5	211,993

Source: Public Service Commission *Annual Report*, 1988.

The situation regarding representation in the management group is not as bleak for Francophones who make up 28.5 per cent of the total public service. Overall, Francophones occupy more than one in five senior management and executive jobs in the federal public service. For example, 21 per cent of SMs and 22.1 per cent of EX-5s are Francophones. Employment equity initiatives may be justified on many grounds. However, the added pressure on the federal government to satisfy its strong commitment to employment equity places an additional hardship on Anglophone men in the federal public service in terms of promotion and other employment opportunities available.

In addition to the combined impact that age profiles, promotions and employment equity regimes have on productivity and worker satisfaction, there are additional pressures that arise from changing demands for different types of jobs. The last of the demographic/institutional data presented here report on anticipated shifts in demand for work performed by the major occupational groups in the federal public service.

A recently released study by the Treasury Board Secretariat contains some provocative data about the potential demand for various types of occupational skills depending on two different scenarios: The first is based on a one per cent growth in the size of the public service between 1988 and the year 2000, and the second is based on a one per cent decline in size during the same time period. The results of the Treasury Board study are summarized in Chart 9.3.

While it is always difficult to predict employment demands, the Treasury Board Secretariat estimates that the demand for employees in two particular groups will grow in size regardless of the growth scenario. It is anticipated that the largest increase in demand during the next few years will be within the administrative and foreign service cadre. It is expected to grow by almost 40 per cent under the one per cent growth scenario and by almost 20 per cent even if the overall size of the public service declines by one per cent. The second occupational group which is expected to grow substantially is the management group which has been projected to grow by 25 per cent under the one per cent growth scenario and by five per cent if the public service declines in size by one per cent.

It is anticipated that both the administrative support and operational groups of public servants will decline quite substantially regardless of the scenario. In the worst case scenario, it is anticipated that by the year 2000, the administrative support group will decline by more than 20 per cent and the operational groups will decline by 30 per cent.

These projections add an additional burden on those working in the public service. Not only do they have to consider the impact of an aging work force, diminishing promotional opportunities, and aggressively administered employment equity programs on their work prospects but they must also deal with society's shifting emphasis away from operational and administrative jobs. The shift in demand in favour of more managerial jobs will serve to multiply the pressure on those public servants who find themselves in the low demand categories.

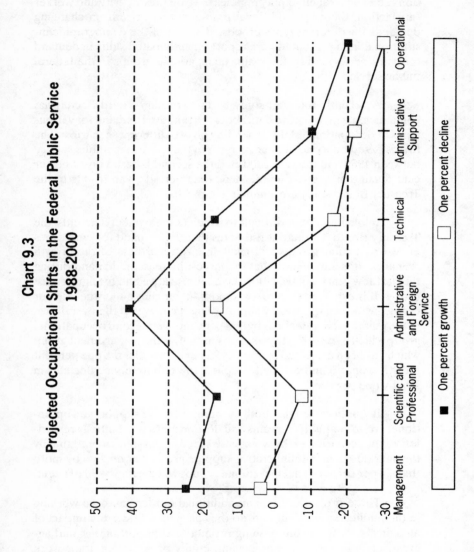

Chart 9.3

Projected Occupational Shifts in the Federal Public Service
1988-2000

The following section turns attention away from the macro forces which are tightening and restricting job opportunities to an analysis of some of the institutional factors that are expected to have an impact on work satisfaction and ultimately productivity. The analysis uses the average score of respondents in the 28 largest federal departments which participated in the 1988 Survey of Managerial Attitudes.[21] A listing of the departments included in this analysis can be found in Appendix 9.1. The Survey of Managerial Attitudes is the second organizational management survey which was undertaken at the University of Ottawa to examine current management practices of federal government managers (i.e. SMs and EXs).

This is the first time that the data from the Survey of Managerial Attitudes have been aggregated on a departmental basis. In all previously published accounts of the survey, individual responses served as the basis for the data analysis. In this instance, five independent variables or predictors have been used to test the general hypothesis that institutional variables have an impact on measures of work satisfaction. These predictors refer to the type of department, the size of department, the number of deputy ministers to have worked in a given department between 1984 and 1988, the average length of a deputy minister's tenure from 1984 to 1988 and the number of assistant deputy ministers who worked, in 1988, in the department of the respondent.

The purpose of these analyses is to demonstrate the existence of a linear relationship between the various independent variables and two measures of work satisfaction: the average level of satisfaction with respondents' departments and the average level of respondents' job satisfaction. Although the 28 scores depend on a sample of different sizes due to the varying size of each department and different response rates, the average response rate was 72 per cent which yielded an average of 104 usable and completed questionnaires for each department. As a result, the data are reliable given the large average sample size for groups.[22]

In Table 9.4, the 28 departments are divided into four different groupings according to criteria established by the Treasury Board Secretariat. The first grouping represents departments which perform only policy work, the second represents five departments which do both policy and operational work, the third includes departments that do only operational work and the last is made up of those departments and agencies which are considered to be central co-ordinating agencies of the federal government.

Overall, the data show that departmental satisfaction was some- what higher for individuals working in operational departments. There was a significant difference in levels of job satisfaction between public servants working in operational departments and those working in central agencies. Job satisfaction was seen to be somewhat lower in central agencies. In addition, there was little to distinguish the level of job satisfaction between those working in operational departments and those working in policy and operations departments.

Table 9.4

The Relationship Between Type of Department and Work Satisfaction

Type of Department	Number	Departmental Satisfaction	Job Satisfaction
Policy	13	4.02	4.22
Policy and Operations	5	4.12	4.32
Operations	6	4.39	4.33
Central Agency	4	3.81	4.04
F score		2.08	1.30

In Table 9.5, the departments have been divided into four different groups depending on their size.

Table 9.5

The Relationship Between Size of Department and Work Satisfaction

Size of Department (1988)	Number	Departmental Satisfaction	Job Satisfaction
1-2000	7	4.01	4.12
2001 - 5000	10	3.95	4.19
5001 - 10,000	6	4.15	4.35
greater than 10,000	5	4.29	4.36
F score		1.46	1.41
Correlation Coefficient		0.41	0.38

Unexpectedly the data demonstrate that departments with the largest number of employees yielded the highest levels of departmental and job satisfaction, although the F value for these groupings did not indicate a very strong level of statistical significance. However, the positive and rather substantial correlation coefficients for these data indicate that the larger departments generally yielded higher levels of departmental and job satisfaction. These results were unexpected since it was predicted that job and departmental satisfaction would be highest in those departments which have shorter lines of communication and more opportunities for interaction. However, our data do not support this view and, in fact, replicate the findings that were found in 1986.

Tables 9.6 and 9.7 look at the importance that deputy minister mobility might play in determining work satisfaction. The first table in this series considers the impact that the traditional practice of changing deputy ministers after only brief lengths of stay in a department might have on work satisfaction. It will be recalled that Gordon Osbaldeston in his study of deputy ministers' accountability suggested that the high turnover rate of deputy ministers has created a number of difficult management problems within the federal government.[23]

Table 9.6
The Relationship Between Number of Deputy Ministers
and Work Satisfaction

Number of Deputy Ministers (1984-1988)	Number	Departmental Satisfaction	Job Satisfaction
1	3	4.32	4.51
2	11	4.17	4.27
3	12	3.94	4.17
4	2	3.93	4.06
Correlation Coefficient		-0.41	-0.42

The negative correlation found in Table 9.6 suggests that the high levels of deputy minister turnover have a detrimental effect on work satisfaction. The data are quite clear, for example, in the case of job satisfaction, where we find that in the instances in which departments had only one deputy minister between 1984 and 1988, the average level of job satisfaction was 4.51, whereas in those cases in which departments had four deputy ministers during the same time period, the average level of job satisfaction for these departments was 4.06. The levels of job satisfaction for those departments having two or three deputy ministers during the same four year period were situated between the two extreme scores.

The additional question of the length of deputy ministers' tenure had less of an impact on work satisfaction (See Table 9.7). In this instance, the data were divided into four groupings: Those departments in which the average stay of deputy ministers was less than or equal to 12 months; those in which the average length of tenure of deputy ministers was between 13 and 24 months; those 11 departments in which the average stay of a deputy minister was between two years and three years; and, finally, those departments in which the average stay of a deputy minister was greater than three years. In this instance, the highest levels of work satisfaction, both departmental and job satisfaction, were found in those departments where the deputy ministers stayed the longest. However, it was not readily apparent that work satisfaction was lowest in those departments where the deputy minister's average length of appointment was less than or equal to one year. Due to the inconsistency of these findings, one can only conclude that the data are somewhat ambiguous and provide a less clear picture than did the "turnover" findings reported in the previous table.

Table 9.7

The Relationship Between the Average Length of Deputy Minister Tenure and Work Satisfaction

Average Length of Deputy Minister Tenure (in months)	Number	Departmental Satisfaction	Job Satisfaction
less than or equal to 12	5	4.21	4.25
13-24	9	3.92	4.16
25-36	11	4.06	4.21
greater than 36	3	4.32	4.51
Correlation Coefficient		0.21	0.33

The final table in this series, Table 9.8, looks at whether the number of assistant deputy ministers who work in a given department might have some detrimental impact on work satisfaction. In this instance, it was hypothesized that the number of assistant deputy ministers in a given department might affect a respondent's level of work satisfaction since a greater number of these ministers may tend to diffuse the quality of communications between deputy ministers and those working lower down in the management ranks. It was therefore expected that job satisfaction would be lowest in those departments which had larger numbers of assistant deputy ministers.

Table 9.8

The Relationship Between Number of Assistant Deputy Ministers and Work Satisfaction

Number of Assistant Deputy Ministers (1984-1988)	Number	Departmental Satisfaction	Job Satisfaction
1 - 4	10	4.08	4.22
5 - 8	9	3.99	4.23
9 or greater	9	4.12	4.25
F score		0.34	0.02
Correlation Coefficient		0.03	0.01

Despite this speculation, the data presented in Table 9.8 clearly suggest that the number of assistant deputy ministers has little to do with managers' perceptions of departmental or job satisfaction. The limited correlation between the number of assistant deputy ministers and work satisfaction, as well as the insignificant differences among the various satisfaction measures, suggest there is little empirical support for the hypothesis that work satisfaction is in some way moderated by the number of assistant deputy ministers who work in the respondent's department.

In a way, this and some of the earlier findings, challenge the general notion that work satisfaction is a function of the directness and length of the lines of communication between the deputy minister and the average manager. This general finding has some relevance to the work of the Public Service 2000 task force since it serves as a reminder that shortened communications, *per se*, do not necessarily appear to produce more satisfied managers.

CONCLUSIONS

Taken as a whole, the data present a rather challenging series of management problems for the future. Given the demographic and institutional nature of many of these problems, solutions are not readily apparent nor will they be easy to implement when they are found. While the private sector literature has much to offer in terms of possible solutions, since similar problems have been addressed during the last decade, we must be mindful that the public service works in a very different and more complex environment than that found in the private sector. It is therefore unreasonable to expect that many of the private sector solutions which have gained some credibility will be entirely appropriate for the federal public service.[24]

One of the most obvious areas of conflict between the public and private sectors is that it is not clear to anyone just who is in charge of managing the federal public service and, in particular, in charge of its management cadre. The distribution of responsibilities among the Public Service Commission, the Treasury Board Secretariat and the Privy Council Office is not defined well enough to present a unified or corporate view of these problems. While not much has been written recently about public sector management, what has appeared now emphasizes a shift away from systems development as a way of managing people to a more humanistic approach. People are now recognized as important to the health of organizations and attendant on this new recognition is a requirement that the human resources function play a more central and proactive role in encouraging, developing and evaluating individual performance in the federal public service.[25] In addition, we should look to the public personnel community for some guidance on ways to improve the issues raised in this macro and micro analysis.

It is also critical that the federal public service recognize the enduring importance of corporate culture. The data from earlier work suggest that public servants, especially those working at the lower end of the management pyramid, are not sufficiently aware of their departmental goals and objectives and are often unclear about the values being inculcated in their departments. This problem, which possibly has its origins in the mobility patterns of deputy ministers, has important ramifications for those who must address the overall problems in the public service. Until the question of values and culture are properly addressed it is likely that morale problems will continue to grow as the knot tightens around the career opportunities of the average public servant. Moreover, although culture is a difficult concept to define and more difficult to successfully implement, it must be recognized that the more employees understand the values of their organization the less they will need explicit rules of behaviour.

There also must be a further recognition that the central agencies should be the facilitators and not the bottlenecks in helping employees deal with impending problems. There must be a fundamental change in attitude towards independent decision-making that permits employees in the field to make decisions without being second-guessed by people in central agencies who often have little experience and a poor perspective on these issues.

Finally, ways must be found to educate politicians about the importance of the public service in Canada. While it is not imperative that politicians support all public service activities, it is critical that politicians acknowledge the role of a professional, non-partisan public service in this country. Starting with this premise, there are ways in which public servants can be held accountable and ways in which parliamentarians can assert their independence without the acrimony and recriminations which appear to characterize their relationship these days.

Unfortunately, the Prime Minister appeared to tip his hand somewhat when he announced the creation of Public Service 2000 by showing his preference for efficiency-type solutions to the problems within the public service. His plans to make the personnel management regime less complicated, to reduce central administrative controls, to clarify the roles of central agencies, and to find ways of encouraging efficiency and improving program delivery are all examples of system solutions to people problems. All of these proposals rely on administrative reform without any particular reference to demographic problems, future demands for specialized jobs, the impact of restricted promotional opportunities on morale, and the effect of rapid deputy minister mobility on employee work satisfaction.

Since the task force has concentrated so much of its attention on administrative reform, there should be some cause for concern among observers of the public service given the significant problems which have been raised in this chapter. One can only hope that in the course of the task force's deliberations, its members will realize that public service reform cannot be effectively dealt with until the problems raised in this chapter are addressed.

Appendix 9.1

	Person Years	Management	Per cent
Agriculture	10,724	218	2.03
Canadian International			
Development Agency	1,178	116	9.85
Communications	2,310	93	4.03
Consumer & Corporate Affairs	2,137	71	3.32
Employment & Immigration	23,357	191	0.82
Energy, Mines and Resources	4,634	162	3.50
Environment	8,811	246	2.79
External Affairs	4,151	446	10.74
Finance	826	91	11.02
Fisheries & Oceans	5,424	147	2.71
Health & Welfare	8,460	163	1.93
Indian & Northern Affairs	4,348	186	4.28
Labour	839	45	5.36
National Defence	31,993	127	0.40
Privy Council Office	365	67	18.36
Public Service Commission	2,192	75	3.42
Public Works	7,768	140	1.80
Regional Industrial Expansion	2,272	252	11.09
Revenue Canada (Customs & Excise)	9,482	106	1.12
Revenue Canada (Taxation)	17,920	152	0.85
Science & Technology	156	35	22.44
Secretary of State	2,860	69	2.41
Statistics Canada	4,388	92	2.10
Supply & Services	9,080	246	2.71
Transport	19,453	275	1.41
Treasury Board (OCG)	131	52	39.69
Treasury Board (Secretariat)	732	176	24.04
Veterans Affairs	3,510	38	1.08
	189,501	4,077	2.15

Notes

1   There was no formal press release. Instead the press was given a private briefing by Paul Tellier.

2   Paul Tellier, *Notes for An Address: The Public Service in a Changing World*, to the Institute of Public Administration of Canada, 40th Annual Conference, August 31, 1988.

3   Honourable Don Mazankowski, *Notes for an Address: A New Commitment to Public Sector Management*, to the Public Policy Forum, Toronto, April 14, 1988.

4   While there have been only a few academic analyses of public sector management, the most comprehensive is *Beyond the Bottom Line: Management in Government*, by T.W. Plumptre, (Halifax: Institute for Research on Public Policy, 1988).

5   See for further details, "Walking the Tightrope," by David Zussman, in Michael J. Prince (ed.), *How Ottawa Spends, 1986* (Toronto: Methuen, 1986), pp. 250-282.

6   Eliminating thousands of jobs does not necessarily mean that government is doing less than it once did. In fact, the increase in regulations and new programs indicates that the overall workload has more than likely increased since 1984.

7   See M. Adams, "Environics Canada overview of changing values," *Environics*, 1989, and D. Yarkalovich and S. Harman, *Starting with the People* (Boston: Houghton-Mifflin, 1988), p. 285.

8   See D. Zussman and J. Jabes, *The Vertical Solitude: Managing in the Public Service* (Montreal: Institute for Research and Public Policy, 1989).

9   *Vertical Solitude*.

10   The fractious exchanges between Mssrs. Jourdanais and Lussier serve as a useful illustration of how much politicians disturb serious public servants.

11   D. Zussman, "Confidence in Public Institutions," (Halifax: Institute for Research on Public Policy, 1987), Working Paper Series.

12   N. Morgan, "Nowhere to Go? Possible Consequences of the Demographic Imbalance in Decision-Making Groups of the Federal Public Service," (Montreal: Institute for Research on Public Policy, 1981), p 160.

13   The management problems which derive from interactions among individuals have been addressed elsewhere. See D. Zussman and J. Jabes, *Vertical Solitute* (Montreal: Institute for Research on Public Policy, 1989), p. 220.

14   For a fascinating analysis of the current situation regarding the deputy minister group, see G.F. Osbaldeston, *Keeping Deputy Ministers Accountable* (London: National Centre for Management Research and Development, 1988), p. 187.

15   In the original study, 13 satisfaction measures were used which were later reduced to five distinct factors on the basis of a factor analysis. Two of these factors, job satisfaction and satisfaction with respondent's department were used in this chapter. The remaining three were intrinsic satisfaction, extrinsic satisfaction and satisfaction with career progress.

16   Evidence from earlier studies has shown that knowledge of goals has an impact on employee work satisfaction. See D. Zussman and J. Jabes, "Motivation, rewards and satisfaction in the Canadian federal public service, *Canadian Public Administration*, Volume 31, No. 2 (Summer), pp. 204-225.

17   Further evidence of the reduced promotional opportunities is the finding that the average public servant, in 1988, has spent 6.4 years in her or his present job classification compared to five years in 1983 — a 28 per cent increase. Quoted from *The Ottawa Citizen*, January 17, 1990. Source: Public Service Commission.

18   The objective set by Michael Wilson to cut the size of the public service by 15,000 jobs has almost been achieved by natural attrition and early retirements.

19   At almost 11 per cent.

20   The federal government has created a management cadre which has six levels and two basic classifications. This system operates throughout the federal public service regardless of size and level of decentralization. The first and lowest level of management is called the Senior Management Group (SM) which is com-

prised of 1,931 employees. The second classification is the Executive Group (EX) which has five levels above the SM group. There are a total of 2,606 EXs of which 959 are EX-1s and 84 are EX-5s. In most cases, the EX-5s are operating at the assistant deputy minister level while the EX-1s are directors.

21   The populations of senior managers (SMs) and executives (EXs) were surveyed in 1988.

22   Both satisfaction scores were based on responses to single item questions using a five point Likert scale. In all of the tables which follow the data have been subjected to an analysis of variance (ANOVA) which is summarized by an F score in those cases where the independent variable is measured by an ordinal scale. Correlation coefficients have also been included where appropriate for the readers' use in interpreting the data.

23   See G.F. Osbaldeston, *Keeping Deputy Ministers Accountable* (London, Ont.: National Centre for Management Research and Development, 1988).

24   The literature on private sector initiatives to improve corporate productivity has concentrated on improving managerial leadership and developing corporate culture and goals. There has been a decrease in emphasis on formal planning models and rules to guide individual behaviour.

25   See, Auditor General of Canada, *Annual Report 1988*, T.M. Plumptre, 1988 and D.R. Zussman and J. Jabes, 1989.

FISCAL FACTS AND TRENDS

This appendix presents an overview of the federal government's fiscal position, includes certain major economic policy indicators for the 1980-89 period, and some international comparisons.

Facts and trends are presented for federal revenue sources, federal expenditures by policy sector, the government's share of the economy, interest and inflation rates, Canadian balance of payments in total and with the United States in particular, and other national economic indicators. In addition, international comparisons on real growth, unemployment, inflation and productivity are reported for Canada, the United States, Japan, Germany and the United Kingdom.

The figures and time series are updated each year, providing readers with an ongoing current record of major budgetary and economic variables.

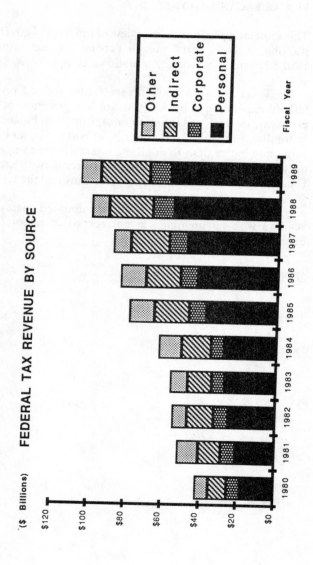

FEDERAL TAX REVENUE BY SOURCE

Other
Indirect
Corporate
Personal

Fiscal Year

($ Billions)

$120
$100
$80
$60
$40
$20
$0

1980 1981 1982 1983 1984 1985 1986 1987 1988 1989

FEDERAL TAX REVENUE BY SOURCE - 1989

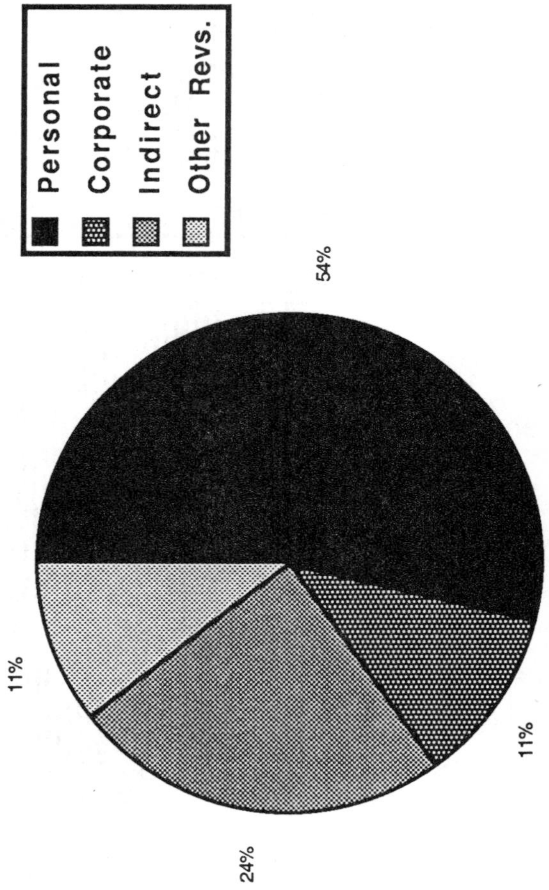

Legend:
- Personal
- Corporate
- Indirect
- Other Revs.

54%

11%

11%

24%

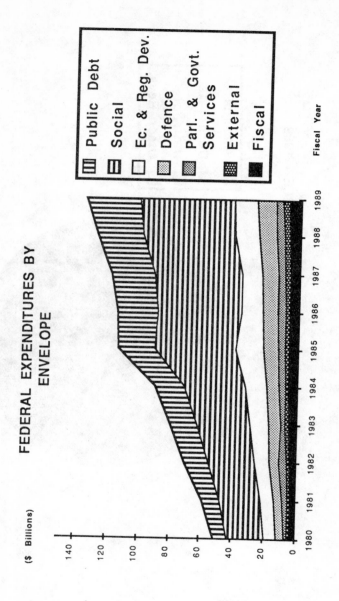

FEDERAL EXPENDITURES BY
ENVELOPE

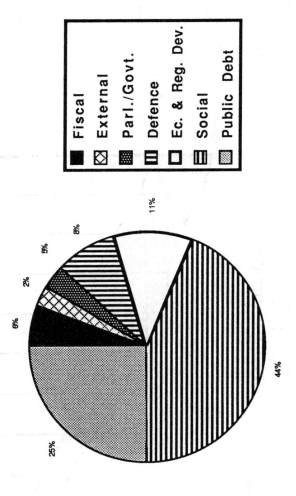

FEDERAL EXPENDITURES BY ENVELOPE - 1989

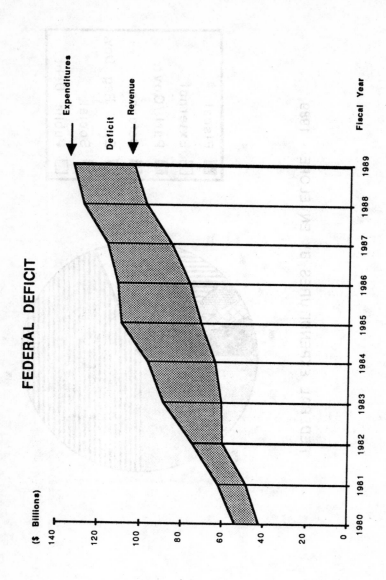

FEDERAL DEFICIT

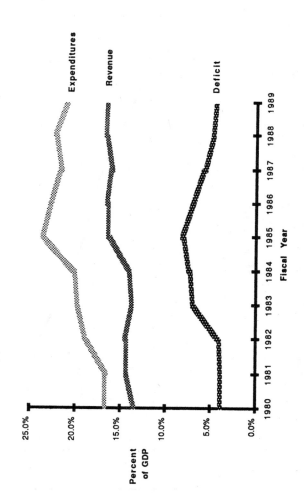

REVENUE, EXPENDITURES, AND DEFICIT AS
PERCENTAGES OF GROSS DOMESTIC PRODUCT

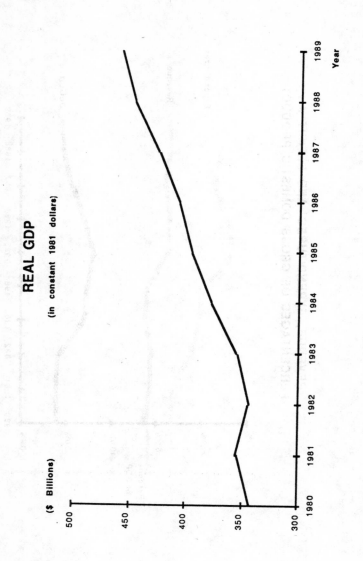

REAL GDP

(in constant 1981 dollars)

($ Billions)

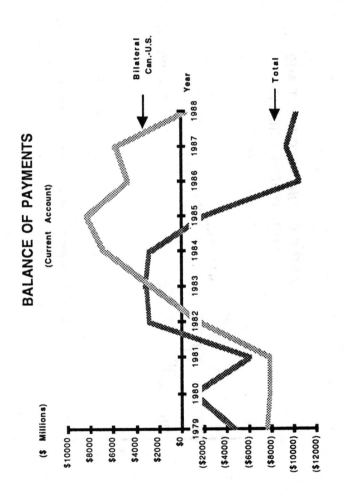

BALANCE OF PAYMENTS
(Current Account)

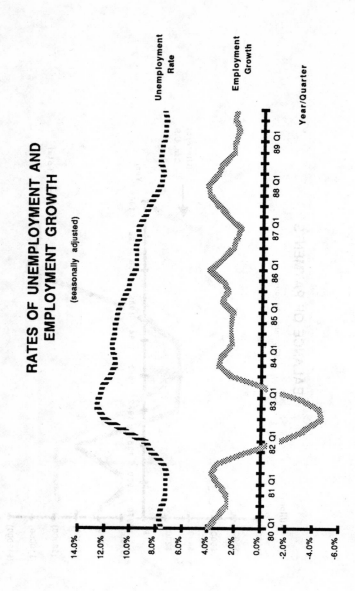

RATES OF UNEMPLOYMENT AND
EMPLOYMENT GROWTH

(seasonally adjusted)

Unemployment
Rate

Employment
Growth

Year/Quarter

14.0%
12.0%
10.0%
8.0%
6.0%
4.0%
2.0%
0.0%
-2.0%
-4.0%
-6.0%

80 Q1   81 Q1   82 Q1   83 Q1   84 Q1   85 Q1   86 Q1   87 Q1   88 Q1   89 Q1

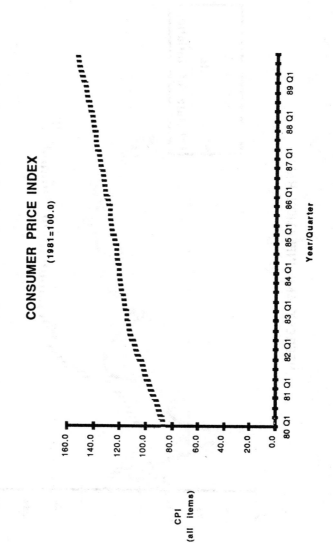

CONSUMER PRICE INDEX
(1981=100.0)

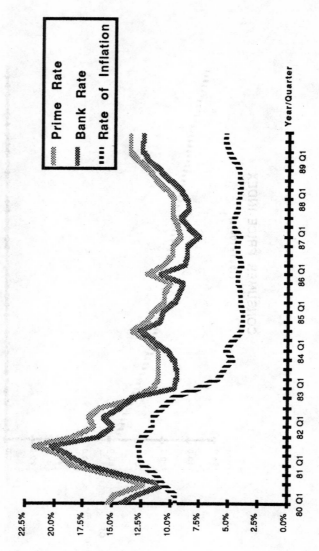

INTEREST AND INFLATION RATES

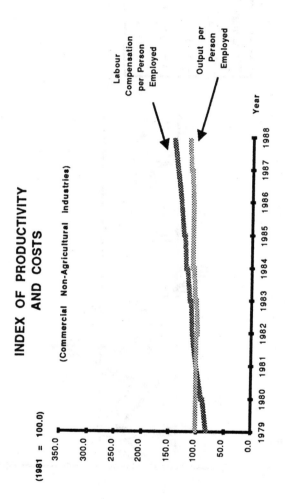

INDEX OF PRODUCTIVITY
AND COSTS

(Commercial Non-Agricultural Industries)

(1981 = 100.0)

Labour
Compensation
per Person
Employed

Output per
Person
Employed

Year

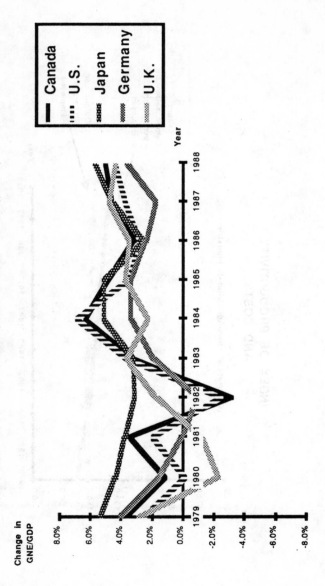

GROWTH IN REAL GNE/GDP

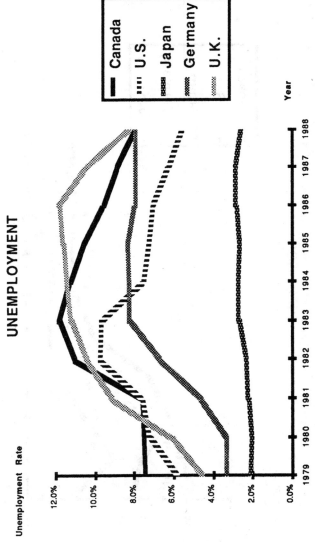

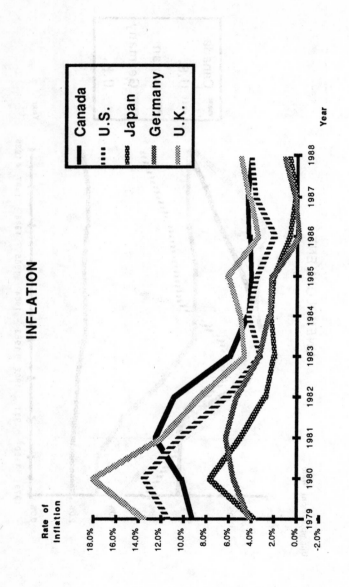

INFLATION

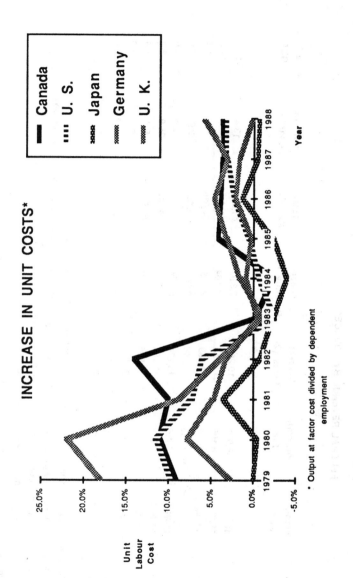

FEDERAL REVENUE BY SOURCE*
($ million)

Fiscal Year	Personal Tax (1)	Corporate Tax	Indirect Taxes (2)	Other Revenue (3)	Total Revenue	Percent Change	As a % of GDP
1980	16,808	6,951	10,266	7,310	41,335	13.4	13.3
1981	19,837	8,106	11,714	11,164	50,821	23.0	14.3
1982	24,046	8,118	13,789	8,115	54,068	6.9	14.4
1983	26,330	7,139	12,748	8,906	55,123	2.0	13.6
1984	26,967	7,286	15,234	12,550	62,037	12.5	14.0
1985	36,807	9,379	18,186	13,702	78,074	25.9	16.3
1986	41,720	9,210	18,896	13,136	82,962	6.3	16.4
1987	47,436	9,885	20,897	9,359	87,577	5.6	15.9
1988	55,550	10,878	23,505	9,661	99,594	13.7	16.6
1989	57,294	11,730	26,167	10,994	106,185	6.6	16.4

1 For the years 1985-88 unemployment insurance contributions are included in the total.
2 Consists of sales taxes, energy taxes (execpt for petroleum & gas revenue tax and incremental oil revenue tax), excise duties, custom imports, and other excise duties and taxes.
3 Consists of non-resident income tax, petroleum and gas revenue tax, incremental oil revenue tax, miscellaneous other taxes, and non-tax revenue.

SOURCE: Public Accounts, various years.

FEDERAL EXPENDITURES BY ENVELOPE*
($ million)

Fiscal Year	Fiscal Arrang.	External Affairs	Parl/Govt Services	Defence	Ec. & Reg. Develop.	Social	Public Debt	Total Outlays	Percent Change	Total As % of GDP
1980	3,635	1,404	2,182	4,389	7,733	23,729	8,524	51,594	8.0	16.6
1981	3,908	1,421	2,962	5,058	8,957	25,846	10,687	58,839	14.0	16.5
1982	4,734	1,702	4,483	6,031	9,457	28,963	15,168	70,538	19.9	18.8
1983	5,661	2,028	2,808	6,990	11,981	33,433	16,971	79,872	13.2	19.7
1984	5,862	2,261	3,493	7,973	13,101	38,704	18,146	89,540	12.1	20.1
1985**	5,985	2,659	4,227	9,021	17,641	50,977	22,455	112,965	26.2	23.6
1986	5,941	2,500	4,797	9,366	13,630	52,264	25,441	113,939	0.8	22.6
1987	6,302	2,912	4,355	10,270	12,625	55,059	26,658	118,182	3.7	21.5
1988	7,007	3,461	4,744	11,074	15,231	57,132	29,028	127,677	8.0	22.2
1989	8,127	3,584	4,714	11,291	14,401	59,619	33,183	134,919	5.7	20.8

* PEMS basis; reflects 1984-85 envelope system; includes loans, investments and advances.
** Expenditure base in Public Accounts modified in 1985.

Source: Economic Review, reference table 51 for 1979-84 data.
        Public Accounts, Table 1.7, various years.

INTERNATIONAL ECONOMIC COMPARISONS*
(PERCENTAGE CHANGES)

	1979	1980	1981	1982	1983	1984	1985	1986	1987	1988
Growth in Real GDP (1)										
Canada	3.7	1.1	3.4	-3.2	3.2	6.3	4.8	3.1	4.5	5.0
U.S.	2.5	-0.2	1.9	-2.5	3.6	6.8	3.4	2.7	3.7	4.4
Japan	5.3	4.3	3.7	3.1	3.2	5.1	5.1	2.5	4.5	5.7
Germany	4.0	1.5	0.0	-1.0	1.9	3.3	3.3	2.3	1.7	3.6
U.K.	2.8	-2.3	-1.2	1.7	3.6	2.2	3.7	3.4	4.7	4.2
Unemployment Rate (2)										
Canada	7.4	7.5	7.6	11.0	11.8	11.2	10.5	9.5	8.8	7.8
U.S.	5.8	7.2	7.6	9.7	9.6	7.5	7.2	7.0	6.2	5.5
Japan	2.1	2.0	2.2	2.3	2.7	2.7	2.6	2.8	2.8	2.5
Germany	3.3	3.3	4.6	6.7	8.2	8.2	8.3	7.9	7.9	7.9
U.K.	4.5	6.1	9.1	10.4	11.2	11.4	11.6	11.8	10.4	8.2
Inflation (3)										
Canada	9.2	10.2	12.5	10.8	5.9	4.3	4.0	4.2	4.4	4.0
U.S.	11.3	13.5	10.3	6.1	3.2	4.3	3.5	1.9	3.7	4.1
Japan	3.7	7.7	4.9	2.7	1.9	2.3	2.0	0.6	0.1	0.7
Germany	4.1	5.5	6.3	5.3	3.3	2.4	2.2	-0.2	0.2	1.2
U.K.	13.4	18.0	11.9	8.6	4.6	5.0	6.1	3.4	4.2	4.9
Unit Labour Costs in Manufact. (4)										
Canada	9.1	11.1	10.0	14.2	-0.1	-2.3	4.3	3.9	3.7	4.0
U.S.	9.8	11.6	7.3	6.1	-2.5	-0.6	0.6	2.4	3.3	3.4
Japan	0.1	-0.4	3.7	-0.8	-2.3	-3.9	-2.2	1.4	-0.5	-0.7
Germany	2.7	7.8	4.8	3.3	-0.5	1.0	0.3	2.2	1.7	0.1
U.K.	18.1	22.1	8.8	3.9	-1.0	1.8	3.3	4.8	3.1	6.0

* According to figures compiled by the OECD.

1. GNE data are reported for the U.S., Japan, Germany, and Canada, while GDP data are reported for the U.K.

2. Unemployment rates are on the basis of national definitions.

3. As measured by the year-to-year variation in the Consumer Price Index.

4. Defined as output at factor cost divided by dependent employment.

Sources: OECD, Historical Statistics 1960-1986 ; OECD Economic Outlook, 1980-88.

FEDERAL DEFICIT*
($ million)

Fiscal Year (end Mar. 31)	Total Revenues	Total Expenditures	Budgetary Deficit	Percent Change	As a % of GDP
1980	41,921	53,422	11,501	-8.2	3.7
1981	48,775	62,297	13,522	17.6	3.8
1982	60,001	74,873	14,872	10.0	4.0
1983	60,705	88,521	27,816	87.0	6.9
1984	64,216	96,615	32,399	16.5	7.3
1985	70,891	109,222	38,324	18.3	8.0
1986	76,833	111,237	34,404	-10.2	6.8
1987	85,784	116,389	30,605	-11.0	5.6
1988	97,452	125,535	28,083	-8.2	4.7
1989	103,981	132,715	28,734	2.3	4.4

* Revenues are calculated on a net basis.

Source: Public Accounts 1988-89, Table 1.2.

Subscribers

We thank the following organizations for assisting in meeting the financial costs of producing *How Ottawa Spends* by subscribing to the 1990-91 edition.

Business Council on National Issues
Ottawa

Canadian Chamber of Commerce
Ottawa

Kinburn Corporation
Ottawa

Ministry of Intergovernmental Affairs
Government of Ontario

The Mutual Group
Waterloo

The Ottawa Citizen
Ottawa

Petro-Canada Inc.
Calgary

Department of the Secretary of State
Government of Canada

Stelco Inc.
Hamilton

Xerox Canada Inc.
North York

The Authors

Lloyd Brown-John is an Associate Professor in the Department of Political Science, University of Windsor.

G. Bruce Doern is a Professor in the School of Public Administration, Carleton University.

Katherine A. Graham is an Associate Professor in the School of Public Administration, Carleton University.

Rianne Mahon is a Professor in the School of Public Administration, Carleton University.

Allan M. Maslove is a Professor in the School of Public Administration, Carleton University.

Allan Moscovitch is an Associate Professor in the School of Social Work, Carleton University.

Michael J. Prince holds the Lansdowne Chair in Social Policy, University of Victoria.

Douglas A. Smith is a Professor in the Department of Economics, Carleton University.

David Zussman is a Professor and Dean in the Faculty of Administration, University of Ottawa.

THE SCHOOL OF PUBLIC ADMINISTRATION
at Carleton University is a national centre for the
study of public policy and public management
in Canada.

The School's Centre for Policy and Program Assessment provides research services and courses to interest groups, businesses, unions and governments in the evaluation of public policies, programs and activities.